Philadelphia's Record Breakers & Legend Makers

Presented by the

PHILADELPHIA DAILY
NEWS

RUNNING PRESS
Philadelphia, Pennsylvania

Canadian representatives: General Publishing Co., Ltd.,
30 Lesmill Road, Don Mills, Ontario M3B 2T6.

International representatives: Worldwide Media Services, Inc.,
115 East Twenty-third Street, New York, New York, 10010.

9   8   7   6   5   4   3   2   1

Digit on right indicates the number of this printing.

Library of Congress Cataloging-in-Publication Number
89-43047 ISBN 0-89471-748-0

Cover design by Toby Schmidt
Front cover photographs of
John B. Kelly Sr. (top), the Kelly Estate
Bernie Parent (lower left), the Philadelphia Flyers
Randall Cunningham (lower right), by Rick Bowmer
Back cover photographs of
Hal Greer (top), the Philadelphia 76ers
Tug McGraw (middle), Norman Y. Lono
Mike Roche (bottom), the *Daily News*
Credits for interior photographs on Page 3

This book may be ordered by mail from the publisher.
Please add $2.50 for postage and handling.

But try your bookstore first!

Running Press Book Publishers
125 South Twenty-second Street
Philadelphia, Pennsylvania 19103

Daily News Executive Sports Editor:
Mike Rathet

Daily News Sports Editor:
Brian Toolan

Editors:
Pat McLoone
Bob Vetrone Jr.

High School Records Provided by:
Ted Silary

**Collegiate Records Provided by
the Sports Information Offices of:**
Drexel University
La Salle Univerisity
University of Pennsylvania
Penn State University
St. Joseph's University
Temple University
Villanova University

**Professional Records Provided by
the Public Relations Departments of:**
Philadelphia Eagles
Philadelphia Flyers
Philadelphia Phillies
Philadelphia 76ers

Profiles Written by:
Tim Kawakami
Pat McLoone
Kevin Mulligan

Interior Photos by:
Associated Press, Pat Bernet, Rick Bowmer, Prentice Cole
W. Everly III, E.W. Faircloth, Bruce Johnson, Matt Lee
Bob Laramie, Norman Y. Lono, Mark Ludak, Ed Mahan
Michael Mercanti, Tom Mihalek, Denis O'Keefe
University of Pennsylvania, Penn State University
Philadelphia *Daily News*, Philadelphia Eagles
Philadelphia Flyers, Philadelphia Phillies, Philadelphia 76ers
Philadelphia Warriors, Sam Psoras, George Reynolds
St. Joseph's University, Elwood P. Smith, Temple University
Villanova University, Susan Winters.

The material in this book was compiled by the Sports Department of the *Philadelphia Daily News* as a statistical history and reference guide to sports in the city of Philadelphia.

The information pertaining to the Phillies, Eagles, scholastic and collegiate football is complete through their 1988 seasons.

The information pertaining to the 76ers, Flyers, scholastic and collegiate basketball is complete through their 1988-89 seasons.

Other information is complete through June, 1988.

Our thanks to everyone who has ever participated in, attended, or inquired about a sports event in or about Philadelphia. It is to them that this book is dedicated.

CONTENTS

We Have Your Numbers

Robin Roberts (left), Del Ennis before 1955 All-Star Game

By RAY DIDINGER

Statistics, baseball's Toby Harrah once said, are like a girl in a bikini.

"They both show a lot," Harrah said, "but not everything."

There is some truth to that. Statistics might appear to be the bottom line in sports, but they aren't always.

Sometimes raw numbers tell part of the story. Sometimes they fool you. And sometimes they flat-out lie.

Take the 1928 Phillies, for example.

Six of their everyday starters batted over .285. Rightfielder Chuck Klein hit .360. The team's home run total (85) was better than half the teams in baseball.

Yet the Phillies finished 43-109 that year, one of their worst seasons ever.

On the flip side, the 1960 Eagles ranked next-to-last among NFL teams in rushing. Their starting backs, Billy Barnes and Ted Dean, averaged less than 3 yards per carry. Meanwhile, their opponents that season averaged 5 yards a crack.

No matter, the '60 Eagles won the NFL championship by defeating Vince Lombardi's Green Bay Packers, 17-13, at Franklin Field.

Sometimes the figures just don't figure, but that doesn't mean they aren't fun. They are.

For trivia freaks, for numerologists, for those of us who just like to spin facts into legend, the statistics of sport are an invaluable resource.

For the nostalgia crowd, the record book is like an old friend. It is a place to visit and reminisce, to browse among the names and achievements — some great, some dubious — that fill the memory like snapshots in a family album.

That is what this book is all about. It is about records — the people who set them and the people who would like to remember them.

There is something for everyone here. The Phillies, Eagles, Sixers and Flyers are included, of course. All the local major college basketball and football teams, including Penn State. Even the high schools.

There is a rundown on Philadelphia-area athletes who have won Olympic gold medals and those who have been elected to various halls of fame.

Boxing fans will find a list of local fighters who held world titles (sorry, Rocky Balboa is not included), as well as the results of every championship bout to take place in the city, dating back to Jack Johnson and Philadelphia Jack O'Brien in 1909.

Some people will use this as a reference book. They now can settle arguments by looking things up rather than calling the *Daily News*. But that isn't why we published this. Really, it's not.

We published it as a fond look back on more than a century of Philadelphia sports, at all levels.

It is all here — the good, the bad and the ugly. Feel free to skip whole decades. (The Phillies in the '20s, for example. Grim stuff.) And linger as long as you like with the Whiz Kids and the Stanley Cup champion Flyers. We understand.

This is the kind of book in which reading between the lines is a must. Who could see the Phillies' 1964 record (92-70, tied for second place) and not think about the September collapse? Who could see Villanova's 1985 basketball box score and not hear the echoes of Lexington, Ky., and the NCAA final?

After all, statistics aren't just numbers. They are a collection of moments and images, sights and sounds. You can feed them through a computer and dissect them however you like, but they still have that emotion attached.

It is the feeling, not the data, that we hold onto.

This Philadelphia time capsule contains some statistics that will surprise you and others that might make you laugh.

For example, did you realize Tony Gonzalez led the Phillies in batting one season with a puny .264 average? Sad but true. The year was 1968.

Did you know Drexel has been playing intercollegiate basketball longer than Penn, La Salle, Villanova and St. Joseph's? It's true. Drexel's hoops program dates back to 1894.

And did you know which former 76er holds the team record for most blocked shots in a game? No, it is not Moses Malone or Darryl Dawkins. And it is not Caldwell Jones or even Bobby Jones.

The answer is Harvey Catchings, with 10 rejections in a 1975 game against Atlanta.

Those are quirks and oddities; every record book has its share. But the great teams and great players rightfully dominate.

We are talking about the likes of Mike Schmidt, Steve Carlton, Steve Van Buren, Harold Carmichael, Bobby Clarke, Bernie Parent, Julius Erving and Wilt Chamberlain. Especially Wilt.

No other Philadelphia athlete, in any sport, had comparable impact. The records the 7-1, 275-pound Chamberlain set, high school through pro, remain virtually untouched today.

Consider:

■ Wilt's high single game at Overbrook: 90 points against Roxborough in 1955.

■ His high school career total: 2,252 points. No other player in the city's prep history is even close.

■ He has the top 10 scoring games in 76ers history. He also has at least the top 15 rebounding games and three of the top five assist games.

■ He has the highest career field goal percentage: 58 percent. Also, the best single-game shooting performance: 18-for-18 against Baltimore in 1967.

It should be noted these records pertain only to the three seasons (1965-66 through 1967-68) Chamberlain played with the 76ers (formerly the Syracuse Nationals). It does not include the three years Chamberlain played with the Philadelphia (now Golden State) Warriors.

That means Wilt's 100-point game, his 55-rebound game and his 50-point scoring average for the 1961-62 season (all NBA records) don't apply here. That makes these numbers all the more remarkable.

Chamberlain starred for the most dominant professional team in Philadelphia history: the Sixers' 1966-67 NBA champions. That club was 68-13 in the regular season, 11-4 in the playoffs, a winning percentage of .823. Wilt averaged an astounding 47.2 minutes per game.

After Chamberlain left in 1968, the Sixers did not win another playoff round until 1977 when Erving and George McGinnis teamed up.

Schmidt and Carlton were the twin towers of Philadelphia baseball from their arrival in 1972 until Carlton's release in 1986. To get an idea just how great these future Hall of Famers were, put their career numbers up against other top players who wore the Phillies uniform. It is no contest.

Schmidt leads the team in 10 of 16 all-time offensive categories. His home run total (542) is more than the next two men, Del Ennis and Chuck Klein, combined (502).

Carlton, meanwhile, had more strikeouts (3,030) than Robin Roberts and Curt Simmons combined (2,923), even though the former Whiz Kids pitched almost 2,000 more innings. That is how overpowering Carlton was in his prime.

A footnote on Schmidt: He led the club in batting average, homers and RBI, but he never led in all three categories the same year. Four Phillies players have done it three times, but all before 1934. Since 1946, other sluggers have done it, including Greg Luzinski, Dick Allen and Del Ennis each twice. Even Don Demeter did it once (1962). But not Schmidt.

Poke around in the Phillies' records and you are likely to come up with any number of interesting tidbits.

Example: For seven consecutive seasons (1936 to '42), the pitcher who led the club in wins finished the year with a losing record. That's what is known as hard times.

The Eagles have suffered, too. They went 28 years without a 1,000-yard rusher before Wilbert Montgomery came along. They have managed just six winning seasons since 1961. But their record book is not without its bright spots.

Start with Van Buren, the halfback they called "Wham Bam" because he ran over anyone who got in his way. Van Buren set a club record with 18 touchdowns in 1945. And that was a 10-game season. Imagine what he might have done with today's 16-game schedule.

The other Eagle whose record stands out is Sonny Jurgensen, the Hall of Fame quarterback. There have been just 15 games in which an Eagles quarterback passed for 350 yards in the team's history: Jurgensen had seven of those, including five in one season (1961).

The club's biggest passing day ever was a surprise: 437 yards by journeyman Bobby Thomason against the New York Giants in 1953. Adrian Burk tied an NFL record with seven touchdown passes in a 1957 game. These two weren't exactly folk heroes in Philadelphia.

Harold Carmichael, a gangly 6-8 receiver drafted on the seventh round in 1971, emerged as the team's most durable and productive player. He finished his Eagles career as the all-time leader in games (180), pass receptions (589) receiving yardage (8,978) and touchdowns (79).

You can have some fun with the Eagles' records if you don't mind mixing eras.

For example, the Eagles, with Van Buren and Bosh Pritchard, rushed for 376 yards in a 1948 game against Washington. That's 25 yards more than Ron Bull gained in the entire 1971 season — and he was the Birds' leading rusher that year.

Also, when Randall Cunningham led the team in both rushing and passing yardage in 1987, it was the first time an Eagles player had pulled off that double since Dave Smukler in 1938.

The Flyers have more off-the-wall statistics than one might expect, given their steady track record (17 consecutive non-losing seasons).

Who holds the club mark for most points in a game? Bobby Clarke, Bill Barber, Reggie Leach . . . one of those guys, right? Wrong. It is Tom Bladon, a defenseman, with eight points (1977).

And who has the record for most penalty minutes in a game? It figures to be either Dave Schultz, Paul Holmgren or Dave Brown. Wrong again. It is Frank Bathe, a willing but artless brawler, with 55 minutes (1979).

More surprises:

The Flyers have not had a scorer reach the 100-point level since 1975-76, yet they have won the Patrick Divison title six times in those 12 years.

Here's another: The Flyers set the club record for most penalty minutes (194) and fewest penalty minutes (zero) in games played exactly one week apart in March 1979. Go figure.

Eagles' Harold Carmichael hauls in another reception

But some numbers glitter. The team went unbeaten for 35 consecutive games (25-0-10) in 1979-80. Bernie Parent won 91 regular-season games with a 1.91 goals-against average in the two Stanley Cup years (1974-75) and was named playoff MVP twice.

No Philadelphia record book would be complete without the Big 5. All five schools have sent at least one team to the NCAA Final Four and two of them — La Salle in 1954 and Villanova in 1985 — came home with the national basketball championship.

The records speak for themselves. La Salle had 19 consecutive winning seasons (1946-65), as did St. Joseph's (1955-74). Penn had 15 consecutive winning seasons (1968-83), as did Temple (1959-74). Villanova had 11 winning seasons in a row twice (1961-72, 1975-86).

The '60s were a golden decade at the Palestra, with packed houses for almost every doubleheader and two, sometimes three city schools in the national rankings.

In those 10 years, the Big 5 schools had a combined record of 897-428, a .677 winning percentage. They sent 27 teams to either the NCAA or National Invitation Tournament and this was when bids still were hard to come by.

There is no gaudier record than the 78.6 field goal percentage (22-for-28) Villanova rang up in the stifling pressure of the NCAA championship game against Georgetown. There was no margin for error as the 'Cats barely squeezed by, 66-64.

Odds and ends in the Big 5 barrel include a curious high-point game: Paul Arizin, of Villanova, scoring 85 against the Naval Air Material Center (whatever that was) in 1949.

Also, Temple's top single-game rebounder is not Tim Perry, John Baum or Jay Norman. It is Fred Cohen, who cleaned 34 boards against Connecticut in 1956. La Salle's Tom Gola still has the top rebounding day overall: 37 against Lebanon Valley in 1955.

Roger Blough, chairman of U.S. Steel, once described his football career at Susquehanna University by saying: "In the three years I played, we won six, lost 17 and tied two. Some statistician with a great capacity for charity calculated that we won 75 percent of the games we didn't lose."

They don't need any such creative accounting at Penn State. Until 1988, the Nittany Lions had not had a losing football season since 1938. They have won two national championships in the last seven years under coach Joe Paterno.

But check the players' individual records. Just like their uniforms: boring. Nobody leads the nation in anything. The school has produced just one Heisman Trophy winner: Upper Darby's John Cappelletti in 1973.

The Nittany Lions are a classic example of the whole being greater than the sum of its parts. Franco Harris is the fourth-leading rusher in NFL history, but he is just the 10th-leading rusher at Penn State.

Clearly, Paterno does not believe in the star system. He believes in winning.

The local football schools have not enjoyed the same big-time success, although Penn capped off its fourth consecutive Ivy League title with a 10-0 season in 1986.

You might want to check the Quakers' football history, which includes a 1916 Rose Bowl appearance (a 14-0 loss to Oregon) and an imposing 222-29-10 record wrapped around the turn of the century, 1891-1910.

Penn was a dynasty in those days, but then so were the Hapsburgs.

The Temple football records reflect the stripping of Paul Palmer's senior year (due to ineligibility). However, Palmer still stands as the school's all-time leader in rushing (3,029 yards) and touchdowns (28).

At Villanova, the record book is dominated by Mike Siani, a wide receiver who was drafted in the first round by the Oakland Raiders in 1971. Siani holds or shares 14 school marks, including 12 catches for 288 yards and five touchdowns in one game against Xavier.

The track and cross-country teams account for most of Villanova's national honors. They have won 78 NCAA championships, carrying on a proud tradition started by coach Jumbo Elliott more than 30 years ago.

In 1988, the Villanova track team produced its first woman Olympian, Vicki Huber, of Wilmington. Huber, the NCAA women's champion at 3,000 meters, placed sixth at that distance in the Seoul Olympics.

More than any other section of this book, the boxing records remind us how things used to be in Philadelphia.

There were a lot of big fights in this city, including three world championship bouts at JFK Stadium, then Municipal Stadium, in one summer (1952). The last one was the Rocky Marciano-Jersey Joe Walcott classic that ended with Marciano knocking Walcott stiff in the 13th round to lift the heavyweight title.

Also, light-heavyweight champion Harold Johnson had three title fights in a little more than three months in Philadelphia (1961). Johnson, who lived in the city, fought once at Convention Hall and twice at the Arena, and won all three.

Today, of course, the big money fights are in Atlantic City. There has not been a title fight in Philadelphia since light-heavyweights Matthew Saad Muhammad and Dwight Braxton met at the Spectrum in August 1982. That's more than six years ago.

And no Philadelphia boxer actually has taken a world title from a champion fighting here since lightweight Ike Williams knocked out Bob Montgomery at Municipal Stadium in August 1947.

In the pages on high schools, it is a name game. Anyone who grew up in this city will recognize them. Gene Banks (West Philadelphia), Michael Brooks (West Catholic), Bobby McNeill (North Catholic), Guy Rodgers (Northeast). Each one has his high point game recorded.

And in football, it is Blair Thomas, of Frankford (and now Penn State), who set the city high school marks for career carries (626), yards (3,941), touchdowns (59) and points (356).

Lawrence Reid, of Cardinal Dougherty (1976), bears special mention. He set the city record for most yards rushing in a prep football game (379) and also set his school's mark for most points in a basketball game (42). In each case, the opposition was Bishop Egan High.

That might be a new record, too. We're still checking.

Words Can Speak Louder

By STAN HOCHMAN

Robin Roberts had a simple philosophy about pitching

"Strike one."

It was 1959, late in a wretched season, my first year of covering big league baseball.

Robin Roberts, aloof, dignified, stingy with words, was a struggling link to the past.

I approached him, hoping to get him to share his hoarded thoughts. Not about the Phillies, who were wretched, but about the art of pitching.

"Robby," I said timidly, "could we talk about your philosophy of pitching?"

"Strike one," Roberts said, summing it up in two eloquent words, distilling all the mumbo jumbo about pitching to the starkest element. Get ahead of the hitter, get the count in your favor.

Twenty-nine years later, pitching coach Claude Osteen goes muttering out the clubhouse door, baffled by Philadelphia pitchers who would not, or could not, throw strikes.

Especially strike one.

"How much?"

Another pitcher, another blunt two-word quote that epitomizes the man who said it.

Jim Bunning pitched that perfect game at Shea Stadium and the writers clogged the area around his locker.

Suddenly, the clubhouse man yelped from the fringe of the media mob, "Got a guy from the Ed Sullivan show on the phone," he shouted. "Wants to know if you'll do the show tonight?"

"How much?" Bunning said bluntly.

The owners held the whip hand back then. Bunning had been traded once, he had a large family, with some of the kids in the stands that afternoon.

Taking a bow on television is nice, but it won't buy groceries at the A & P. Bunning got his price, made his appearance, upstaged Ken Venturi, who had won the U.S. Open that day, and went on to be part of the tragic 1964 collapse of the Phillies.

Bunning is a Republican congressman now. He was a blue-collar workman then.

Roberts is there, in this record book, for pitching 529 games for the Phillies, for winning 234 of them, for throwing 35 shutouts. Bunning is there, too, for whiffing 1,197 hitters, for 23 shutouts in 89 wins, for that perfect game, 6/21/64.

The games are a blur, the numbers fuzzy. What I remember are the words. Roberts saying "strike one." Bunning asking, "How much?"

I remember Eddie Sawyer letting Roberts hit for himself midway through the 1960 opener in Cincinnati.

All three beat writers second-guessed Sawyer. He quit the next day, saying, "I'm 49 and I

Gene Mauch meets fans at airport after the Phillies failed to secure the National League Championship in 1964

want to live to be 50."

Andy Cohen managed the second game of the season. And then Gene Mauch arrived, young, brash, handsome.

"Why," Mauch asked that day, "is everybody so gloomy?"

"You'll find out, you'll find out," the writers choused.

He found out. The Phillies lost 23 in a row the next year. In the spring of '62, Mauch said that the record-breaking losing streak had crystallized the Phillies, given them an identity. They were no longer ex-Orioles or ex-Cardinals.

He was always doing verbal tricks like that, softening a hitter's slump by saying, "Think of all the fun he's going to have, getting to .300."

Not enough of his hitters did, but Mauch won 645 games and he deserves a prominent place in the record book, in the memory book.

"Extraordinary people do extraordinary things," Mauch said, over and over, but somehow he could not solve the riddle of the most extraordinary player he managed, Dick Allen.

Allen said some memorable things in his controversial career here, including the flip comment about playing on Astroturf: "If my horse can't eat it, I don't want to play on it."

Sadly, he will be remembered most for his graffiti, scrawling sorrowful messages in the dirt around first base.

"Boo" for the harsh treatment he got from the fans. "Coke" for the cruel expectations that he hit the ball over the Coca-Cola sign atop the leftfield roof every time up.

And then, coach George Myatt's raspy comment, the day Bob Skinner got fired, the day the Phillies played an exhibition in Reading that Allen wanted to miss: "The Good Lord his self couldn't manage Allen."

And then, there was the conversation I had with Hank Allen, Dick's brother, and now a respected horse trainer in Maryland.

Dick's lifetime average was .311 when we talked and I suggested to Hank that Dick might hit .351 if he conformed.

"And maybe," Hank said sternly, "he might hit .251."

There are other, lighter memories. Don Demeter shares the record for most runs in one game, five.

Demeter was a lanky, taciturn Oklahoman, traded here by the Dodgers. Looked me in the eye one day and said, "I read the *Daily News* and eat a bowl of Rice Krispies every night.

Sonny Liston connects with a right hand to Albert Westphal in the first round of their 1961 fight at Convention Hall

That way I don't have anything on my stomach or my mind when I go to sleep."

Sonny Liston put Albert Westphal to sleep in the first round at Convention Hall one night.

The writers were awed by Liston and no one wanted to ask the first postfight question.

Finally, I asked Liston about the sight of Westphal, chalk-pale, sprawled on the canvas, his leg twitching. How did Westphal look to him?

"He looked *gooood,*" Liston said.

Liston ought to be in our listing of home-town champions, because he lived in Philadelphia while champ.

Later, after being hounded out of town, he would say, "I'd rather be a lamppost in Denver than mayor of Philadelphia."

Muhammad Ali belongs, too, because he lived on City Avenue for a while. I visited him there one day and he did 25 minutes of dialogue from "Big Time Buck White," a

show he performed in, during his conscientious objector exile from the ring.

Joe Frazier is there, and I can still hear him say, after whipping Ali at Madison Square Garden, talking through lumpy lips about the punch that knocked Ali down, "I got that left hook from down home."

The *Daily News* set a record the next day, doubling its normal circulation. No other paper in the world did that.

Ali was the most charismatic athlete I've ever been around. Wilt Chamberlain was not far behind.

And although he could be moody at times, Wilt was willing to share his insights into the game of basketball.

Yet it is not something he said that sticks with me, but something he did.

He commissioned a rug to be made from the fur of Arctic wolves, the softest fur from the area around the nose.

He was proud of that exotic rug, and when I

wrote about it, we both got a stack of angry mail from animal lovers who did not understand the ecology.

I wonder if Wilt still has that rug. And I wonder if he ever will compromise his feelings about the 76ers' organization and consent to have his number retired.

I see Don Looney in the Eagles' section, for catching 14 passes for 180 yards in one game, 12/1/40.

Many years later I interviewed his son, Joe Don, after a game in Philadelphia. Joe Don, the quintessential blithe spirit, said, "I never met a man I didn't like, until I met Will Rogers."

Joe Kuharich was the Eagles' coach back then. Before he stopped talking to the media, he would say wonderful things like, "Trading quarterbacks is rare, but not unusual."

He described one player "as a horse of a another fire department" and he was always talking about how games "teeter-totter."

I suppose the best one word quote I ever got was uttered by kicker Sam Baker after a loss that included three botched field goals.

Baker's impression of that game?

"Dastardly."

Dastardly, that rhymes with something Bobby Clarke said on the eve of the Flyers-Russians hockey game.

"I hate the bastards," Clarke said. He played like it, too.

Before Clarke, before the Broad Street Bullies, the Flyers had little guys like Andre Lacroix.

Ed Conrad covered the Flyers for us then. And he wrote: "Andre Lacroix got his baptism of fire last night, and although he is still wet behind the ears, he proved he could cut the mustard."

New Yorker magazine reprinted the paragraph and Conrad carried it around proudly in his wallet. And when I became sports editor I took Conrad and his orange blazer off the hockey beat and the fan club draped nasty banners about me from the Spectrum railings and threatened to boycott the paper.

Bernie Parent helped me forget all that garbage with his grace under fire, with his undentable good humor, with his trademark quote, "Some fun, eh?"

It has been some fun, watching so many of the record-breakers for the past 29 years. And if the mug shot looks too solemn, let me remind you of the exclusive quote I got from Duane Thomas after the Super Bowl game, the one he preceded with a week of silence.

"Duane," I asked, "are you happy?"

He nodded.

Desperate, I said, "Well, you don't look happy."

"Happiness," Thomas said, tapping his chest, "is in here."

Bless them all, the introverted ones such as Wilbert Montgomery and the silent Steve Carlton as well as the extroverts such as the gabby Tug McGraw and always approachable Julius Erving.

For the records they have set, for the pleasure they have given us.

Dallas Cowboys running back Duane Thomas gets tackled by three Miami defenders in Super Bowl VI at New Orleans

PHILLIES

Season	Manager	W- L-T	Pct.	Pos.	GB
1883	Bob Ferguson	4- 13	.235	8	NA
	Bill Purcell	13- 68	.160	—	—
	Total	17- 81	.173	8	46
1884	Harry Wright	39- 73	.348	6	45
1885	Harry Wright	56- 54	.509	3	30
1886	Harry Wright	71- 43	.623	4	14
1887	Harry Wright	75- 48	.610	2	3½
1888	Harry Wright	69- 61	.531	3	14½
1889	Harry Wright	63- 64	.496	4	20½
1890	Harry Wright	78- 54	.591	3	9½
1891	Harry Wright	68- 69	.496	4	18½
1892	Harry Wright	87- 66	.569	4	16½
1893	Harry Wright	72- 57	.558	4	14
1894	Arthur Irwin	71- 57	.555	4	18
1895	Arthur Irwin	78- 53	.595	3	9½
1896	Billy Nash	62- 68	.477	8	18½
1897	George Stallings	55- 77	.417	10	38
1898	George Stallings	19- 27	.413	8	NA
	Bill Shettsline	59- 44	.573	—	—
	Total	78- 71	.523	6	24
1899	Bill Shettsline	94- 58-2	.617	3	9
1900	Bill Shettsline	75- 63-3	.543	3	7½
1901	Bill Shettsline	83- 57-0	.593	2	7½
1902	Bill Shettsline	56- 81-2	.410	7	46
1903	Chief Zimmer	49- 86-4	.367	7	39½
1904	Hugh Duffy	52-100-3	.345	8	53½
1905	Hugh Duffy	83- 69-3	.545	4	21½
1906	Hugh Duffy	71- 82-1	.464	4	45½
1907	Bill Murray	83- 64-2	.564	3	21½
1908	Bill Murray	83- 71-1	.539	4	16
1909	Bill Murray	74- 79-1	.484	5	36½
1910	Red Dooin	78- 75-4	.510	4	25½
1911	Red Dooin	79- 73-1	.520	4	19½
1912	Red Dooin	73- 79-0	.480	5	30½
1913	Red Dooin	88- 63-8	.579	2	12½
1914	Red Dooin	74- 80-0	.481	6	20½
1915	Pat Moran	90- 62-1	.592	1	—
1916	Pat Moran	91- 62-1	.594	2	2½
1917	Pat Moran	87- 65-2	.571	2	10
1918	Pat Moran	55- 68-2	.448	6	26

Season	Manager	W- L-T	Pct.	Pos.	GB
1919	Jack Coombs	18- 44-0	.290	8	NA
	Gavvy Cravath	29- 46-1	.388	—	—
	Total	47- 90-1	.344	8	47½
1920	Gavvy Cravath	62- 91-0	.405	8	30½
1921	Bill Donovan	31- 71-0	.304	8	NA
	Kaiser Wilhelm	20- 32-0	.385	—	—
	Total	51-103-0	.331	8	43½
1922	Kaiser Wilhelm	57- 96-1	.373	7	35½
1923	Art Fletcher	50-104-1	.326	8	45½
1924	Art Fletcher	55- 96-1	.365	7	37
1925	Art Fletcher	68- 85-0	.444	6	27
1926	Art Fletcher	58- 93-1	.385	8	29½
1927	Stuffy McInnis	51-103-1	.332	8	43
1928	Burt Shotton	43-109-0	.283	8	51
1929	Burt Shotton	71- 82-1	.464	5	27½
1930	Burt Shotton	52-102-2	.340	8	40
1931	Burt Shotton	66- 88-1	.429	6	35
1932	Burt Shotton	78- 76-0	.506	4	12
1933	Burt Shotton	60- 92-0	.395	7	31
1934	Jimmy Wilson	56- 93-0	.376	7	37
1935	Jimmy Wilson	64- 89-3	.420	7	35½
1936	Jimmy Wilson	54-100-0	.351	8	38
1937	Jimmy Wilson	61- 92-2	.400	7	34½
1938	Jimmy Wilson	45-103-1	.305	8	NA
	Hans Lobert	0- 2-0	.000	—	—
	Total	45-105-1	.301	8	43
1939	Doc Prothro	45-106-1	.299	8	50½
1940	Doc Prothro	50-103-0	.327	8	50
1941	Doc Prothro	43-111-1	.281	8	57
1942	Hans Lobert	42-109-0	.278	8	62½
1943	Bucky Harris	40- 53-2	.432	5	NA
	Fred Fitzsimmons	24- 37-1	.395	—	—
	Total	64- 90-3	.417	7	41
1944	Fred Fitzsimmons	61- 92-1	.399	8	43½
1945	Fred Fitzsimmons	17- 50-0	.254	8	NA
	Ben Chapman	29- 58-0	.333	—	—
	Total	46-108-0	.299	8	52
1946	Ben Chapman	69- 85-1	.448	5	28
1947	Ben Chapman	62- 92-1	.403	7	32
1948	Ben Chapman	37- 42-1	.469	7	NA
	Dusty Cooke	6- 6-1	.500	6	NA
	Eddie Sawyer	23- 40-0	.365	—	—
	Total	66- 88-1	.429	6	25½

YEAR-BY-YEAR RECORDS

Season	Manager	W- L-T	Pct.	Pos.	GB
1949	Eddie Sawyer	81- 73-0	.526	3	16
1950	Eddie Sawyer	91- 63-3	.589	1	—
1951	Eddie Sawyer	73- 81-0	.474	5	23½
1952	Eddie Sawyer	28- 35-0	.444	6	NA
	Steve O'Neill	59- 32-0	.648	—	—
	Total	87- 67-0	.565	4	9½
1953	Steve O'Neill	83- 71-2	.538	3	22
1954	Steve O'Neill	40- 37-0	.519	3	NA
	Terry Moore	35- 42-0	.455	—	—
	Total	75- 79-0	.487	4	22
1955	Mayo Smith	77- 77-0	.500	4	21½
1956	Mayo Smith	71- 83-0	.461	5	22
1957	Mayo Smith	77- 77-2	.500	5	19
1958	Mayo Smith	39- 44-0	.470	7	NA
	Eddie Sawyer	30- 41-0	.423	—	—
	Total	69- 85-0	.448	8	23

Season	Manager	W- L-T	Pct.	Pos.	GB
1959	Eddie Sawyer	64- 90-1	.416	8	23
1960	Eddie Sawyer	0- 1-0	.000	6	NA
	Andy Cohen	1- 0-0	1.000	4	NA
	Gene Mauch	58- 94-0	.382	—	—
	Total	59- 95-0	.383	8	36
1961	Gene Mauch	47-107-1	.307	8	46
1962	Gene Mauch	81- 80-0	.503	7	20
1963	Gene Mauch	87- 75-0	.537	4	12
1964	Gene Mauch	92- 70-0	.568	2	1
1965	Gene Mauch	85- 76-1	.528	6	11½
1966	Gene Mauch	87- 75-0	.537	4	8
1967	Gene Mauch	82- 80-0	.506	5	19½
1968	Gene Mauch	26- 27-0	.491	4	NA
	George Myatt	2- 0-0	1.000	5	NA
	Bob Skinner	48- 59-0	.449	—	—
	Total	76- 86-0	.469	7	21
1969	Bob Skinner	44- 64-0	.407	5	24½
	George Myatt	19- 35-0	.352	—	—
	Total	63- 99-0	.389	5	37
1970	Frank Lucchesi	73- 88-0	.453	5	15½
1971	Frank Lucchesi	67- 95-0	.414	6	30
1972	Frank Lucchesi	26- 50-0	.342	6	21½
	Paul Owens	33- 47-0	.413	—	—
	Total	59- 97-0	.378	6	37½
1973	Danny Ozark	71- 91-0	.438	6	11½
1974	Danny Ozark	80- 82-0	.494	3	8
1975	Danny Ozark	86- 76-0	.531	2	6½
1976	Danny Ozark	101- 61-0	.623	1	—
1977	Danny Ozark	101- 61-0	.623	1	—
1978	Danny Ozark	90- 72-0	.556	1	—
1979	Danny Ozark	65- 67-1	.493	5	13
	Dallas Green	19- 11-0	.633	—	—
	Total	84- 78-1	.518	4	14
1980	Dallas Green	91- 71-0	.562	1	—
1981	Dallas Green (1st Half)	34- 21-0	.618	1	—
	(2nd Half)	25- 27-0	.481	3	4½
	Total	59- 48-0	.551	—	—
1982	Pat Corrales	89- 73-0	.549	2	3
1983	Pat Corrales	43- 42-1	.506	1	—
	Paul Owens	47- 30-0	.610	—	—
	Total	90- 72-1	.555	1	—
1984	Paul Owens	81- 81-0	.500	4	15½
1985	John Felske	75- 87-0	.463	5	26
1986	John Felske	86- 75-0	.534	2	21½
1987	John Felske	29- 32-0	.475	5	9½
	Lee Elia	51- 50-0	.505	—	—
	Total	80- 82-0	.494	4	15
1988	Lee Elia	60- 92-1	.396	6	34½
	John Vukovich	5- 4-0	.556	—	—
	Total	65- 96-1	.404	6	35½

Danny Ozark: 1973-79

MANAGERS' RECORDS

Dallas Green addresses Phils during 1980 spring training

Seasons	Manager	W- L- T	Pct.
1883	Bob Ferguson	4- 13- 0	.235
1883	Bill Purcell	13- 68- 1	.165
1884-93	Harry Wright	678-589-25	.534
1894-95	Arthur Irwin	149-110- 4	.574
1896	Billy Nash	62- 68- 1	.477
1897-98	George Stallings	74-104- 2	.417
1898-02	Bill Shettsline	367-303- 7	.547
1903	Chief Zimmer	49- 86- 4	.367
1904-06	Hugh Duffy	206-251- 7	.452
1907-09	Bill Murray	240-214- 4	.528
1910-14	Red Dooin	392-370-13	.514
1915-18	Pat Moran	323-257- 6	.556
1919	Jack Coombs	18- 44- 0	.290
1919-20	Gavvy Cravath	91-137- 1	.400
1921	Bill Donovan	31- 71- 0	.304
1921-22	Kaiser Wilhelm	77-128- 1	.376
1923-26	Art Fletcher	231-378- 3	.380
1927	Stuffy McInnis	51-103- 1	.332
1928-33	Burt Shotton	370-549- 4	.403
1934-38	Jimmy Wilson	280-477- 6	.371
1938	Hans Lobert	0- 2- 0	.000
1942	Hans Lobert	42-109- 0	.278
	Totals	42-111- 0	.275
1939-41	Doc Prothro	138-320- 2	.302
1943	Bucky Harris	40- 53- 2	.432
1943-45	Fred Fitzsimmons	102-179- 2	.364
1945-48	Ben Chapman	197-277- 2	.416
1948	Dusty Cooke	6- 6- 1	.500
1948-52	Eddie Sawyer	296-292- 3	.503
1958-60	Eddie Sawyer	94-132- 1	.416
	Totals	390-424- 4	.479
1952-54	Steve O'Neill	182-140- 2	.565
1954	Terry Moore	35- 42- 0	.455
1955-58	Mayo Smith	264-281- 2	.484
1960	Andy Cohen	1- 0- 0	1.000
1960-68	Gene Mauch	645-684- 2	.485
1968	George Myatt	2- 0- 0	1.000
1969	George Myatt	19- 35- 0	.352
	Totals	21- 35- 0	.375
1968-69	Bob Skinner	92-123- 0	.428
1970-72	Frank Lucchesi	166-233- 0	.416
1972	Paul Owens	33- 47- 0	.413
1983-84	Paul Owens	128-111- 0	.536
	Totals	161-158- 0	.505
1973-79	Danny Ozark	594-510- 1	.538
1979-81	Dallas Green	169-130- 0	.565
1982-83	Pat Corrales	132-115- 1	.534
1985-87	John Felske	190-194- 0	.495
1987-88	Lee Elia	111-142- 1	.439
1988	John Vukovich	5- 4- 0	.556

Manager Paul Owens plants a kiss on pitcher Charles Hudson after Game 3 victory in 1983 NL Championship Series

POSTSEASON RESULTS

(Home team in CAPS)

1915

WORLD SERIES
Boston 4, Philadelphia 1
10/ 8: PHILLIES 3, Boston 1
10/ 9: Boston 2, PHILLIES 1
10/11: BOSTON 2, Phillies 1
10/12: BOSTON 2, Phillies 1
10/13: Boston 5, PHILLIES 4

1950

WORLD SERIES
New York 4, Phillies 0
10/ 4: New York 1, PHILLIES 0
10/ 5: New York 2, PHILLIES 1
10/ 6: NEW YORK 3, Phillies 2
10/ 7: NEW YORK 5, Phillies 2

1976

NATIONAL LEAGUE CHAMPIONSHIP SERIES
Cincinnati 3, Phillies 0
10/ 9: Cincinnati 6, PHILLIES 3
10/10: Cincinnati 6, PHILLIES 2
10/12: CINCINNATI 7, Phillies 6

1977

NATIONAL LEAGUE CHAMPIONSHIP SERIES
Los Angeles 3, Phillies 1
10/ 4: Phillies 7, LOS ANGELES 5
10/ 5: LOS ANGELES 7, Phillies 1
10/ 7: Los Angeles 6, PHILLIES 5
10/ 8: Los Angeles 4, PHILLIES 1

1978

NATIONAL LEAGUE CHAMPIONSHIP SERIES
Los Angeles 3, Phillies 1
10/ 4: Los Angeles 9, PHILLIES 5
10/ 5: Los Angeles 4, PHILLIES 0
10/ 6: Phillies 9, LOS ANGELES 4
10/ 7: LOS ANGELES 4, Phillies 3 (10 inn.)

1980

NATIONAL LEAGUE CHAMPIONSHIP SERIES
Phillies 3, Houston 2
10/ 7: PHILLIES 3, Houston 1
10/ 8: Houston 7, PHILLIES 4 (10 inn.)
10/10: HOUSTON 1, Phillies 0 (11 inn.)
10/11: Phillies 5, HOUSTON 3 (10 inn.)
10/12: Phillies 8, HOUSTON 7 (10 inn.)
WORLD SERIES
Phillies 4, Kansas City 2
10/14: PHILLIES 7, Kansas City 6
10/15: PHILLIES 6, Kansas City 4
10/17: KANSAS CITY 4, Phillies 3 (10 inn.)
10/18: KANSAS CITY 5, Phillies 3
10/19: Phillies 4, KANSAS CITY 3
10/21: PHILLIES 4, Kansas City 1

1981

NATIONAL LEAGUE EAST DIVISION SERIES
Montreal 3, Phillies 2
10/ 7: MONTREAL 3, Phillies 1
10/ 8: MONTREAL 3, Phillies 1
10/ 9: PHILLIES 6, Montreal 2
10/10: PHILLIES 6, Montreal 5
10/11: Montreal 3, PHILLIES 0

1983

NATIONAL LEAGUE CHAMPIONSHIP SERIES
Phillies 3, Los Angeles 1
10/ 4: Phillies 1, LOS ANGELES 0
10/ 5: LOS ANGELES 4, Phillies 1
10/ 7: PHILLIES 7, Los Angeles 2
10/ 8: PHILLIES 7, Los Angeles 2
WORLD SERIES
Baltimore 4, Phillies 1
10/11: Phillies 2, BALTIMORE 1
10/12: BALTIMORE 4, Phillies 1
10/14: Baltimore 3, PHILLIES 2
10/15: Baltimore 5, PHILLIES 4
10/16: Baltimore 5, PHILLIES 0

INDIVIDUAL BATTING RECORDS

	GAME	SEASON
Games	—	163: Pete Rose, 1979
At-bats	(Nine-Inning Game) 7: Rick Schu, vs. New York, 6/11/85 Juan Samuel, vs. New York, 6/11/85	701: Juan Samuel, 1984
Runs	5: Silent John Titus, vs. Pittsburgh, 6/4/12 Denny Sothern, vs. Cincinnati, 6/6/30 Lou Chiozza, vs. New York, 4/19/35 Don Demeter, at Los Angeles, 9/21/61	196: Billy Hamilton, 1894 158: Chuck Klein, 1930
Hits	6: Connie Ryan, at Pittsburgh, 4/16/53	254: Lefty O'Doul, 1929
Singles	5: Mel Clark, at Chicago (2nd), 8/24/52 Cookie Rojas, at Cincinnati, 6/16/66 Richie Hebner, at Cincinnati, 7/30/78 Lonnie Smith, vs. Houston, 7/14/80 Bake McBride, vs. Houston, 7/29/80 Bob Dernier, at Atlanta, 7/21/83	181: Lefty O'Doul, 1929 Richie Ashburn, 1951
Doubles	4: Sherry Magee, vs. St. Louis, 6/17/14 Gavvy Cravath, at Cincinnati, 8/8/15 Gavvy Cravath, vs. Boston, 6/23/19 Denny Sothern, vs. Cincinnati, 6/6/30 Dick Bartell, vs. Boston, 4/25/33 Willie Jones, at Boston, 4/20/49	59: Chuck Klein, 1930
Triples	3: Harry Wolverton, at Pittsburgh, 7/13/00	26: Sam Thompson, 1894 19: Juan Samuel, 1984
Home Runs	4: Ed Delahanty, at Chicago, 7/13/96 Chuck Klein, at Pittsburgh (10 inn.), 7/10/36 Mike Schmidt, at Chicago, 4/17/76	48: Mike Schmidt, 1980
Runs Batted In	8: Kitty Bransfield, at Pittsburgh, 7/11/10 Gavvy Cravath, vs. Pittsburgh, 8/18/15 Willie Jones, at St. Louis, 8/20/58	170: Chuck Klein, 1930
Walks	5: Dick Allen, vs. San Francisco, 8/16/68	128: Mike Schmidt, 1983
Strikeouts	5: Dick Allen, at St. Louis (1st), 6/28/64 Sherry Magee, vs. New York, 8/31/06	180: Mike Schmidt, 1975
Batting Avg.	—	.408: Ed Delahanty, 1899 .398: Lefty O'Doul, 1929

MISCELLANEOUS

HITTING FOR THE CYCLE

Lave Cross, at Brooklyn, 4/24/94
Sam Thompson, vs. Louisville, 8/17/94
Cy Williams, at Pittsburgh, 8/5/27
Chuck Klein, vs. Chicago, 7/1/31
Chuck Klein, at St. Louis, 5/26/33
Johnny Callison, at Pittsburgh, 6/27/63

LONGEST HITTING STREAKS

36: Billy Hamilton, 1894
31: Ed Delahanty, 1899
26: Chuck Klein, 1930 (twice)
24: Willie Montanez, 1974
23: Goldie Rapp, 1921
    Johnny Moore, 1934
    Richie Ashburn, 1948
    Pete Rose, 1979
    Lonnie Smith, 1981
22: Chuck Klein, 1931
    Chick Fullis, 1933
21: Danny Litwhiler, 1940
    Pete Rose, 1982
20: Chuck Klein, 1932
    Richie Ashburn, 1951
    Pancho Herrera, 1960
    Garry Maddox, 1978
19: Gavvy Cravath, 1917
    Del Ennis, 1947

Juan Samuel slides in safely with a triple

Kent Tekulve set a team record by appearing in 90 games for the Phillies in 1987

INDIVIDUAL PITCHING RECORDS

	GAME	SEASON
Innings Pitched	20: Tully Sparks, vs. Chicago, 8/24/05 Joe Oeschger, vs. Brooklyn, 4/30/19	3,740: Robin Roberts, 1948-61
Hits	Not Available	3,661: Robin Roberts, 1948-61
Runs	NA	1,501: Robin Roberts, 1948-61
Earned Runs	NA	1,437: Robin Roberts, 1948-61
Home Runs	6: Wayman Kerksieck, at New York (1st), 8/13/39	NA
Walks	12: Fred Mitchell, vs. Brooklyn, 7/27/03 Curt Simmons, vs. St. Louis, 9/6/48	1,252: Steve Carlton, 1972-86
Strikeouts	18: Chris Short, at New York (2nd, 15 inn.), 10/2/65 17: Art Mahaffey, vs. Chicago (2nd, 9 inn.), 4/23/61	3,030: Steve Carlton, 1972-86

	SEASON
Innings Pitched	389: Grover Alexander, 1916
Hits	348: Claude Passeau, 1937
Runs	175: Ray Benge, 1930
Earned Runs	147: Robin Roberts, 1956
Home Runs	46: Robin Roberts, 1956
Walks	164: Earl Moore, 1911
Strikeouts	310: Steve Carlton, 1972
Wins	33: Grover Alexander, 1916 (33-12)
Losses	24: Chick Fraser, 1904 (14-24)
Saves	40: Steve Bedrosian, 1987
Games	90: Kent Tekulve, 1987
Games Started	45: Grover Alexander, 1916
Complete Games	38: Grover Alexander, 1916
Shutouts	16: Grover Alexander, 1916
Earned Run Avg.	1.22: Grover Alexander, 1915
Winning Pct.	.800: Robin Roberts, 1952 (28-7)

MISCELLANEOUS

NO-HITTERS

Charles Ferguson
    vs. Providence, Aug. 29, 1885
Red Donahue
    vs. Boston, July 8, 1898
Chick Fraser
    at Chicago, Sept. 18, 1903
John Lush
    at Brooklyn, May 1, 1906
Jim Bunning
    at New York, June 21, 1964
Rick Wise
    at Cincinnati, June 23, 1971

LONGEST WINNING STREAKS

15: Steve Carlton, 1972
12: Charles Ferguson, 1886
10: Charles Pittinger, 1905
    Earl Moore, 1910
    Grover Alexander, 1913
 9: Tully Sparks, 1907
    Grover Alexander, 1915
    Ken Heintzelman, 1949
    Robin Roberts, 1952

YEAR-BY-YEAR BATTING LEADERS

	BATTING AVG. (Minimum: 300 AB)		HOME RUNS		RUNS BATTED IN	
1883	Emil Gross	.307	Four tied	1	Not Available	
1884	Jack Manning	.271	Jack Manning	5	N/A	
1885	Charlie Ferguson	.306	Joe Mulvey	6	N/A	
1886	Jim Fogarty	.293	Sid Farrar	5	Joe Mulvey	53
1887	Ed Andrews	.325	George Wood	14	Charlie Ferguson	85
1888	Ben Sanders	.246	George Wood	6	Sid Farrar	53
1889	Sam Thompson	.296	Sam Thompson	20	Sam Thompson	111
1890	Billy Hamilton	.325	Jack Clements	7	Sam Thompson	102
1891	Billy Hamilton	.340	Sam Thompson	8	Sam Thompson	90
1892	Billy Hamilton	.330	Roger Connor	12	Sam Thompson	104
1893	Billy Hamilton	.380	Ed Delahanty	19	Ed Delahanty	146
1894	Tuck Turner	.416	Sam Thompson	13	Sam Thompson	141
1895	Ed Delahanty	.399	Sam Thompson	18	Sam Thompson	165
1896	Ed Delahanty	.397	Ed Delahanty	13	Ed Delahanty	126
1897	Ed Delahanty	.377	Nap Lajoie	10	Nap Lajoie	127
1898	Ed Delahanty	.334	Elmer Flick	7	Nap Lajoie	127
1899	Ed Delahanty	.408	Ed Delahanty	9	Ed Delahanty	137
1900	Elmer Flick	.378	Elmer Flick	11	Elmer Flick	110
1901	Ed Delahanty	.357	Ed Delahanty Elmer Flick	8 8	Ed Delahanty	108
1902	Shad Barry	.287	Shad Barry	3	Shad Barry	57
1903	Roy Thomas	.327	Bill Keister	3	Bill Keister	63
1904	Silent John Titus	.294	Red Dooin	6	Sherry Magee	57
1905	Roy Thomas	.317	Sherry Magee	5	Sherry Magee	98
1906	Sherry Magee	.282	Sherry Magee	6	Sherry Magee	67
1907	Sherry Magee	.328	Sherry Magee	4	Sherry Magee	85
1908	Kitty Bransfield	.304	Kitty Bransfield	3	Kitty Bransfield	71
1909	John Bates	.293	Silent John Titus	3	Sherry Magee	66
1910	Sherry Magee	.331	Sherry Magee	6	Sherry Magee	123
1911	Red Dooin	.328	Fred Luderus	16	Fred Luderus	99
1912	Hans Lobert	.327	Gavvy Cravath	11	Sherry Magee	72
1913	Gavvy Cravath	.341	Gavvy Cravath	19	Gavvy Cravath	128
1914	Beals Becker	.325	Gavvy Cravath	19	Sherry Magee	103
1915	Fred Luderus	.315	Gavvy Cravath	24	Gavvy Cravath	115
1916	Gavvy Cravath	.283	Gavvy Cravath	11	Gavvy Cravath	70
1917	Gavvy Cravath George Whitted	.280 .280	Gavvy Cravath	12	Gavvy Cravath	83
1918	Fred Luderus	.288	Gavvy Cravath	8	Irish Meusel	62
1919	Gavvy Cravath	.341	Gavvy Cravath	12	Irish Meusel	59
1920	Cy Williams	.325	Cy Williams	15	Cy Williams	72
1921	Irish Meusel	.353	Cy Williams	18	Cy Williams	75
1922	Curt Walker	.337	Cy Williams	26	Cy Williams	92
1923	Butch Henline	.324	Cy Williams	41	Cy Williams	114
1924	Cy Williams	.328	Cy Williams	24	Cy Williams	93
1925	George Harper	.349	George Harper	18	George Harper	97
1926	Cy Williams	.345	Cy Williams	18	Fred Leach	71

20

YEAR-BY-YEAR BATTING LEADERS

	BATTING AVG.		HOME RUNS		RUNS BATTED IN	
1927	Russ Wrightstone Fred Leach	.306 .306	Cy Williams	30	Cy Williams	98
1928	Fred Leach	.304	Don Hurst	19	Pinky Whitney	103
1929	Lefty O'Doul	.398	Chuck Klein	43	Chuck Klein	145
1930	Chuck Klein	.386	Chuck Klein	40	Chuck Klein	170
1931	Chuck Klein	.337	Chuck Klein	31	Chuck Klein	121
1932	Chuck Klein	.348	Chuck Klein	38	Don Hurst	143
1933	Chuck Klein	.368	Chuck Klein	28	Chuck Klein	120
1934	Johnny Moore	.343	Dolf Camilli	12	Johnny Moore	93
1935	Johnny Moore	.323	Dolf Camilli	25	Johnny Moore	93
1936	Johnny Moore	.328	Dolf Camilli	28	Dolf Camilli	102
1937	Pinky Whitney	.341	Dolf Camilli	27	Dolf Camilli	80
1938	Phil Weintraub	.311	Chuck Klein	8	Morrie Arnovich	72
1939	Morrie Arnovich	.324	Joe Marty Emmett Mueller	9 9	Morrie Arnovich	67
1940	Pinky May	.293	Johnny Rizzo	20	Johnny Rizzo	53
1941	Nick Etten	.311	Danny Litwhiler	18	Nick Etten	79
1942	Danny Litwhiler	.271	Danny Litwhiler	9	Danny Litwhiler	56
1943	Babe Dahlgren	.287	Ron Northey	16	Ron Northey	68
1944	Ron Northey	.288	Ron Northey	22	Ron Northey	104
1945	Jimmy Wasdell	.300	Vince DiMaggio	19	Vince DiMaggio	84
1946	Del Ennis	.313	Del Ennis	17	Del Ennis	73
1947	Harry Walker	.371	Andy Seminick	13	Del Ennis	81
1948	Richie Ashburn	.333	Del Ennis	30	Del Ennis	95
1949	Eddie Waitkus	.306	Del Ennis	25	Del Ennis	110
1950	Del Ennis	.311	Del Ennis	31	Del Ennis	126
1951	Richie Ashburn	.344	Willie Jones	22	Willie Jones	81
1952	Smoky Burgess	.296	Del Ennis	20	Del Ennis	107
1953	Richie Ashburn	.330	Del Ennis	29	Del Ennis	125
1954	Smoky Burgess	.368	Del Ennis	25	Del Ennis	119
1955	Richie Ashburn	.338	Del Ennis	29	Del Ennis	120
1956	Richie Ashburn	.303	Stan Lopata	32	Del Ennis Stan Lopata	95 95
1957	Richie Ashburn	.297	Rip Repulski	20	Ed Bouchee	76
1958	Richie Ashburn	.350	Harry Anderson	23	Harry Anderson	97
1959	Dave Philley	.291	Gene Freese	23	Wally Post	94
1960	Tony Gonzalez	.299	Pancho Herrera	17	Pancho Herrera	71
1961	Lee Walls	.280	Don Demeter	20	Don Demeter	68
1962	Don Demeter	.307	Don Demeter	29	Don Demeter	107
1963	Tony Gonzalez	.306	Johnny Callison	26	Don Demeter	83
1964	Dick Allen	.318	Johnny Callison	31	Johnny Callison	104
1965	Cookie Rojas	.303	Johnny Callison	32	Johnny Callison	101
1966	Dick Allen	.317	Dick Allen	40	Dick Allen	110
1967	Tony Gonzalez	.339	Dick Allen	23	Dick Allen	77
1968	Tony Gonzalez	.264	Dick Allen	33	Dick Allen	90
1969	Dick Allen	.288	Dick Allen	32	Dick Allen	89

Dick Allen (left) and Greg Luzinski each led the Phils in homers, runs batted in and batting average in the same season

Garry Maddox led the Phillies in batting average twice, seven years apart: .330 in 1976 and .275 in 1983

YEAR-BY-YEAR BATTING LEADERS

	BATTING AVG.		HOME RUNS		RUNS BATTED IN	
1970	Tony Taylor	.301	Deron Johnson	27	Deron Johnson	93
1971	Tim McCarver	.278	Deron Johnson	34	Willie Montanez	99
1972	Greg Luzinski	.281	Greg Luzinski	18	Greg Luzinski	68
1973	Del Unser	.289	Greg Luzinski	29	Greg Luzinski	97
1974	Willie Montanez	.304	Mike Schmidt	36	Mike Schmidt	116
1975	Dave Cash Larry Bowa	.305 .305	Mike Schmidt	38	Greg Luzinski	120
1976	Garry Maddox	.330	Mike Schmidt	38	Mike Schmidt	107
1977	Greg Luzinski	.309	Greg Luzinski	39	Greg Luzinski	130
1978	Larry Bowa	.294	Greg Luzinski	35	Greg Luzinski	101
1979	Pete Rose	.331	Mike Schmidt	45	Mike Schmidt	114
1980	Bake McBride	.309	Mike Schmidt	48	Mike Schmidt	121
1981	Pete Rose	.325	Mike Schmidt	31	Mike Schmidt	91
1982	Bo Diaz	.288	Mike Schmidt	35	Mike Schmidt	87
1983	Garry Maddox	.275	Mike Schmidt	40	Mike Schmidt	109
1984	Von Hayes	.292	Mike Schmidt	36	Mike Schmidt	106
1985	Mike Schmidt	.277	Mike Schmidt	33	Glenn Wilson	102
1986	Von Hayes	.305	Mike Schmidt	37	Mike Schmidt	119
1987	Milt Thompson	.302	Mike Schmidt	35	Mike Schmidt	113
1988	Milt Thompson	.288	Chris James	19	Juan Samuel	67

YEAR-BY-YEAR PITCHING LEADERS

	WINS		EARNED RUN AVG. (Minimum: 100 IP)		STRIKEOUTS	
1883	John Coleman	12-48	John Coleman	4.87	John Coleman	159
1884	Charles Ferguson	21-24	Bill Vinton	2.23	Charles Ferguson	194
1885	Ed Daily Charles Ferguson	26-22 26-19	Ed Daily Charles Ferguson	2.21 2.22	Ed Daily	140
1886	Charles Ferguson	32- 9	Charles Ferguson	1.98	Charles Ferguson	212
1887	Dan Casey	28-13	Dan Casey	2.86	Charlie Buffinton	160
1888	Charlie Buffinton	28-17	Ben Sanders	1.90	Charlie Buffinton	199
1889	Charlie Buffinton	26-17	Charlie Buffinton	3.24	Charlie Buffinton	153
1890	Kid Gleason	38-16	Kid Gleason	2.63	Kid Gleason	222
1891	Kid Gleason	24-19	Kid Gleason	3.51	Duke Esper	108
1892	Gus Weyhing	28-18	Tim Keefe	2.36	Gus Weyhing	202
1893	Gus Weyhing	24-16	Jack Taylor	4.24	Gus Weyhing	101
1894	Jack Taylor	22-11	Jack Taylor	4.08	Gus Weyhing	81
1895	Jack Taylor	26-13	Al Orth	3.89	Jack Taylor	93
1896	Jack Taylor	21-20	Al Orth	4.41	Jack Taylor	97
1897	Jack Taylor	16-20	George Wheeler	3.96	Jack Taylor	88
1898	Wiley Piatt	24-14	Al Orth	3.02	Wiley Piatt	121
1899	Wiley Piatt	23-15	Al Orth	2.49	Wiley Piatt	89
1900	Chick Fraser	16-10	Chick Fraser	3.14	Al Orth	68
1901	Al Orth Red Donahue	20-12 20-13	Al Orth	2.27	Bill Duggleby	94
1902	Doc White	16-20	Doc White	2.53	Doc White	185
1903	Bill Duggleby	13-18	Tully Sparks	2.72	Chick Fraser	104
1904	Chick Fraser	14-24	Frank Corridon	2.19	Chick Fraser	127
1905	Charles Pittinger	23-14	Tully Sparks	2.18	Charles Pittinger	136
1906	Tully Sparks	19-16	Tully Sparks	2.16	Johnny Lush	151
1907	Tully Sparks	22- 8	Lewis Richie	1.77	Frank Corridon	131
1908	George McQuillan	23-17	George McQuillan	1.53	George McQuillan	114
1909	Earl Moore	18-12	Earl Moore	2.10	Earl Moore	173
1910	Earl Moore	22-15	George McQuillan	1.60	Earl Moore	185
1911	Grover Alexander	28-13	Grover Alexander	2.57	Grover Alexander	227
1912	Grover Alexander	19-17	Eppa Rixey	2.50	Grover Alexander	195
1913	Tom Seaton	27-12	Ad Brennan	2.39	Tom Seaton	168
1914	Grover Alexander	27-15	Grover Alexander	2.38	Grover Alexander	214
1915	Grover Alexander	31-10	Grover Alexander	1.22	Grover Alexander	241
1916	Grover Alexander	33-12	Grover Alexander	1.55	Grover Alexander	167
1917	Grover Alexander	30-13	Chief Bender	1.67	Grover Alexander	201
1918	Mike Prendergast Brad Hogg	13-14 13-13	Elmer Jacobs	2.41	Brad Hogg	81
1919	Lee Meadows	8-10	Lee Meadows	2.47	Lee Meadows	88
1920	Lee Meadows	16-14	Lee Meadows	2.84	Eppa Rixey	109
1921	Lee Meadows	11-16	Jesse Winters	3.63	Jim Ring	88
1922	Lee Meadows Jim Ring	12-18 12-18	Phil Weinert	3.40	Jim Ring	116
1923	Jim Ring	18-16	Jim Ring	3.76	Jim Ring	112
1924	Jim Ring Bill Hubbell	10-12 10- 9	Jim Ring	3.97	Jim Ring	72

YEAR-BY-YEAR PITCHING LEADERS

	WINS		EARNED RUN AVG.		STRIKEOUTS	
1925	Jim Ring	14-16	Hal Carlson	4.23	Jim Ring	93
1926	Hal Carlson	17-12	Hal Carlson	3.23	Hal Carlson	55
1927	Jack Scott	9-21	Dutch Ulrich	3.17	Hub Pruett	90
1928	Ray Benge	8-18	Ray Benge	4.55	Jim Ring	72
1929	Claude Willoughby	15-14	Claude Willoughby	4.99	Ray Benge	78
1930	Phil Collins	16-11	Phil Collins	4.78	Phil Collins	87
1931	Jumbo Elliott	19-14	Ray Benge	3.17	Ray Benge	117
1932	Phil Collins	14-12	Snipe Hansen	3.72	Ray Benge	89
1933	Ed Holley	13-15	Ed Holley	3.53	Ed Holley	56
1934	Curt Davis	19-17	Curt Davis	2.95	Curt Davis	99
1935	Curt Davis	16-14	Syl Johnson	3.56	Syl Johnson	89
1936	Bucky Walters Claude Passeau	11-21 11-15	Claude Passeau	3.48	Claude Passeau	85
1937	Wayne LaMaster	15-19	Claude Passeau	4.34	Wayne LaMaster Claude Passeau	135 135
1938	Claude Passeau	11-18	Al Hollingsworth	3.82	Claude Passeau	100
1939	Kirby Higbe	10-14	Syl Johnson	3.81	Kirby Higbe	95
1940	Kirby Higbe	14-19	Hugh Mulcahy	3.60	Kirby Higbe	137
1941	John Podgajny Tom Hughes	9-12 9-14	Ike Pearson	3.57	Si Johnson	80
1942	Tom Hughes	12-18	Tom Hughes	3.06	Rube Melton	107
1943	Schoolboy Rowe	14- 8	Dick Barrett	2.39	Al Gerheauser	92
1944	Ken Raffensberger Charley Schanz	13-20 13-16	Ken Raffensberger	3.06	Ken Raffensberger	136
1945	Andy Karl	9- 8	Andy Karl	2.99	Dick Barret	72
1946	Schoolboy Rowe Oscar Judd	11- 4 11-12	Schoolboy Rowe	2.12	Ken Raffensberger	73
1947	Dutch Leonard	17-12	Dutch Leonard	2.68	Dutch Leonard	103
1948	Dutch Leonard	12-17	Dutch Leonard	2.51	Dutch Leonard	92
1949	Ken Heintzelman	17-10	Ken Heintzelman	3.02	Robin Roberts	95
1950	Robin Roberts	20-11	Jim Konstanty	2.66	Robin Roberts Curt Simmons	146 146
1951	Robin Roberts	21-15	Robin Roberts	3.03	Robin Roberts	127
1952	Robin Roberts	28- 7	Robin Roberts	2.59	Robin Roberts	148
1953	Robin Roberts	23-16	Robin Roberts	2.75	Robin Roberts	198
1954	Robin Roberts	23-15	Curt Simmons	2.81	Robin Roberts	185
1955	Robin Roberts	23-14	Robin Roberts	3.28	Robin Roberts	160
1956	Robin Roberts	19-18	Bob Miller	3.24	Robin Roberts	157
1957	Jack Sanford	19- 8	Jack Sanford	3.08	Jack Sanford	188
1958	Robin Roberts	17-14	Robin Roberts	3.24	Robin Roberts	130
1959	Robin Roberts	15-17	Gene Conley	3.00	Robin Roberts	137
1960	Robin Roberts	12-16	Dick Farrell	2.70	Robin Roberts	122
1961	Art Mahaffey	11-19	Don Ferrarese	3.76	Art Mahaffey	158
1962	Art Mahaffey	19-14	Chris Short	3.42	Art Mahaffey	177
1963	Ray Culp	14-11	John Klippstein	1.93	Ray Culp	176
1964	Jim Bunning	19- 8	Chris Short	2.20	Jim Bunning	219
1965	Jim Bunning	19- 9	Jim Bunning	2.60	Jim Bunning	268
1966	Chris Short	20-10	Jim Bunning	2.41	Jim Bunning	252

Jim Lonborg's 17 wins and 3.21 earned run average led the Phillies in 1974

Rick Wise led the Phillies in victories three straight years. He was 15-13 in 1969, 13-14 in '70 and 17-14 in '71.

YEAR-BY-YEAR PITCHING LEADERS

	WINS		EARNED RUN AVG.		STRIKEOUTS	
1967	Jim Bunning	17-15	Jim Bunning	2.29	Jim Bunning	253
1968	Chris Short	19-13	Larry Jackson	2.77	Chris Short	202
1969	Rick Wise	15-13	Rick Wise	3.23	Grant Jackson	180
1970	Rick Wise	13-14	Dick Selma	2.75	Dick Selma	153
1971	Rick Wise	17-14	Rick Wise	2.88	Rick Wise	155
1972	Steve Carlton	27-10	Steve Carlton	1.98	Steve Carlton	310
1973	Wayne Twitchell Ken Brett Jim Lonborg Steve Carlton	13- 9 13- 9 13-16 13-20	Wayne Twitchell	2.50	Steve Carlton	223
1974	Jim Lonborg	17-13	Jim Lonborg	3.21	Steve Carlton	240
1975	Steve Carlton	15-14	Tug McGraw	2.97	Steve Carlton	192
1976	Steve Carlton	20- 7	Ron Reed	2.46	Steve Carlton	195
1977	Steve Carlton	23-10	Gene Garber	2.36	Steve Carlton	198
1978	Steve Carlton	16-13	Ron Reed	2.23	Steve Carlton	161
1979	Steve Carlton	18-11	Steve Carlton	3.62	Steve Carlton	213
1980	Steve Carlton	24- 9	Steve Carlton	2.34	Steve Carlton	286
1981	Steve Carlton	13- 4	Steve Carlton	2.42	Steve Carlton	179
1982	Steve Carlton	23-11	Steve Carlton	3.10	Steve Carlton	286
1983	John Denny	19- 6	John Denny	2.37	Steve Carlton	275
1984	Jerry Koosman	14-15	John Denny	2.45	Steve Carlton	163
1985	Kevin Gross	15-13	Shane Rawley	3.31	Kevin Gross	151
1986	Kevin Gross	12-12	Bruce Ruffin	2.46	Kevin Gross	154
1987	Shane Rawley	17-11	Kent Tekulve	3.09	Don Carman	125
1988	Kevin Gross	12-14	Greg Harris	2.36	Kevin Gross	162

CAREER BATTING LEADERS

GAMES		BATTING AVG.		HOME RUNS		RUNS BATTED IN	
Mike Schmidt	2,362	Billy Hamilton	.362	Mike Schmidt	542	Mike Schmidt	1,567
Richie Ashburn	1,794	Ed Delahanty	.348	Del Ennis	259	Ed Delahanty	1,286
Larry Bowa	1,739	Elmer Flick	.345	Chuck Klein	243	Del Ennis	1,124
Tony Taylor	1,669	Sam Thompson	.335	Greg Luzinski	223	Chuck Klein	983
Del Ennis	1,630	Chuck Klein	.326	Cy Williams	217	Sam Thompson	958
Ed Delahanty	1,544	Spud Davis	.321	Dick Allen	204	Sherry Magee	889
Sherry Magee	1,521	Fred Leach	.312	Johnny Callison	185	Greg Luzinski	811
Willie Jones	1,520	Richie Ashburn	.311	Willie Jones	180	Cy Williams	796
Granny Hamner	1,501	Pinky Whitney	.307	Andy Seminick	123	Willie Jones	753
Cy Williams	1,463	Cy Williams	.306	Gavvy Cravath	117	Pinky Whitney	734

HITS		RUNS		DOUBLES		TRIPLES	
Richie Ashburn	2,217	Mike Schmidt	1,487	Ed Delahanty	432	Ed Delahanty	151
Ed Delahanty	2,211	Ed Delahanty	1,365	Mike Schmidt	401	Sherry Magee	127
Mike Schmidt	2,204	Richie Ashburn	1,114	Sherry Magee	337	Sam Thompson	103
Del Ennis	1,812	Chuck Klein	963	Chuck Klein	336	Richie Ashburn	97
Larry Bowa	1,798	Sam Thompson	928	Del Ennis	310	Johnny Callison	84
Chuck Klein	1,705	Roy Thomas	916	Richie Ashburn	287	Larry Bowa	81
Sherry Magee	1,647	Sherry Magee	898	Granny Hamner	271	Gavvy Cravath	72
Cy Williams	1,553	Del Ennis	891	Johnny Callison	265	Juan Samuel	70
Granny Hamner	1,518	Billy Hamilton	877	Sam Thompson	258	Del Ennis	65
Tony Taylor	1,511	Cy Williams	825	Greg Luzinski	253	(Four tied)	64

SINGLES		EXTRA-BASE HITS		TOTAL BASES		WALKS	
Richie Ashburn	1,811	Mike Schmidt	1,002	Mike Schmidt	4,349	Mike Schmidt	1,486
Ed Delahanty	1,544	Ed Delahanty	667	Ed Delahanty	3,197	Richie Ashburn	946
Larry Bowa	1,498	Chuck Klein	643	Del Ennis	3,029	Roy Thomas	946
Roy Thomas	1,236	Del Ennis	634	Chuck Klein	2,898	Willie Jones	693
Mike Schmidt	1,202	Sherry Magee	539	Richie Ashburn	2,764	Ed Delahanty	643
Del Ennis	1,178	Johnny Callison	534	Cy Williams	2,557	Greg Luzinski	572
Tony Taylor	1,178	Cy Williams	503	Sherry Magee	2,463	Billy Hamilton	551
Sherry Magee	1,108	Greg Luzinski	497	Johnny Callison	2,426	Cy Williams	551
Granny Hamner	1,083	Dick Allen	472	Greg Luzinski	2,263	Sherry Magee	547
Chuck Klein	1,062	Sam Thompson	456	Willie Jones	2,236	Del Ennis	539

STOLEN BASES		SACRIFICE FLIES		AT-BATS		STRIKEOUTS	
Sherry Magee	387	Mike Schmidt	105	Mike Schmidt	8,204	Mike Schmidt	1,866
Larry Bowa	288	Greg Luzinski	53	Richie Ashburn	7,122	Greg Luzinski	1,098
Juan Samuel	238	Garry Maddox	51	Larry Bowa	6,815	Dick Allen	1,023
Richie Ashburn	199	Bob Boone	43	Ed Delahanty	6,352	Johnny Callison	854
Garry Maddox	189	Larry Bowa	36	Del Ennis	6,327	Tony Taylor	818
Mike Schmidt	174	Dick Allen	32	Tony Taylor	5,799	Juan Samuel	780
Roy Thomas	164	Willie Jones	32	Granny Hamner	5,772	Del Ennis	622
Von Hayes	149	Tony Gonzalez	29	Sherry Magee	5,505	Andy Seminick	591
Dode Paskert	149	Willie Montanez	29	Willie Jones	5,419	Tony Gonzalez	549
Tony Taylor	136	Johnny Callison	28	Johnny Callison	5,306	Gavvy Cravath	528

Steve Bedrosian passed Tug McGraw in 1988 to become the Phillies all-time leader in saves

CAREER PITCHING LEADERS

GAMES		WINS		SHUTOUTS		COMPLETE GAMES	
Robin Roberts	529	Steve Carlton	241	Grover Alexander	61	Robin Roberts	272
Steve Carlton	499	Robin Roberts	234	Steve Carlton	39	Grover Alexander	220
Tug McGraw	463	Grover Alexander	190	Robin Roberts	35	Steve Carlton	185
Chris Short	459	Chris Short	132	Chris Short	24	Tully Sparks	150
Ron Reed	458	Curt Simmons	115	Jim Bunning	23	Al Orth	149
Dick Farrell	359	Al Orth	101	Tully Sparks	18	Bill Duggleby	137
Grover Alexander	338	Tully Sparks	94	Earl Moore	18	Curt Simmons	112
Jack Baldschun	333	Bill Duggleby	91	Curt Simmons	18	Jim Ring	102
Curt Simmons	325	Jim Bunning	89	George McQuillan	17	Eppa Rixey	100
Jim Konstanty	314	Eppa Rixey	87	(Two tied)	16	Chris Short	88

SAVES		INNINGS PITCHED		STRIKEOUTS		LOSSES	
Steve Bedrosian	97	Robin Roberts	3,740	Steve Carlton	3,030	Robin Roberts	199
Tug McGraw	94	Steve Carlton	3,696	Robin Roberts	1,871	Steve Carlton	161
Ron Reed	90	Grover Alexander	2,513	Chris Short	1,585	Chris Short	127
Dick Farrell	65	Chris Short	2,252	Grover Alexander	1,409	Curt Simmons	110
Jack Baldschun	59	Curt Simmons	1,939	Jim Bunning	1,197	Eppa Rixey	103
Al Holland	55	Tully Sparks	1,691	Curt Simmons	1,052	Bill Duggleby	100
Jim Konstanty	54	Bill Duggleby	1,642	Larry Christenson	781	Jim Ring	98
Gene Garber	51	Eppa Rixey	1,604	Kevin Gross	727	Tully Sparks	95
Dick Selma	26	Jim Bunning	1,520	Rick Wise	717	Grover Alexander	91
Kent Tekulve	25	Al Orth	1,505	Dick Ruthven	717	Ray Benge	85

Steve Carlton

At first blush, Phillie fans hooted the 1972 trade that brought Steve Carlton to Philadelphia from the Cardinals for popular righthander Rick Wise.

But it took just a single, scintillating season to end any questions about Carlton and make Wise just a vague footnote to history. Eventually, after 14½ years in Phillie pinstripes, Carlton became the definition of a milestone pitcher.

His Phillie career ended with his release on June 24, 1986, and after brief stints with four other teams in '86 and '87, Carlton ended his career having amassed a pitching record of Hall of Fame proportions.

He won an unprecedented four Cy Young awards (1972, 1977, 1980 and 1982), garnered 329 career victories (putting him ninth on the all-time list), totaled 4,131 career strikeouts (ranking him second all-time behind Nolan Ryan), and collected a National League-record six one-hitters, 10 All-Star Game appearances, and six 20-win seasons.

Carlton holds the Phillies' record for most victories (241) and most strikeouts (3,031); he's No. 2 on the team list in shutouts and innings pitched.

And Carlton's 3,522nd strikeout, which came on June 7, 1983, temporarily moved him past Nolan Ryan atop baseball's all-time strikout list.

Carlton was born in Miami, Fla., on Dec. 22, 1944. He graduated from North Miami High School and attended Miami Dade South Community College.

He was signed as a free agent by the St. Louis Cardinals on Oct. 8, 1963.

He spent eight years in the St. Louis organization, compiling a major league record of 77-62, before being dealt for Wise on Feb. 25, 1972.

That season, working for a dreary team that would win just 59 games, Carlton went 27-10, earning his first Cy Young trophy.

In what might have been the greatest pitching season in modern history, Carlton posted a 1.97 ERA and a career-high, league-leading 310 strikeouts, winning 15 straight games in the process, a team record.

In the next three years, Carlton dipped back down to earth, posting a 44-47 record.

But in 1976, Carlton led the Phils to a division title with a 20-7 record. In 1977 the club won another division title, and Carlton earned his second Cy Young with a 23-10 mark.

Three years later, in the Phils' 1980 World Series championship season, Carlton was a dominant 24-9, winning his third Cy Young.

To cap his career off, in 1982, at age 37, he was the league's only 20-game winner, registering a 23-11 record. That got him his milestone fourth Cy Young award.

"Catching him was almost scary," said Tim McCarver, Carlton's longtime special catcher. "He was that good. On nights when he had his No. 1 slider, he was almost unhittable.

"Lefty pitched through hitters. He didn't even see him. It was just some guy stopping by with a bat in his hand. He was irrelevant."

Mike Schmidt

Chris James . . . Randy Ready . . . it really doesn't matter. No matter who the Phillies trot out to the position, and no matter how well any given player performs, third base in Philadelphia just won't be the same without Mike Schmidt.

Michael Jack Schmidt announced his sudden retirement from baseball on May 29, 1989. He stepped down as the greatest player in Phillies history and, in the opinion of most, as the finest third baseman in the history of the game.

"He's a great ballplayer, a tremendous ballplayer," said Hank Aaron, baseball's all-time home run leader. "I'm sure that when the time comes, he'll be voted into the Hall of Fame. I'd be ashamed if he didn't go in as a first-timer."

The folks at Cooperstown will come knocking in 1995. When they do, they will admit a ballplayer who ranks seventh on the all-time list of home runs. Schmidt's magic number was 548, which places him just above Mickey Mantle (536) and just below Reggie Jackson (563).

Schmidt also is 17th in career RBI (1,595), 15th in extra-base hits (1,015), 13th in walks (1,507) and third, behind only Brooks Robinson (2,870) and Graig Nettles (2,412), in games played at third base (2,212).

Schmidt handled third base, baseball's "hot corner," with uncommon skill. In fact, he won a National League-record 10 Gold Gloves at the position.

Schmidt was born in Dayton, Ohio, on Sept. 27, 1949. He was picked in the second round of the June 1971 draft out of Ohio University.

After brief stints at Double-A Reading (1971) and Triple-A Eu-

gene (1972) and a cup of coffee with the Phils at the end of '72, Schmidt made it to the majors for good at the start of the 1973 season. He struggled that year with a .196 average, but his troubles would not last long.

A year later, Schmidt led the National League with 36 home runs. He would win or share seven more home run titles.

Schmidt's best year came in 1980 when he hit .286 and had career-highs of 48 home runs and 121 runs batted in. Not so coincidentally, the Phillies won the only World Series title in franchise history that season.

"I longed to be a great major league ballplayer and have people want my autograph," Schmidt said the day after he announced his retirement. "But I wasn't sure I had the confidence . . . I wasn't sure I could do the things I needed to do to stay in the big leagues, to be one of the Philadelphia Phillies forever. I really wasn't sure."

Now, of course, there is no doubt about it.

EAGLES

Year	Head Coach	W- L- T	Pct.	Pos.
1933	Lud Wray	3- 5- 1	.389	4
1934	Lud Wray	4- 7- 0	.364	T3
1935	Lud Wray	2- 9- 0	.182	5
1936	Bert Bell	1-11- 0	.083	5
1937	Bert Bell	2- 8- 1	.227	5
1938	Bert Bell	5- 6- 0	.455	4
1939	Bert Bell	1- 9- 1	.136	T4
1940	Bert Bell	1-10- 0	.091	5
1941	Greasy Neale	2- 8- 1	.227	4
1942	Greasy Neale	2- 9- 0	.182	5
1943	Greasy Neale and Walt Kiesling	5- 4- 1	.550	3
1944	Greasy Neale	7- 1- 2	.800	2
1945	Greasy Neale	7- 3- 0	.700	2
1946	Greasy Neale	6- 5- 0	.545	2
1947	Greasy Neale	8- 4- 0	.667	T1
1948	Greasy Neale	9- 2- 1	.792	1
1949	Greasy Neale	11- 1- 0	.917	1
1950	Greasy Neale	6- 6- 0	.500	T3
1951	Bo McMillin	2- 0- 0	1.000	—
	Wayne Millner	2- 8- 0	.200	—
	Totals	4- 8- 0	.333	5
1952	Jim Trimble	7- 5- 0	.583	T2
1953	Jim Trimble	7- 4- 1	.625	2
1954	Jim Trimble	7- 4- 1	.625	2
1955	Jim Trimble	4- 7- 1	.375	T4
1956	Hugh Devore	3- 8- 1	.292	6
1957	Hugh Devore	4- 8- 0	.333	5
1958	Buck Shaw	2- 9- 1	.208	T5
1959	Buck Shaw	7- 5- 0	.583	T2
1960	Buck Shaw	10- 2- 0	.833	1
1961	Nick Skorich	10- 4- 0	.714	2
1962	Nick Skorich	3-10- 1	.250	7
1963	Nick Skorich	2-10- 2	.214	7
1964	Joe Kuharich	6- 8- 0	.429	T3
1965	Joe Kuharich	5- 9- 0	.357	T5
1966	Joe Kuharich	9- 5- 0	.643	T2
1967	Joe Kuharich	6- 7- 1	.464	2
1968	Joe Kuharich	2-12- 0	.143	4
1969	Jerry Williams	4- 9- 1	.321	4
1970	Jerry Williams	3-10- 1	.250	5
1971	Jerry Williams	0- 3- 0	.000	—
	Ed Khayat	6- 4- 1	.591	—
	Totals	6- 7- 1	.464	3
1972	Ed Khayat	2-11- 1	.179	5

Year	Head Coach	W- L- T	Pct.	Pos.
1973	Mike McCormack	5- 8- 1	.393	3
1974	Mike McCormack	7- 7- 0	.500	4
1975	Mike McCormack	4-10- 0	.286	5
1976	Dick Vermeil	4-10- 0	.286	4
1977	Dick Vermeil	5- 9- 0	.357	T4
1978	Dick Vermeil	9- 7- 0	.563	2
1979	Dick Vermeil	11- 5- 0	.688	T1
1980	Dick Vermeil	12- 4- 0	.750	1
1981	Dick Vermeil	10- 6- 0	.625	2
1982	Dick Vermeil	3- 6- 0	.333	5
1983	Marion Campbell	5-11- 0	.313	4
1984	Marion Campbell	6- 9- 1	.406	5
1985	Marion Campbell	6- 9- 0	.400	—
	Fred Bruney	1- 0- 0	1.000	—
	Totals	7- 9- 0	.438	4
1986	Buddy Ryan	5-10- 1	.344	4
1987	Buddy Ryan	7- 8- 0	.467	4
1988	Buddy Ryan	10- 6- 0	.625	1

POSTSEASON RESULTS
(Home team in CAPS)

1947 DIVISIONAL PLAYOFF
12/21/47: Eagles 21, PITTSBURGH 0
NFL CHAMPIONSHIP
12/28/47: CHICAGO CARDS, 28, Eagles 21

1948 NFL CHAMPIONSHIP
12/19/48: EAGLES 7, Chicago Cardinals 0

1949 NFL CHAMPIONSHIP
12/18/49: Eagles 14, LOS ANGELES 0

1960 NFL CHAMPIONSHIP
12/26/60: EAGLES 17, Green Bay 13

1961 PLAYOFF BOWL (at Miami)
1/ 6/62: Detroit 38, Eagles 10

1966 PLAYOFF BOWL (at Miami)
1/ 8/67: Baltimore 20, Eagles 14

1978 NFC WILD CARD PLAYOFF
12/24/78: ATLANTA 14, Eagles 13

1979 NFC WILD CARD PLAYOFF
12/23/79: EAGLES 27, Chicago 17
NFC DIVISIONAL PLAYOFF
12/29/79: TAMPA BAY 24, Eagles 17

1980 NFC DIVISIONAL PLAYOFF
1/ 3/81: EAGLES 31, Minnesota 16
NFC CHAMPIONSHIP
1/11/81: EAGLES 20, Dallas 7
SUPER BOWL XV (At New Orleans)
1/25/81: Oakland 27, Eagles 10

1981 NFC WILD CARD PLAYOFF
12/27/81: New York Giants 27, EAGLES 21

1988 NFC DIVISIONAL PLAYOFF
12/31/88: Chicago 20, EAGLES 12

COACHES' RECORDS

Seasons	Head Coach	W- L- T	Pct.
1933-35	Lud Wray	9-21- 1	.306
1936-40	Bert Bell	10-44- 2	.196
1941-50	Greasy Neale	66-44- 5	.596
1951	Bo McMillin	2- 0- 0	1.000
1951	Wayne Millner	2- 8- 0	.200
1952-55	Jim Trimble	25-20- 3	.552
1956-57	Hugh Devore	7-16- 1	.313
1958-60	Buck Shaw	20-16- 1	.554
1961-63	Nick Skorich	15-25- 3	.384
1964-68	Joe Kuharich	28-42- 1	.401
1969-71	Jerry Williams	7-22- 2	.258
1971-72	Ed Khayat	8-15- 2	.360
1973-75	Mike McCormack	16-25- 1	.393
1976-82	Dick Vermeil	57-51- 0	.528
1983-85	Marion Campbell	17-29- 1	.372
1985	Fred Bruney	1- 0- 0	1.000
1986-88	Buddy Ryan	22-25- 1	.469

Buddy Ryan has 22 wins in three years with Eagles

Dick Vermeil's intensity helped steer the Eagles to 57 wins and their only Super Bowl appearance on Jan. 25, 1981

BEST SINGLE-GAME PERFORMANCES

RUSHING YARDAGE

205: Steve Van Buren, vs. Pittsburgh, 11/27/49

197: Wilbert Montgomery, vs. Cleveland, 11/4/79

196: Steve Van Buren, at Los Angeles, 12/18/49

194: Wilbert Montgomery, vs. Dallas, 1/11/81

190: Swede Hanson, vs. Cincinnati, 11/6/34

186: Timmy Brown, at Cleveland, 11/7/65

180: Timmy Brown, at St. Louis, 11/28/65

174: Steve Van Buren, vs. NY Bulldogs, 11/20/49

171: Steve Van Buren, vs. Washington, 11/21/48

169: Wilbert Montgomery, at Minnesota, 9/14/80

163: Billy Barnes, vs. Washington, 11/1/59

162: Earnest Jackson, at St. Louis, 11/17/85

156: Tom Sullivan, vs. New York Giants, 11/25/73

155: Tom Sullivan, at Buffalo, 10/7/73

147: Wilbert Montgomery, vs. Houston, 12/19/82

144: Wilbert Montgomery, at Baltimore, 10/1/78

143: Steve Van Buren, at New York Giants, 11/7/48

138: Steve Van Buren, at Washington, 11/2/47

137: Steve Van Buren, vs. Boston Yanks, 11/14/48
Leroy Harris, vs. Green Bay, 11/25/79
Wilbert Montgomery, vs. New England, 9/13/81

136: Frank Ziegler, at Washington, 12/2/51

RECEIVING YARDAGE

237: Tommy McDonald, vs. New York Giants, 12/10/61

204: Pete Retzlaff, vs. Washington, 11/14/65

203: Bud Grant, vs. Dallas Texans, 12/7/52

199: Timmy Brown, at St. Louis, 12/16/62

197: Ben Hawkins, at St. Louis, 10/22/67

194: Harold Jackson, at New York Giants, 10/11/70

187: Tommy McDonald, vs. St. Louis, 10/1/61
Ben Hawkins, vs. Pittsburgh, 10/1/67
Harold Carmichael, at St. Louis, 10/14/73

186: Bud Grant, at Chicago Cardinals, 11/30/52

184: Jack Ferrante, vs. Detroit, 12/12/48

180: Don Looney, at Washington, 12/1/40

179: Tommy McDonald, vs. Pittsburgh, 9/15/63

176: Bobby Walston, vs. New York Giants, 11/8/53

174: Timmy Brown, at Minnesota, 10/28/62

170: Mike Quick, vs. St. Louis, 10/28/84

166: Jerry Williams, at Chicago Cardinals, 10/3/54

163: Jerry Williams, vs. Washington, 11/28/54

162: Tommy McDonald, at St. Louis, 12/16/62
Cris Carter, vs. NY Giants, 10/10/88

161: Harold Jackson, at Dallas, 9/17/72

160: Timmy Brown, vs. New York Giants, 9/23/62

156: Pete Pihos, at Chicago Cardinals, 10/25/53

153: Tommy McDonald (9-3), at Washington, 12/6/59

PASSING YARDAGE

437: Bobby Thomason, vs. NY Giants, 11/8/53

436: Sonny Jurgensen, at Washington, 10/29/61

419: Sonny Jurgensen, at St. Louis, 12/16/62

407: Randall Cunningham, at Chicago, 12/31/88

403: Sonny Jurgensen, at Detroit, 12/17/61

399: Sonny Jurgensen, vs. St. Louis, 10/1/61

396: Sonny Jurgensen, vs. NY Giants, 9/23/62

394: Ron Jaworski, at San Francisco, 11/3/85

380: Ron Jaworski, vs. Dallas, 10/20/85

379: Roman Gabriel, at St. Louis, 10/14/73

371: Ron Jaworski, vs. Washington, 9/12/82

369: Randall Cunningham, vs. NY Giants, 10/10/88

367: Sonny Jurgensen, vs. NY Giants, 12/10/61

362: Norm Snead, at Cleveland, 11/7/65

351: Sonny Jurgensen, vs. Dallas, 11/26/61

349: Bobby Thomason, vs. Washington, 10/1/55

345: Adrian Burk, vs. Washington, 11/28/54
Ron Jaworski, at Minnesota, 10/18/81

342: Sonny Jurgensen, vs. Dallas, 11/25/62

340: Ron Jaworski, vs. St. Louis, 10/28/84

338: Scott Tinsley, at Dallas, 10/11/87

335: Norm Snead, vs. Pittsburgh, 9/28/69

Randall Cunningham threw for 407 yards in Chicago

34

MILESTONE GAMES

100 YARDS RUSHING

Wilbert Montgomery	26
Steve Van Buren	19
Tom Woodeshick	7
Timmy Brown	6
Swede Hanson	4
Tom Sullivan	4
Earl Gros	3
Mike Hogan	3
Earnest Jackson	3
Frank Ziegler	3
Billy Barnes	2
Keith Byars	2
Jack Hinkle	2
Don Johnson	2
Bosh Pritchard	2
(11 tied with 1)	

400 YARDS PASSING

Sonny Jurgensen	3
Randall Cunningham	1
Bobby Thomason	1

300 YARDS PASSING

Ron Jaworski	12
Sonny Jurgensen	10
Norm Snead	8
Randall Cunningham	4
Bobby Thomason	4
Roman Gabriel	3
Adrian Burk	1
King Hill	1
Pete Liske	1
Davey O'Brien	1
Joe Pisarcik	1
Scott Tinsley	1
Norm Van Brocklin	1

100 YARDS RECEIVING

Pete Retzlaff	24
Harold Carmichael	20
Mike Quick	20
Tommy McDonald	17
Pete Pihos	14
Ben Hawkins	13
Harold Jackson	13
Bobby Walston	10
Timmy Brown	8
Jack Ferrante	6
Charle Young	6
Charles Smith	5
Bud Grant	4
(Two tied with 3)	
(Four tied with 2)	
(21 tied with 1)	

INDIVIDUAL RECORDS

	SINGLE GAME
Rushing Yardage	205: Steve Van Buren, vs. Pittsburgh, 11/27/49
Rushing Attempts	35: Steve Van Buren, vs. New York Bulldogs, 11/20/49
Rushing TDs	3: Swede Hansen, vs. Cincinnati Reds, 11/6/34 Steve Van Buren, vs. Boston Yanks, 12/9/45 Clarence Peaks, vs. Chicago Cardinals, 11/16/58 Tom Sullivan, vs. New York Giants, 10/13/74 Wilbert Montgomery, at Washington, 9/10/78 Wilbert Montgomery, vs. Washington, 10/7/79 Wilbert Montgomery, vs. Houston, 12/19/82
Longest Run	90: Wilbert Montgomery (TD), vs. Houston, 12/19/82
Passing Yardage	437: Bobby Thomason, vs. New York Giants, 11/8/53
Passes Attempted	60: Davey O'Brien, at Washington, 12/1/40
Passes Completed	33: Davey O'Brien, at Washington, 12/1/40 Sonny Jurgensen, vs. New York Giants, 9/23/62
Passing TDs	7: Adrian Burk, at Washington, 10/17/54
Longest Pass Play	99: Ron Jaworski to Mike Quick (TD), vs. Atlanta, 11/10/85
Interceptions	6: Bobby Thomason, vs. Chicago Cardinals, 10/21/56 Pete Liske, vs. Dallas, 9/26/71
Receiving Yardage	237: Tommy McDonald, vs. New York Giants, 12/10/61
Receptions	14: Don Looney, at Washington, 12/1/40
Receiving TDs	4: Joe Carter, vs. Cincinnati, 11/6/34 Ben Hawkins, vs. Pittsburgh, 9/28/69
Points	25: Bobby Walston, at Washington, 10/17/54
Touchdowns	4: Joe Carter, vs. Cincinnati, 11/6/34 Clarence Peaks, vs. Chicago Cardinals, 11/16/58 Tommy McDonald, vs. New York Giants, 10/4/59 Ben Hawkins, vs. Pittsburgh, 9/28/69 Wilbert Montgomery, at Washington, 9/10/78 Wilbert Montgomery, vs. Washington, 10/7/79
PATs Made	8: Cliff Patton, vs. Los Angeles Rams, 10/7/50 Bobby Walston, at Chicago Cardinals, 10/25/53
Field Goals Made	6: Tom Dempsey, at Houston, 11/12/72
Interceptions By	4: Russ Craft, at Chicago Cardinals, 9/24/50
Punts	15: John Teltschik, vs. New York Giants (ot), 12/6/87
Punt Returns	9: Larry Marshall, vs. Tampa Bay, 9/18/77
Kickoff Return Yardage	247: Timmy Brown, vs. Dallas, 11/6/66

INDIVIDUAL RECORDS

	INDIVIDUAL, SEASON	INDIVIDUAL, CAREER
Rushing Yardage	1,512: Wilbert Montgomery, 1979	6,538: Wilbert Montgomery, 1977-84
Rushing Attempts	338: Wilbert Montgomery, 1979	1,465: Wilbert Montgomery, 1977-84
Rushing TDs	15: Steve Van Buren, 1945	69: Steve Van Buren, 1944-51
Passing Yardage	3,808: Randall Cunningham, 1988	26,963: Ron Jaworski, 1977-86
Passes Attempted	560: Randall Cunningham, 1988	3,918: Ron Jaworski, 1977-86
Passes Completed	301: Randall Cunningham, 1988	2,088: Ron Jaworski, 1977-86
Passing TDs	32: Sonny Jurgensen, 1961	175: Ron Jaworski, 1977-86
Interceptions	26: Sonny Jurgensen, 1962	151: Ron Jaworski, 1977-86
Receiving Yardage	1,409: Mike Quick, 1983	8,978: Harold Carmichael, 1971-83
Receptions	81: Keith Jackson, 1988	589: Harold Carmichael, 1971-83
Receiving TDs	13: Tommy McDonald, 1960, '61 Mike Quick, 1983	79: Harold Carmichael, 1971-83
Points	116: Paul McFadden, 1984	881: Bobby Walston, 1951-62
Touchdowns	18: Steve Van Buren, 1945	79: Harold Carmichael, 1971-83
PATs Made	50: Cliff Patton, 1948	365: Bobby Walston, 1951-62
Field Goals Made	30: Paul McFadden, 1984	91: Paul McFadden, 1984-87
Interceptions By	11: Bill Bradley, 1971	34: Bill Bradley, 1969-76
Punts	108: John Teltschik, 1986	393: Adrian Burk, 1951-56
Punt Returns	54: Wally Henry, 1981	148: Wally Henry, 1977-82
Punt Ret. Yardage	489: Larry Marshall, 1977	1,231: Wally Henry, 1977-82
Kickoff Returns	48: Herman Hunter, 1985	169: Timmy Brown, 1960-67
Kickoff Ret. Yardage	1,047: Herman Hunter, 1985	4,483: Timmy Brown, 1960-67

As a rookie, Keith Jackson hauled in 81 balls to set the Eagles' team record for pass receptions in a season

TEAM RECORDS

	GAME	OPPONENT
Rushing Yardage	376: vs. Washington, 10/21/48	370: at Detroit, 9/20/35
Rushing Attempts	64: Four times; Last done at Chicago Cardinals, 10/25/53	60: New York Giants, 11/20/83
Passing Yardage	460: vs. New York Giants, 11/8/53	440: at Dallas, 10/9/66
Passes Attempted	60: at Washington, 12/1/40	55: Los Angeles Rams, 10/7/50
Passes Completed	33: at Washington, 12/1/40 vs. New York Giants, 9/23/62	34: at New England (ot), 11/29/87
Total Yards	582: at Cleveland, 11/7/65	652: at Dallas, 10/9/66
First Downs	34: vs. Baltimore, 11/15/81	37: Green Bay, 11/11/62
Penalties	19: vs. Houston, 10/2/88	22: Chicago, 11/26/44
Points Scored	64: vs. Cincinnati Reds, 11/6/34	62: at New York Giants, 11/26/72

OPPONENT'S INDIVIDUAL RECORDS

	SINGLE GAME
Rushing Yardage	237: Jim Brown, at Cleveland, 11/19/61
Rushing Attempts	43: Butch Woolfolk, New York Giants, 11/20/83
Rushing TDs	4: Jim Brown, at Cleveland, 11/19/61; Jim Taylor, Green Bay, 11/11/62
Passing Yardage	409: Phil Simms, at New York Giants, 9/2/84
Passes Attempted	53: Tom Ramsey, at New England (ot), 11/29/87
Passes Completed	34: Tom Ramsey, at New England (ot), 11/29/87
Passing TDs	5: Frank Filchock, Washington, 10/8/44; Sammy Baugh, Washington, 9/28/47; Sonny Jurgensen, at Washington, 10/11/64; Don Meredith, at Dallas, 10/9/66; Dallas, 9/29/68; Craig Morton, at Dallas, 10/19/69
Interceptions	8: Jim Hardy, at Chicago Cardinals, 9/24/50
Receiving Yardage	212: Hugh Taylor, Washington, 9/28/47
Receptions	12: Bobby Mitchell, at Washington, 10/11/64
Receiving TDs	3: Frank Liebel, at New York Giants, 12/2/45; Hugh Taylor, Washington, 9/28/47; Del Shofner, New York Giants, 12/10/61; Bob Hayes, at Dallas, 10/9/66; Woodley Lewis, Chicago Cardinals, 12/14/57; Ron Johnson, New York Giants, 10/2/72; Larry Brown, at Washington, 12/16/73
Points	24: (See Touchdowns)
Touchdowns	4: Jim Brown, at Cleveland, 11/19/61; Jim Taylor, Green Bay, 11/11/62; John David Crow, at St. Louis, 12/16/62; Ron Johnson, New York Giants, 10/2/72; Larry Brown, at Washington, 12/16/73
PATs Made	8: Danny Villanueva, at Dallas, 10/9/66; Pete Gogolak, at New York Giants, 11/26/73
Field Goals Made	5: Jim Bakken, at St. Louis, 12/13/64; Mac Percival, Chicago, 10/20/68; Raul Allegre, Baltimore, 10/30/83
Interceptions By	3: Ward Cuff, New York Giants, 9/13/41; Ray Ramsey, at Chicago Cardinals, 9/30/51; Johnny Sample, Pittsburgh, 10/8/61; Dick Lynch, New York Giants, 9/29/63; Jim Bradshaw, Pittsburgh, 10/24/65; Herb Adderley, Dallas, 9/26/71; Dave Waymer, at New Orleans, 10/6/85
Punts	14: Sammy Baugh, at Washington, 11/5/39
Punt Returns	9: Leon Bright, New York Giants, 12/11/82; Pete Shaw, New York Giants, 11/20/83; Phil McConkey, New York Giants (ot), 12/6/87

YEAR-BY-YEAR LEADERS

YEAR	RUSHING YARDAGE		PASSING YARDAGE		RECEPTIONS	
1933	Swede Hanson	494	Reds Kirkman	354	Swede Hanson	9
1934	Swede Hanson	805	Ed Matesic	272	Joe Carter	16
1935	Swede Hanson	209	Ed Storm	372	Joe Carter	11
1936	Swede Hanson	359	Dave Smukler	345	Ed Manske	17
1937	Emmett Mortell	312	Dave Smukler	432	Bill Hewitt	16
1938	Dave Smukler	313	Dave Smukler	524	Joe Carter	27
1939	Dave Smukler	218	Davey O'Brien	1,324	Herschel Ramsey	31
1940	Dick Riffle	238	Davey O'Brien	1,290	Don Looney	58
1941	Jim Castiglia	183	Tommy Thompson	974	Dick Humbert	29
1942	Bob Davis	207	Tommy Thompson	1,410	Fred Meyer	16
1943	Jack Hinkle	571	Roy Zimmerman	846	Tony Bova	17
1944	Steve Van Buren	444	Roy Zimmerman	785	Larry Cabrelli	13
1945	Steve Van Buren	832	Roy Zimmerman	991	Jack Ferrante	21
1946	Steve Van Buren	529	Tommy Thompson	745	Jack Ferrante	28
1947	Steve Van Buren	1,008	Tommy Thompson	1,680	Pete Pihos	23
1948	Steve Van Buren	945	Tommy Thompson	1,965	Pete Pihos	46
1949	Steve Van Buren	1,146	Tommy Thompson	1,727	Jack Ferrante Pete Pihos	34 34
1950	Frank Ziegler	733	Tommy Thompson	1,608	Pete Pihos	38
1951	Frank Ziegler	418	Adrian Burk	1,329	Pete Pihos	35
1952	John Huzvar	349	Bobby Thomason	1,334	Bud Grant	56
1953	Don Johnson	439	Bobby Thomason	2,462	Pete Pihos	63
1954	Jim Palmer	408	Adrian Burk	1,740	Pete Pihos	60
1955	Harold Giancanelli	385	Adrian Burk Bobby Thomason	1,359 1,337	Pete Pihos	62
1956	Ken Keller	433	Bobby Thomason	1,119	Bobby Walston	39
1957	Billy Barnes	529	Bobby Thomason	630	Billy Barnes	19
1958	Billy Barnes	551	Norm Van Brocklin	2,409	Pete Retzlaff	56
1959	Billy Barnes	687	Norm Van Brocklin	2,617	Tommy McDonald	47
1960	Clarence Peaks	465	Norm Van Brocklin	2,471	Pete Retzlaff	46
1961	Clarence Peaks	471	Sonny Jurgensen	3,723	Tommy McDonald	64
1962	Timmy Brown	545	Sonny Jurgensen	3,261	Tommy McDonald	58
1963	Timmy Brown	841	Sonny Jurgensen	1,413	Pete Retzlaff	57
1964	Earl Gros	748	Norm Snead	1,906	Pete Retzlaff	51

Pete Retzlaff

Sonny Jurgensen

Clarence Peaks

YEAR-BY-YEAR LEADERS

YEAR	RUSHING YARDAGE		PASSING YARDAGE		RECEPTIONS	
1965	Timmy Brown	861	Norm Snead	2,346	Pete Retzlaff	66
1966	Timmy Brown	548	Norm Snead	1,275	Pete Retzlaff	40
1967	Tom Woodeshick	670	Norm Snead	3,399	Ben Hawkins	59
1968	Tom Woodeshick	947	Norm Snead	1,655	Ben Hawkins	42
1969	Tom Woodeshick	831	Norm Snead	2,768	Harold Jackson	65
1970	Cyril Pinder	657	Norm Snead	2,323	Lee Bouggess	50
1971	Ron Bull	351	Pete Liske	1,937	Harold Jackson	47
1972	"Po" James	565	John Reaves	1,508	Harold Jackson	62
1973	Tom Sullivan	968	Roman Gabriel	3,219	Harold Carmichael	67
1974	Tom Sullivan	760	Roman Gabriel	1,867	Charle Young	63
1975	Tom Sullivan	632	Roman Gabriel	1,644	Charle Young / Harold Carmichael	49 / 49
1976	Mike Hogan	561	Mike Boryla	1,247	Harold Carmichael	42
1977	Mike Hogan	546	Ron Jaworski	2,183	Harold Carmichael	46
1978	Wilbert Montgomery	1,220	Ron Jaworski	2,487	Harold Carmichael	55
1979	Wilbert Montgomery	1,512	Ron Jaworski	2,669	Harold Carmichael	52
1980	Wilbert Montgomery	778	Ron Jaworski	3,529	Wilbert Montgomery	50
1981	Wilbert Montgomery	1,402	Ron Jaworski	3,095	Harold Carmichael	61
1982	Wilbert Montgomery	515	Ron Jaworski	2,076	Harold Carmichael	35
1983	Hubie Oliver	434	Ron Jaworski	3,315	Mike Quick	69
1984	Wilbert Montgomery	789	Ron Jaworski	2,754	John Spagnola	65
1985	Earnest Jackson	1,028	Ron Jaworski	3,450	Mike Quick	73
1986	Keith Byars	577	Ron Jaworski	1,405	Mike Quick	60
1987	Randall Cunningham	505	Randall Cunningham	2,786	Mike Quick	46
1988	Randall Cunningham	624	Randall Cunningham	3,808	Keith Jackson	81

POINTS SCORED

Year	Player	Pts	Year	Player	Pts	Year	Player	Pts
1933	Swede Hanson	24	1951	Bobby Walston	94	1970	Mark Moseley	67
1934	Swede Hanson	50	1952	Bobby Walston	82	1971	Tom Dempsey	49
1935	Ed Manske	24	1953	Bobby Walston	87	1972	Tom Dempsey	71
1936	Hank Reese	9	1954	Bobby Walston	114	1973	Tom Dempsey	106
1937	Bill Hewitt	30	1955	Dick Bielski	56	1974	Tom Sullivan	72
1938	Joe Carter	48	1956	Bobby Walston	53	1975	Horst Muhlmann	81
1939	Franny Murray	26	1957	Bobby Walston	53	1976	Horst Muhlmann	51
1940	Dick Riffle / Don Looney	30 / 30	1958	Bobby Walston	67	1977	Harold Carmichael	42
1941	Jim Castiglia	24	1959	Tommy McDonald	66	1978	Wilbert Montgomery	60
1942	Bob Davis	18	1960	Bobby Walston	105	1979	Tony Franklin	105
1943	Ernie Steele / Bob Thurbon	36 / 36	1961	Bobby Walston	97	1980	Tony Franklin	96
1944	Roy Zimmerman	62	1962	Timmy Brown	78	1981	Tony Franklin	101
1945	Steve Van Buren	110	1963	Timmy Brown	66	1982	Wilbert Montgomery	54
1946	Augie Lio	51	1964	Sam Baker	84	1983	Mike Quick	78
1947	Steve Van Buren	84	1965	Sam Baker	65	1984	Paul McFadden	116
1948	Cliff Patton	74	1966	Sam Baker	92	1985	Paul McFadden	104
1949	Steve Van Buren	72	1967	Sam Baker	81	1986	Paul McFadden	86
1950	Cliff Patton	56	1968	Sam Baker	74	1987	Paul McFadden	84
			1969	Sam Baker	79	1988	Luis Zendejas	87

CAREER LEADERS

PASSES ATTEMPTED

Ron Jaworski	3,918
Norm Snead	2,236
Tommy Thompson	1,396
Randall Cunningham	1,256
Roman Gabriel	1,185
Bobby Thomason	1,113
Sonny Jurgensen	1,107

PASS COMPLETIONS

Ron Jaworski	2,088
Norm Snead	1,154
Tommy Thompson	723
Randall Cunningham	669
Roman Gabriel	661
Sonny Jurgensen	602
Bobby Thomason	556

PASSING YARDS

Ron Jaworski	26,963
Norm Snead	15,672
Tommy Thompson	10,255
Sonny Jurgensen	9,639
Randall Cunningham	8,533
Bobby Thomason	8,124
Norm Van Brocklin	7,497

Ron Jaworski is Eagles' all-time leader in three passing categories

SEASONS

Chuck Bednarik	14
Harold Carmichael	14
Frank Kilroy	13
Vic Sears	13
Bobby Walston	12
Jerry Sisemore	12

RUSHING YARDS

Wilbert Montgomery	6,538
Steve Van Buren	5,860
Timmy Brown	3,703
Tom Woodeshick	3,563
Tom Sullivan	3,135
Clarence Peaks	2,927

PASS RECEPTIONS

Harold Carmichael	589
Pete Retzlaff	452
Pete Pihos	373
Mike Quick	341
Bobby Walston	311
Tommy McDonald	287

GAMES

Harold Carmichael	180
Chuck Bednarik	169
Randy Logan	159
Guy Morriss	157
Jerry Sisemore	156

RUSHING ATTEMPTS

Wilbert Montgomery	1,465
Steve Van Buren	1,320
Tom Sullivan	871
Timmy Brown	850
Tom Woodeshick	831

RECEIVING YARDS

Harold Carmichael	8,978
Pete Retzlaff	7,412
Mike Quick	6,101
Pete Pihos	5,619
Tommy McDonald	5,499

CONSECUTIVE GAMES

Harold Carmichael	162
Randy Logan	159
Bobby Walston	148
Ken Clarke	139
Herman Edwards	135
Frank LeMaster	129

POINTS

Bobby Walston	881
Sam Baker	475
Harold Carmichael	474
Steve Van Buren	464
Tony Franklin	412
Tommy McDonald	402

TOUCHDOWNS

Harold Carmichael	79
Steve Van Buren	77
Tommy McDonald	67
Pete Pihos	63
Timmy Brown	62
Wilbert Montgomery	58

PROFILE

Wilbert Montgomery

If one performance by one player is the essence of the Eagles' rise from mediocrity under Dick Vermeil in the late '70s and early '80s, Wilbert Montgomery's 194-yard afternoon on Jan. 11, 1981, in the 1980 NFC Championship game over the Cowboys, is it.

Montgomery, the slashing, crashing little (5-10, 195) tailback out of tiny Abilene Christian, wobbled into that game already banged up with hip, ankle and knee injuries.

But he carried the ball 26 times that day, including a mood-setting 42-yard touchdown burst on the Eagles' second play from scrimmage.

"All we did was wind him up, he took care of the rest," said Eagles head trainer Otho Davis of that day.

Behind Montgomery, the Eagles beat the Cowboys 20-7 and went on to their only Super Bowl appearance.

Montgomery was born in Greenville, Miss., on Sept. 16, 1954. He came to the Eagles as a little-known sixth-round pick from the NAIA school, the 154th pick in the draft. He was small and quiet, but by 1978 Vermeil saw enough to give him the ball 259 times. Montgomery responded with 1,220 yards — a robust 4.7-per-carry average.

In those years, with the Eagles not quite able to put together a consistent passing attack, Montgomery carried a ferocious offensive load.

By the time he was traded to the Lions in 1985 preseason, Montgomery's amazing production had built up an impressive array of team records.

Montgomery holds the team record for most career rushing yards (6,538), most rushing yards in a season (1,512 in 1979), most attempts in a career (1,465), most attempts in a season (338 in 1979), most 100-career games (26) and longest run from scrimmage (a 90-yard TD against Houston on Dec. 19, 1982).

He also registered the second-most (1,402 in 1981) and third-most (1,220 in 1978) rushing yards in the season. In addition, Montgomery is second to Steve Van Buren for most yards gained in a game (205 by Van Buren, 197 by Montgomery), and also to Van Buren for most rushing touchdowns in a career (69 to 45). Montgomery is seventh on the Eagle all-time receptions list with 266.

In 1979, Montgomery had perhaps the greatest individual season in recent Eagle history, leading the NFL with 2,012 all-purpose yards (rushing, receiving and returns).

But all those carries and all those hits and all those times he hurled his body back into the line cost him. And by his eighth season, his body had had enough.

He retired in 1985 as the NFL's No. 17 all-time rusher, having gained a total of 6,789 yards on 1,540 carries.

"When Wilbert is healthy," Ron Jaworski said during Montgomery's career, "he's the finest player in the game. Some backs might run better, some might catch a pass better, some might do other things better. But overall, nobody's better than Wilbert."

PROFILE

Norm Van Brocklin

Norm Van Brocklin, the legendary "Dutchman," was traded to the Eagles from the Rams before the 1958 season; he was 32 years old, and near the end of his career.

But in three years, the Eagles' quarterback took the team from last place to the 1960 NFL Championship. In that season, Van Brocklin threw 24 touchdown passes, averaged 43.1 yards a punt, won the league's Most Valuable Player award and was unquestionably the morale leader of the underdog team.

After the championship game, Van Brocklin threw three touchdown passes in the Pro Bowl. Then he retired.

"Van Brocklin might have been the best pure passer of modern times," said George Allen.

"He could throw a ball almost the length of the football field and hit a fast receiver in full stride right in the hands. He could throw bullets to the sidelines. He could throw right through defenses. He had strength, touch and tremendous timing."

He was born in Eagle Butte, S.D., on March 15, 1926, and attended the University of Oregon. The Rams drafted him in the fourth round of the 1949 draft.

During nine years in Los Angeles — including the Rams' 1951 championship season — he battled Bobby Waterfield and then Billy Wade for playing time. Finally, Van Brocklin got his wish and was traded to the Eagles.

He completed the pass that won the championship for the Rams in 1951 and on Sept. 28 of that year, he threw for what stands still as the NFL single-game record 554 yards against the old New York Yankees. In his nine seasons, the Rams won four division titles.

Overall in his career, he won three league passing titles. Still, he never was the starter in LA for long.

But with the Eagles, things were entirely different. In his three seasons, Van Brocklin was the only quarterback the Eagles would need. He made the Pro Bowl twice.

And in the 1960 season, whenever the Eagles found themselves trailing in the fourth quarter — as they often did — they would turn to their quarterback to will them to victory.

"I never played with anyone like Van Brocklin," said receiver Pete Retzlaff. "We respected him, we were in awe of him, we were constantly seeking approval. We all felt his wrath at one time or another, but we trusted him. If he said, 'We're going to get it going,' we believed him."

Van Brocklin announced his retirement after that season, then went on to coach two teams — the 1961 expansion Vikings (through 1966) and the 1968 Falcons (into the '74 season).

He died on May 2, 1983, survived by his wife, Gloria, six children and six grandchildren.

SIXERS

SYRACUSE NATIONALS (NBL)

Season	Head Coach	W- L	Pct.	Pos.	GB
1946-47	Benny Borgmann	21-23	.477	T3	10
1947-48	Benny Borgmann	24-36	.400	4	20
1948-49	Al Cervi	40-23	.638	2	8½

SYRACUSE NATIONALS (NBA)

Season	Head Coach	W- L	Pct.	Pos.	GB
1949-50	Al Cervi	51-13	.797	1	—
1950-51	Al Cervi	32-34	.485	4	8
1951-52	Al Cervi	40-26	.606	1	—
1952-53	Al Cervi	47-24	.662	2	½
1953-54	Al Cervi	42-30	.583	T2	2
1954-55	Al Cervi	43-29	.597	1	—
1955-56	Al Cervi	35-37	.486	3	10
1956-57	Al Cervi	4- 8	.333	—	—
	Paul Seymour	34-26	.567	—	—
	Total	38-34	.528	2	6
1957-58	Paul Seymour	41-31	.569	2	8
1958-59	Paul Seymour	35-37	.486	3	17
1959-60	Paul Seymour	45-30	.600	3	14
1960-61	Alex Hannum	38-41	.481	3	19
1961-62	Alex Hannum	41-39	.512	3	19
1962-63	Alex Hannum	48-32	.600	2	10

TEAM MOVED TO PHILADELPHIA AND BECAME 76ERS

Season	Head Coach	W- L	Pct.	Pos.	GB
1963-64	Dolph Schayes	34-46	.425	3	25
1964-65	Dolph Schayes	40-40	.500	3	22
1965-66	Dolph Schayes	55-25	.688	1	—
1966-67	Alex Hannum	68-13	.840	1	—
1967-68	Alex Hannum	62-20	.756	1	—
1968-69	Jack Ramsay	55-27	.671	2	2

Season	Head Coach	W- L	Pct.	Pos.	GB
1969-70	Jack Ramsay	42-40	.512	4	18
1970-71	Jack Ramsay	47-35	.573	2	5
1971-72	Jack Ramsay	30-52	.366	3	26
1972-73	Roy Rubin	4-47	.078	—	—
	Kevin Loughery	5-26	.161	—	—
	Totals	9-73	.110	4	59
1973-74	Gene Shue	25-57	.305	4	26
1974-75	Gene Shue	34-48	.415	4	31
1975-76	Gene Shue	46-36	.561	T2	8
1976-77	Gene Shue	50-32	.610	1	—
1977-78	Gene Shue	2- 4	.333	—	—
	Bill Cunningham	53-23	.697	—	—
	Totals	55-27	.671	1	—
1978-79	Bill Cunningham	47-35	.573	2	7
1979-80	Bill Cunningham	59-23	.720	2	2
1980-81	Bill Cunningham	62-20	.756	T1	—
1981-82	Bill Cunningham	58-24	.707	2	5
1982-83	Bill Cunningham	65-17	.793	1	—
1983-84	Bill Cunningham	52-30	.634	2	10
1984-85	Bill Cunningham	58-24	.707	2	5
1985-86	Matt Guokas	54-28	.659	2	13
1986-87	Matt Guokas	45-37	.549	2	14
1987-88	Matt Guokas	20-23	.465	—	—
	Jim Lynam	16-23	.410	—	—
	Totals	36-46	.439	4	21
1988-89	Jim Lynam	46-36	.561	2	6

COACHES' RECORDS

		Regular Season			Playoffs		
Seasons	Coach	W- L	Pct.		W- L	Pct.	
1946-48	Benny Borgmann	45- 59	.433		1- 6	.143	
1948-56	Al Cervi	334-224	.599		35-29	.547	
1956-60	Paul Seymour	155-124	.556		9-11	.450	
1960-63	Alex Hannum	127-112	.531		8-12	.400	
1966-68	Alex Hannum	130- 33	.798		18- 6	.750	
	Total	257-145	.639		26-20	.565	
1963-66	Dolph Schayes	129-111	.537		9-12	.429	
1968-72	Jack Ramsay	174-154	.530		5-12	.294	
1972-73	Roy Rubin	4- 47	.078		0- 0	—	
1973	Kevin Loughery	5- 26	.161		0- 0	—	
1973-77	Gene Shue	157-177	.470		11-11	.500	
1977-85	Bill Cunningham	454-196	.698		66-39	.629	
1985-88	Matt Guokas	119- 88	.575		8- 9	.471	
1988-89	Jim Lynam	62- 59	.512		0- 3	.000	

Matty Guokas

Jimmy Lynam

43

Maurice Cheeks has risen above every other Sixer on the club's all-time assists and steals lists

CAREER LEADERS

GAMES		POINTS		REBOUNDS		ASSISTS	
Hal Greer	1,122	Hal Greer	21,586	Dolph Schayes	11,256	Maurice Cheeks	6,212
Dolph Schayes	1,059	Dolph Schayes	19,249	John Kerr	9,517	Hal Greer	4,540
Maurice Cheeks	853	Julius Erving	18,364	Bill Cunningham	6,638	Julius Erving	3,224
Julius Erving	836	Bill Cunningham	13,626	Wilt Chamberlain	6,632	Dolph Schayes	3,072
John Kerr	834	John Kerr	11,699	Julius Erving	5,601	Larry Costello	2,902
Paul Seymour	690	Maurice Cheeks	10,429	Hal Greer	5,564	Bill Cunningham	2,625
Al Bianchi	687	Chet Walker	9,043	Charles Barkley	4,660	Paul Seymour	2,335
Steve Mix	668	Charles Barkley	8,616	Luke Jackson	4,613	Wilt Chamberlain	1,879
Bill Cunningham	654	Larry Costello	7,957	Caldwell Jones	4,454	John Kerr	1,779
Bobby Jones	617	Fred Carter	7,673	Chet Walker	4,426	Fred Carter	1,720

FIELD GOALS MADE		FREE THROWS MADE		STEALS		BLOCKED SHOTS	
Hal Greer	8,504	Dolph Schayes	6,979	Maurice Cheeks	1,942	Julius Erving	1,293
Julius Erving	7,237	Hal Greer	4,578	Julius Erving	1,508	Caldwell Jones	926
Dolph Schayes	6,135	Julius Erving	3,844	Steve Mix	851	Bobby Jones	693
Bill Cunningham	5,116	Bill Cunningham	3,394	Bobby Jones	727	Darryl Dawkins	635
John Kerr	4,623	Moses Malone	2,499	Charles Barkley	612	Charles Barkley	479
Maurice Cheeks	4,192	John Kerr	2,453	Doug Collins	518	Moses Malone	461
Chet Walker	3,318	Chet Walker	2,407	George McGinnis	498	Harvey Catchings	404
Fred Carter	3,248	Larry Costello	2,231	Andrew Toney	369	Maurice Cheeks	272
Wilt Chamberlain	3,105	Maurice Cheeks	2,005	Fred Carter	343	Clemon Johnson	200
Charles Barkley	3,032	Charles Barkley	1,894	Henry Bibby	333	Mike Gminski	191

YEAR-BY-YEAR LEADERS

(Rebounds Not Kept Before 1950-51; Assists Not Kept Before 1949-50)					
	POINTS		**REBOUNDS**		**ASSISTS**
1948-49	Dolph Schayes	811	Not Available		NA
1949-50	Dolph Schayes	1,072	NA		Al Cervi	264
1950-51	Dolph Schayes	1,121	Dolph Schayes	1,080	Fred Scolari	255
1951-52	Dolph Schayes	868	Dolph Schayes	773	George King	244
1952-53	Dolph Schayes	1,262	Dolph Schayes	920	George King	364
1953-54	Dolph Schayes	1,228	Dolph Schayes	870	Paul Seymour	364
1954-55	Dolph Schayes	1,333	Dolph Schayes	887	Paul Seymour	483
1955-56	Dolph Schayes	1,472	Dolph Schayes	891	George King	410
1956-57	Dolph Schayes	1,617	Dolph Schayes	1,008	Dolph Schayes	229
1957-58	Dolph Schayes	1,791	Dolph Schayes	1,022	Larry Costello	317
1958-59	Dolph Schayes	1,534	John Kerr	1,008	Larry Costello	379
1959-60	Dolph Schayes	1,689	Dolph Schayes	959	Larry Costello	449
1960-61	Dolph Schayes	1,868	Dolph Schayes	960	Larry Costello	413
1961-62	Hal Greer	1,619	John Kerr	1,176	Larry Costello	358
1962-63	Hal Greer	1,562	John Kerr	1,049	Larry Costello	334
1963-64	Hal Greer	1,865	John Kerr	1,018	Hal Greer	374
1964-65	Hal Greer	1,413	Luke Jackson	980	Hal Greer	313
1965-66	Wilt Chamberlain	2,649	Wilt Chamberlain	1,943	Wilt Chamberlain	414
1966-67	Wilt Chamberlain	1,956	Wilt Chamberlain	1,957	Wilt Chamberlain	630
1967-68	Wilt Chamberlain	1,992	Wilt Chamberlain	1,952	Wilt Chamberlain	702
1968-69	Bill Cunningham	2,034	Bill Cunningham	1,050	Hal Greer	414
1969-70	Bill Cunningham	2,114	Bill Cunningham	1,101	Hal Greer	405
1970-71	Bill Cunningham	1,859	Bill Cunningham	946	Archie Clark	440
1971-72	Bill Cunningham	1,744	Bill Cunningham	918	Bill Cunningham	443
1972-73	Fred Carter	1,617	LeRoy Ellis	744	Fred Carter	349
1973-74	Fred Carter	1,666	LeRoy Ellis	890	Fred Carter	443
1974-75	Fred Carter	1,686	Bill Cunningham	726	Bill Cunningham	442
1975-76	George McGinnis	1,769	George McGinnis	967	Fred Carter	372
1976-77	Julius Erving	1,770	George McGinnis	911	Henry Bibby	356
1977-78	George McGinnis	1,587	George McGinnis	810	Henry Bibby	464
1978-79	Julius Erving	1,803	Caldwell Jones	747	Maurice Cheeks	431
1979-80	Julius Erving	2,100	Caldwell Jones	950	Maurice Cheeks	556
1980-81	Julius Erving	2,014	Caldwell Jones	813	Maurice Cheeks	560
1981-82	Julius Erving	1,974	Caldwell Jones	708	Maurice Cheeks	667
1982-83	Moses Malone	1,908	Moses Malone	1,194	Maurice Cheeks	543
1983-84	Julius Erving	1,727	Moses Malone	950	Maurice Cheeks	478
1984-85	Moses Malone	1,941	Moses Malone	1,031	Maurice Cheeks	497
1985-86	Moses Malone	1,759	Charles Barkley	1,026	Maurice Cheeks	753
1986-87	Charles Barkley	1,564	Charles Barkley	994	Maurice Cheeks	538
1987-88	Charles Barkley	2,264	Charles Barkley	951	Maurice Cheeks	635
1988-89	Charles Barkley	2,037	Charles Barkley	986	Maurice Cheeks	554

INDIVIDUAL RECORDS

	SINGLE-GAME
Points	68: Wilt Chamberlain, vs. Chicago, 12/16/67
Field Goals Made	30: Wilt Chamberlain, vs. Chicago, 12/16/67
Field Goals Attempted	43: Wilt Chamberlain, vs. Los Angeles, 2/7/66
Field Goal Percentage	100.0: Wilt Chamberlain, vs. Baltimore, 2/24/67 (18-18) Wilt Chamberlain, vs. Baltimore, 3/19/67 (16-16) Wilt Chamberlain, vs. Los Angeles, 1/20/67 (15-15)
Three-Point FG Made	4: Andrew Toney, vs. Boston, 3/21/82 Charles Barkley, vs. Dallas, 12/20/88 Scott Brooks, vs. Atlanta, 1/13/89, vs. Chicago, 1/25/89
Three-Point FG Attempted	10: Charles Barkley, vs. Dallas, 12/20/88
Three-Point FG Percentage	100.0: Many times
Free Throws Made	23: Dolph Schayes, vs. Minneapolis, 1/17/52
Free Throws Attempts	27: Dolph Schayes, vs. Minneapolis, 1/17/52
Free Throw Percentage	100.0: Dolph Schayes, vs. Minneapolis, 1/10/57 (18-18) Dolph Schayes, vs. Boston, 3/9/57 (18-18) Dolph Schayes, vs. Los Angeles, 10/29/60 (18-18)
Rebounds	43: Wilt Chamberlain, vs. Boston, 3/6/65
Assists	21: Wilt Chamberlain, vs. Detroit, 2/2/68 21: Maurice Cheeks, vs. New Jersey, 10/30/82
Blocked Shots	10: Harvey Catchings, vs. Atlanta, 3/21/75
Steals	9: Maurice Cheeks, vs. LA Clippers, 1/5/87
Personal Fouls	7: Alex Hannum, vs. Boston, 12/26/60
Disqualifications	—
Turnovers	10: Julius Erving, vs. Atlanta, 11/15/77 10: Darryl Dawkins, vs. Phoenix, 3/4/79 10: Charles Barkley, vs. New Jersey, 3/27/87
Minutes	63: Larry Costello, vs. Cincinnati (3 ot), 1/8/59

Charles Barkley holds record for three-point attempts

OPPONENT (GAME)

Points:
70: Wilt Chamberlain, San Francisco, 3/10/63

Field Goals Made:
27: Wilt Chamberlain, San Francisco,
12/11/62, 3/10/63, 11/26/64

Free Throws Made:
30: Bob Cousy, Boston (4 ot), 3/12/53

Rebounds:
51: Bill Russell, Boston, 2/5/60

Assists:
23: Jerry West, Los Angeles, 2/1/67

SPECTRUM (GAME)

Points:
52: Michael Jordan, Chicago, 11/16/88

Field Goals Made:
24: Michael Jordan, Chicago, 11/16/88

Rebounds:
35: Wilt Chamberlain, vs. Baltimore, 1/21/68

Assists:
21: Wilt Chamberlain, vs. Detroit, 2/2/68
Maurice Cheeks, vs. New Jersey, 10/30/82

Steals:
10: Fred Brown, Seattle, 12/3/76
Eddie Jordan, New Jersey, 3/23/79

Blocked Shots:
10: Harvey Catchings, vs. Atlanta, 3/21/75

INDIVIDUAL RECORDS

	SEASON	CAREER
Points	2,649: Wilt Chamberlain, 1965-66	21,586: Hal Greer, 1958-73
FG Made	1,074: Wilt Chamberlain, 1965-66	8,504: Hal Greer, 1958-73
FG Attempted	1,990: Wilt Chamberlain, 1965-66	18,811: Hal Greer, 1958-73
FG Pct.	68.3: Wilt Chamberlain, 1966-67 (785-1,150)	58.3: Wilt Chamberlian, 1964-68 (3,105-5,325)
3-Pt. FG Made	71: Hersey Hawkins, 1988-89	138: Andrew Toney, 1980-88
3-Pt. FG Att.	166: Hersey Hawkins, 1988-89	403: Andrew Toney, 1980-88
3-Pt. FG Pct.	44.8: Leon Wood, 1985-86 (13-29)	34.2: Andrew Toney, 1980-88 (138-403)
FT Made	737: Moses Malone, 1984-85	6,979: Dolph Schayes, 1948-64
FT Attempted	976: Wilt Chamberlain, 1965-66	8,273: Dolph Schayes, 1948-64
FT Pct.	90.45: Dolph Schayes, 1956-57 (625-691)	84.6: Larry Costello, 1957-67 (2,231-2,637)
Rebounds	1,957: Wilt Chamberlain, 1966-67	11,256: Dolph Schayes, 1948-64
Assists	753: Maurice Cheeks, 1985-86	6,212: Maurice Cheeks, 1978-89
Blocked Shots	200: Caldwell Jones, 1976-77	1,293: Julius Erving, 1976-87
Steals	212: Steve Mix, 1973-74	1,942: Maurice Cheeks, 1978-89
Personal Fouls	334: George McGinnis, 1975-76	3,855: Hal Greer, 1958-73
Disqualifications	16: Alex Hannum, 1950-51	90: Dolph Schayes, 1948-64
Turnovers	350: Charles Barkley, 1985-86	2,323: Julius Erving, 1976-87
Minutes	3,836: Wilt Chamberlain, 1967-68	39,788: Hal Greer, 1958-73

Andrew Toney holds career records for three-pointers

BEST PERFORMANCES

POINTS

68: Wilt Chamberlain, vs. Chicago, 12/16/67
65: Wilt Chamberlain, vs. Los Angeles, 2/17/66
62: Wilt Chamberlain, vs. San Francisco, 3/3/66
58: Wilt Chamberlain, vs. Cincinnati, 2/13/67
53: Wilt Chamberlain, vs. Detroit, 10/23/65 Wilt Chamberlain, vs. Los Angeles, 1/25/66 Wilt Chamberlain, vs. Seattle, 12/20/67 Wilt Chamberlain, vs. Los Angeles, 3/18/67
52: Wilt Chamberlain, vs. Seattle, 12/1/67
51: Wilt Chamberlain, vs. Baltimore, 3/14/65 Moses Malone, vs. Detroit (ot), 11/14/84

REBOUNDS

43: Wilt Chamberlain, vs. Boston, 3/6/65
42: Wilt Chamberlain, vs. Boston, 1/14/66
41: Wilt Chamberlain, vs. Boston, 4/5/67
40: Wilt Chamberlain, vs. Boston, 12/28/65
39: Wilt Chamberlain, vs. Boston, 4/6/65

ASSISTS

21: Wilt Chamberlain, vs. Detroit, 2/2/68 Maurice Cheeks, vs. New Jersey, 10/30/82
19: Wilt Chamberlain, vs. Cincinnati, 3/24/67 Wilt Chamberlain, vs. Cincinnati (ot), 3/19/68 Maurice Cheeks, vs. Washington, 4/13/87
18: Paul Seymour, vs. Philadelphia, 1/26/55 Larry Costello, vs. Boston, 3/3/60 Maurice Cheeks, vs. San Antonio, 11/7/86

The Sixers' team records for highest field goal percentage were set with the help of Bobby Jones's surehandedness

TEAM RECORDS

	GAME	SEASON
Points	163: vs. San Francisco, 3/10/63	10,143: 1966-67 (125.2/Game)
FG Made	69: vs. San Francisco, 3/10/63	3,965: 1967-68 (48.4/Game)
FG Attempted	140: vs. Philadelphia, 3/1/61	8,885: 1961-62 (111.1/Game)
FG Pct.	68.6: vs. New Jersey, 3/22/86 (48-70)	51.8: 1981-82 (3,616-6,974)
FT Made	59: vs. Anderson (5 ot), 11/24/49	2,350: 1962-63 (29.4/Game)
FT Attempted	86: vs. Anderson (5 ot), 11/24/49	3,411: 1966-67 (42.1/Game)
FT Pct.	100.0: vs. Boston, 11/2/57 (29-29) vs. Indiana, 3/10/81 (15-15)	79.4: 1956-57 (2,075-2,613)
Rebounds	101: vs. San Francisco, 4/16/67	5,914: 1967-68 (72.1/Game)
Assists	45: vs. Denver, 12/7/88	2,369: 1980-81 (28.9/Game)
Steals	24: vs. Detroit, 11/11/78	862: 1985-86 (10.5/Game)
Blocked Shots	20: vs. Milwaukee, 4/5/81 vs. Seattle, 3/9/84	653: 1983-84 (8.0/Game)
Personal Fouls	60: vs. Baltimore (ot), 11/15/52	2,344: 1961-62 (29.3/Game)
Disqualifications	8: vs. Baltimore (ot), 11/15/52	64: 1950-51
Turnovers	38: vs. Phoenix, 3/4/79	1,915: 1976-77 (23.4/Game)

POSTSEASON RESULTS

(Home team in CAPS)

1950

EASTERN DIVISION SEMIFINALS
Syracuse 2, Philadelphia 0
3/22: SYRACUSE 93, Philadelphia 76
3/23: Syracuse 59, PHILADELPHIA 53
EASTERN DIVISION FINALS
Syracuse 2, New York 1
3/26: SYRACUSE 91, New York 83 (ot)
3/30: NEW YORK 80, Syracuse 76
4/ 2: SYRACUSE 91, New York 80
CHAMPIONSHIP SERIES
Minneapolis 4, Syracuse 2
4/ 8: Minneapolis 68, SYRACUSE 66
4/ 9: SYRACUSE 91, Minneapolis 85
4/14: MINNEAPOLIS 91, Syracuse 77
4/16: MINNEAPOLIS 77, Syracuse 69
4/20: SYRACUSE 83, Minneapolis 76
4/23: MINNEAPOLIS 110, Syracuse 95

1951

EASTERN DIVISION SEMIFINALS
Syracuse 2, Philadelphia 0
3/20: Syracuse 91, PHILA. 89 (ot)
3/22: SYRACUSE 90, Philadelphia 78
EASTERN DIVISION FINALS
New York 3, Syracuse 2
3/28: NEW YORK 103, Syracuse 92
3/29: SYRACUSE 102, New York 80
3/31: NEW YORK 97, Syracuse 75
4/ 1: SYRACUSE 90, New York 83
4/ 4: NEW YORK 83, Syracuse 81

1952

EASTERN DIVISION SEMIFINALS
Syracuse 2, Philadelphia 1
3/20: SYRACUSE 102, Philadelphia 83
3/22: PHILADELPHIA 100, Syracuse 95
3/23: SYRACUSE 84, Philadelphia 73
EASTERN DIVISON FINALS
New York 3, Syracuse 1
4/ 2: New York 87, SYRACUSE 85
4/ 3: SYRACUSE 102, New York 92
4/ 4: NEW YORK 99, Syracuse 92
4/ 8: NEW YORK 100, Syracuse 93

1953

EASTERN DIVISION SEMIFINALS
Boston 2, Syracuse 0
3/19: Boston 87, SYRACUSE 81
3/21: BOSTON 111, Syracuse 105 (4 ot)

1954

EASTERN DIVISION ROUND-ROBIN
3/16: Boston 93, NEW YORK 71
3/17: Syracuse 96, BOSTON 95 (ot)
3/18: SYRACUSE 75, New York 68
3/20: BOSTON 79, New York 78
3/21: Syracuse 103, NEW YORK 99
3/22: SYRACUSE 98, Boston 85
EASTERN DIVISION FINALS
Syracuse 2, Boston 0
3/25: SYRACUSE 109, Boston 94
3/27: Syracuse 83, BOSTON 76
CHAMPIONSHIP SERIES
Minneapolis 4, Syracuse 3
3/31: MINNEAPOLIS 79, Syracuse 68
4/ 3: Syracuse 62, MINNEAPOLIS 60
4/ 4: Minneapolis 81, SYRACUSE 67
4/ 8: SYRACUSE 80, Minneapolis 69
4/10: Minneapolis 84, SYRACUSE 73
4/11: Syracuse 65, MINNEAPOLIS 63
4/12: MINNEAPOLIS 87, Syracuse 80

1955

EASTERN DIVISION FINALS
Syracuse 3, Boston 1
3/22: SYRACUSE 110, Boston 100
3/24: SYRACUSE 116, Boston 110
3/26: BOSTON 100, Syracuse 97 (ot)
3/27: Syracuse 110, BOSTON 94
CHAMPIONSHIP SERIES
Syracuse 4, Fort Wayne 3
3/31: SYRACUSE 86, Fort Wayne 82
4/ 2: SYRACUSE 87, Fort Wayne 84
4/ 3: FORT WAYNE 96, Syracuse 89
4/ 5: FORT WAYNE 109, Syracuse 102
4/ 7: FORT WAYNE 74, Syracuse 71
4/ 9: SYRACUSE 109, Fort Wayne 104
4/10: SYRACUSE 92, Fort Wayne 91

1956

EASTERN DIVISION 3RD-PLACE GAME
3/15: SYRACUSE 82, New York 77
EASTERN DIVISION SEMIFINALS
Syracuse 2, Boston 1
3/17: BOSTON 110, Syracuse 93
3/19: SYRACUSE 101, Boston 98
3/21: Syracuse 102, BOSTON 97
EASTERN DIVISON FINALS
Philadelphia 3, Syracuse 2
3/23: PHILADELPHIA 109, Syracuse 87
3/25: SYRACUSE 122, Philadelphia 118
3/27: PHILADELPHIA 119, Syracuse 96
3/28: SYRACUSE 108, Philadelphia 104
3/29: PHILA. 109, Syracuse 104

1957

EASTERN DIVISION SEMIFINALS
Syracuse 2, Philadelphia 0
3/16: Syracuse 103, PHILADELPHIA 96
3/18: SYRACUSE 91, Philadelphia 80
EASTERN DIVISION FINALS
Boston 3, Syracuse 0
3/21: BOSTON 108, Syracuse 90
3/23: Boston 120, SYRACUSE 105
3/24: BOSTON 83, Syracuse 80

1958

EASTERN DIVISION SEMIFINALS
Philadelphia 2, Syracuse 1
3/15: SYRACUSE 86, Philadelphia 82
3/16: PHILADELPHIA 95, Syracuse 93
3/18: Philadelphia 101, SYRACUSE 88

1959

EASTERN DIVISION SEMIFINALS
Syracuse 2, New York 0
3/13: Syracuse 129, NEW YORK 123
3/15: SYRACUSE 131, New York 115
EASTERN DIVISION FINALS
Boston 4, Syracuse 3
3/18: BOSTON 131, Syracuse 109
3/21: SYRACUSE 120, Boston 118
3/22: BOSTON 133, Syracuse 111
3/25: SYRACUSE 119, Boston 107
3/28: BOSTON 129, Syracuse 108
3/29: SYRACUSE 133, Boston 121
4/ 1: BOSTON 130, Syracuse 125

1960

EASTERN DIVISION SEMIFINALS
Philadelphia 2, Syracuse 1
3/11: PHILADELPHIA 115, Syracuse 92
3/13: SYRACUSE 125, Philadelphia 119
3/14: PHILA. 132, Syracuse 112

1961

EASTERN DIVISION SEMIFINALS
Syracuse 3, Philadelphia 0
3/14: Syracuse 115, PHILA. 107
3/16: SYRACUSE 115, Philadelphia 114
3/18: Syracuse 106, Philadelphia 103
EASTERN DIVISON FINALS
Boston 4, Syracuse 1
3/19: BOSTON 128, Syracuse 115
3/21: SYRACUSE 115, Boston 98
3/23: BOSTON 133, Syracuse 110
3/25: Boston 120, SYRACUSE 107
3/26: BOSTON 123, Syracuse 101

1962

EASTERN DIVISION SEMIFINALS
Philadelphia 3, Syracuse 2
3/16: PHILA. 110, Syracuse 103
3/18: Philadelphia 97, SYRACUSE 82
3/19: Syracuse 101, PHILA. 100
3/20: Philadelphia 106, Syracuse 99
3/22: PHILA. 121, Syracuse 104

1963

EASTERN DIVISION SEMIFINALS
Cincinnati 3, Syracuse 2
3/19: SYRACUSE 123, Cincinnati 120
3/21: CINCINNATI 133, Syracuse 115
3/23: SYRACUSE 121, Cincinnati 117
3/24: CINCINNATI 125, Syracuse 118
3/26: Cincinnati 131, SYRACUSE 127 (ot)

1964

EASTERN DIVISION SEMIFINALS
Cincinnati 3, Sixers 2
3/22: CINCINNATI 127, Sixers 102
3/24: SIXERS 122, Cincinnati 114
3/25: CINCINNATI 101, Sixers 89
3/28: SIXERS 129, Cincinnati 120
3/29: CINCINNATI 130, Sixers 124

1965

EASTERN DIVISION SEMIFINALS
Sixers 3, Cincinnati 1
3/24: Sixers 119, CINCINNATI 117
3/26: Cincinnati 121, SIXERS 120
3/28: Sixers 108, CINCINNATI 94 (ot)
3/31: SIXERS 119, Cincinnati 112
EASTERN DIVISION FINALS
Boston 4, Sixers 3
4/ 4: BOSTON 108, Sixers 98
4/ 6: SIXERS 109, Boston 103
4/ 8: BOSTON 112, Sixers 94
4/ 9: SIXERS 134, Boston 131 (ot)
4/11: BOSTON 114, Sixers 108
4/13: SIXERS 112, Boston 106
4/15: BOSTON 110, Sixers 109

1966

EASTERN DIVISION FINALS
Boston 4, Sixers 1
4/ 3: Boston 115, SIXERS 96
4/ 6: BOSTON 114, Sixers 93
4/ 7: SIXERS 111, Boston 105
4/10: BOSTON 114, Sixers 108 (ot)
4/12: Boston 120, Sixers 112

1967

EASTERN DIVISION SEMIFINALS
Sixers 3, Cincinnati 1
3/21: Cincinnati 120, Sixers 116
3/22: Sixers 123, CINCINNATI 102
3/24: SIXERS 121, Cincinnati 106
3/25: Sixers 112, CINCINNATI 94

POSTSEASON RESULTS

1967

EASTERN DIVISION FINALS
Sixers 4, Boston 1
3/31: SIXERS 127, Boston 113
4/ 2: Sixers 107, BOSTON 102
4/ 5: SIXERS 115, Boston 104
4/ 9: BOSTON 121, Sixers 117
4/11: SIXERS 140, Boston 116

CHAMPIONSHIP SERIES
Sixers 4, San Francisco 2
4/14: SIXERS 141, San Fran. 135 (ot)
4/16: SIXERS 126, San Francisco 95
4/18: SAN FRANCISCO 130, Sixers 124
4/20: Sixers 122, SAN FRANCISCO 108
4/23: San Francisco 117, SIXERS 109
4/24: Sixers 125, SAN FRANCISCO 122

1968

EASTERN DIVISION SEMIFINALS
Sixers 4, New York 2
3/22: SIXERS 118, New York 110
3/23: NEW YORK 128, Sixers 117
3/27: SIXERS 138, New York 132 (2ot)
3/30: NEW YORK 107, Sixers 98
3/31: SIXERS 123, New York 107
4/ 1: Sixers 113, NEW YORK 97

EASTERN DIVISION FINALS
Boston 4, Sixers 3
4/ 5: Boston 127, SIXERS 118
4/10: Sixers 115, BOSTON 106
4/11: SIXERS 122, Boston 114
4/14: Sixers 110, BOSTON 105
4/15: Boston 122, SIXERS 104
4/17: BOSTON 114, Sixers 106
4/19: Boston 100, SIXERS 96

1969

EASTERN DIVISION SEMIFINALS
Boston 4, Sixers 1
3/26: Boston 114, SIXERS 100
3/28: BOSTON 134, Sixers 103
3/30: Boston 125, SIXERS 118
4/ 1: Sixers 119, BOSTON 116
4/ 4: Boston 93, SIXERS 90

1970

EASTERN DIVISION SEMIFINALS
Milwaukee 4, Sixers 1
3/25: MILWAUKEE 125, Sixers 118
3/27: Sixers 112, MILWAUKEE 105
3/30: Milwaukee 156, SIXERS 120
4/ 1: Milwaukee 118, SIXERS 111
4/ 3: MILWAUKEE 115, Sixers 106

1971

EASTERN CONFERENCE SEMIFINALS
Baltimore 4, Sixers 3
3/24: Sixers 126, BALTIMORE 112
3/26: Baltimore 119, SIXERS 107
3/28: BALTIMORE 111, Sixers 103
3/30: Baltimore 120, Sixers 105
4/ 1: Sixers 104, BALTIMORE 103
4/ 3: SIXERS 98, Baltimore 94
4/ 4: BALTIMORE 128, Sixers 120

1976

FIRST ROUND
Buffalo 2, Sixers 1
4/15: Buffalo 95, SIXERS 89
4/16: Sixers 131, BUFFALO 106
4/18: Buffalo 124, SIXERS 123 (ot)

1977

EASTERN CONFERENCE SEMIFINALS
Sixers 4, Boston 3
4/17: Boston 113, SIXERS 111
4/20: SIXERS 113, Boston 101
4/22: Sixers 109, BOSTON 100
4/24: BOSTON 124, Sixers 119
4/27: SIXERS 110, Boston 91
4/29: BOSTON 113, Sixers 108
5/ 1: SIXERS 83, Boston 77

EASTERN CONFERENCE FINALS
Sixers 4, Houston 2
5/ 5: SIXERS 128, Houston 117
5/ 8: SIXERS 106, Houston 97
5/11: HOUSTON 118, Sixers 94
5/13: Sixers 107, HOUSTON 95
5/15: Houston 118, SIXERS 115
5/17: Sixers 112, HOUSTON 109

CHAMPIONSHIP FINALS
Portland 4, Sixers 2
5/22: SIXERS 107, Portland 101
5/26: SIXERS 107, Portland 89
5/29: PORTLAND 129, Sixers 107
5/31: PORTLAND 130, Sixers 98
6/ 3: Portland 110, SIXERS 104
6/ 5: PORTLAND 109, Sixers 107

1978

EASTERN CONFERENCE SEMIFINALS
Sixers 4, New York 0
4/16: SIXERS 130, New York 90
4/18: SIXERS 119, New York 100
4/20: Sixers 137, NEW YORK 126
4/23: Sixers 112, NEW YORK 107

EASTERN CONFERENCE FINALS
Washington 4, Sixers 2
4/30: Washington 122, SIXERS 117
5/ 3: SIXERS 110, Washington 104
5/ 5: WASHINGTON 123, Sixers 108
5/ 7: WASHINGTON 121, Sixers 105
5/10: SIXERS 107, Washington 94
5/12: WASHINGTON 101, Sixers 99

1979

FIRST ROUND
Sixers 2, New Jersey 0
4/11: SIXERS 122, New Jersey 114
4/13: Sixers 111, NEW JERSEY 101

EASTERN CONFERENCE SEMIFINALS
San Antonio 4, Sixers 3
4/15: SAN ANTONIO 119, Sixers 106
4/17: SAN ANTONIO 121, Sixers 120
4/20: SIXERS 123, San Antonio 115
4/22: San Antonio 115, SIXERS 112
4/26: Sixers 120, SAN ANTONIO 97
4/29: SIXERS 92, San Antonio 90
5/ 2: SAN ANTONIO 111, Sixers 108

Dave Cowens shoots over Darryl Dawkins in one of many Sixer-Celtic playoffs

POSTSEASON RESULTS

1980

FIRST ROUND
Sixers 2, Washington 0
4/ 2: SIXERS 111, Washington 96
4/ 4: Sixers 112, WASHINGTON 104

EASTERN CONFERENCE SEMIFINALS
Sixers 4, Atlanta 1
4/ 6: SIXERS 107, Atlanta 104
4/ 9: SIXERS 99, Atlanta 92
4/10: ATLANTA 105, Sixers 93
4/13: Sixers 107, ATLANTA 83
4/15: SIXERS 105, Atlanta 100

EASTERN CONFERENCE FINALS
Sixers 4, Boston 1
4/18: Sixers 96, BOSTON 93
4/20: BOSTON 96, Sixers 90
4/23: SIXERS 99, Boston 97
4/24: SIXERS 102, Boston 90
4/27: Sixers 105, BOSTON 94

CHAMPIONSHIP FINALS
Los Angeles 4, Sixers 2
5/ 4: LOS ANGELES 109, Sixers 102
5/ 7: Sixers 107, LOS ANGELES 104
5/10: Los Angeles 111, SIXERS 101
5/11: SIXERS 105, Los Angeles 102
5/14: LOS ANGELES 108, Sixers 103
5/16: Los Angeles 123, SIXERS 107

1981

FIRST ROUND
Sixers 2, Indiana 0
3/31: SIXERS 124, Indiana 108
4/ 2: Sixers 96, INDIANA 85

EASTERN CONFERENCE SEMIFINALS
Sixers 4, Milwaukee 3
4/ 5: SIXERS 125, Milwaukee 122
4/ 7: Milwaukee 109, SIXERS 99
4/10: Sixers 108, MILWAUKEE 103
4/12: MILWAUKEE 109, Sixers 98
4/15: SIXERS 116, Milwaukee 99
4/17: MILWAUKEE 109, Sixers 86
4/19: SIXERS 99, Milwaukee 98

EASTERN CONFERENCE FINALS
Boston 4, Sixers 3
4/21: Sixers 105, BOSTON 104
4/22: BOSTON 118, Sixers 99
4/24: SIXERS 110, Boston 100
4/26: SIXERS 107, Boston 105
4/29: BOSTON 111, Sixers 109
5/ 1: Boston 100, SIXERS 98
5/ 3: BOSTON 91, Sixers 90

1982

FIRST ROUND
Sixers 2, Atlanta 0
4/21: SIXERS 111, Atlanta 76
4/23: Sixers 98, ATLANTA 95

EASTERN CONFERENCE SEMIFINALS
Sixers 4, Milwaukee 2
4/25: SIXERS 125, Milwaukee 122
4/28: SIXERS 120, Milwaukee 108
5/ 1: MILWAUKEE 92, Sixers 91
5/ 2: Sixers 100, MILWAUKEE 93
5/ 5: Milwaukee 110, SIXERS 98
5/ 7: Sixers 102, MILWAUKEE 90

EASTERN CONFERENCE FINALS
Sixers 4, Boston 3
5/ 9: BOSTON 121, Sixers 81
5/12: Sixers 121, BOSTON 113
5/15: SIXERS 99, Boston 97
5/16: SIXERS 119, Boston 94
5/19: BOSTON 114, Sixers 85
5/21: Boston 88, SIXERS 75
5/23: Sixers 120, BOSTON 106

CHAMPIONSHIP SERIES
Los Angeles 4, Sixers 2
5/27: Los Angeles 124, SIXERS 117
5/30: SIXERS 110, Los Angeles 94
6/ 1: LOS ANGELES 129, Sixers 108
6/ 3: LOS ANGELES 111, Sixers 101
6/ 6: SIXERS 135, Los Angeles 102
6/ 8: LOS ANGELES 114, Sixers 104

1983

EASTERN CONFERENCE SEMIFINALS
Sixers 4, New York 0
4/24: SIXERS 112, New York 102
4/27: SIXERS 98, New York 91
4/30: Sixers 107, NEW YORK 105
5/ 1: Sixers 105, NEW YORK 102

EASTERN CONFERENCE FINALS
Sixers 4, Milwaukee 1
5/ 8: SIXERS 111, Milwaukee 109
5/11: SIXERS 87, Milwaukee 81
5/14: Sixers 104, MILWAUKEE 96
5/15: MILWAUKEE 100, Sixers 94
5/18: SIXERS 115, Milwaukee 103

CHAMPIONSHIP SERIES
Sixers 4, Los Angeles 0
5/22: SIXERS 113, Los Angeles 107
5/26: SIXERS 103, Los Angeles 93
5/29: Sixers 111, LOS ANGELES 94
5/31: Sixers 115, LOS ANGELES 108

1984

FIRST ROUND
New Jersey 3, Sixers 2
4/18: New Jersey 116, SIXERS 101
4/20: New Jersey 116, SIXERS 102
4/22: Sixers 108, NEW JERSEY 100
4/24: Sixers 110, NEW JERSEY 102
4/26: New Jersey 101, SIXERS 98

1985

FIRST ROUND
Sixers 3, Washington 1
4/17: SIXERS 104, Washington 97
4/21: SIXERS 113, Washington 94
4/24: WASHINGTON 118, Sixers 100
4/26: Sixers 106, WASHINGTON 98

EASTERN CONFERENCE SEMIFINALS
Sixers 4, Milwaukee 0
4/28: Sixers 127, MILWAUKEE 105
4/30: Sixers 112, MILWAUKEE 108
5/ 3: SIXERS 109, Milwaukee 104
5/ 5: SIXERS 121, Milwaukee 112

EASTERN CONFERENCE FINALS
Boston 4, Sixers 1
5/12: BOSTON 108, Sixers 93
5/14: BOSTON 106, Sixers 98
5/18: Boston 105, SIXERS 94
5/19: SIXERS 115, Boston 104
5/22: BOSTON 102, Sixers 100

1986

FIRST ROUND
Sixers 3, Washington 2
4/18: Washington 95, SIXERS 94
4/20: SIXERS 102, Washington 97
4/22: Sixers 91, WASHINGTON 86
4/24: WASHINGTON 116, Sixers 111
4/27: SIXERS 134, Washington 109

EASTERN CONFERENCE SEMIFINALS
Milwaukee 4, Sixers 3
4/29: Sixers 118, MILWAUKEE 112
5/ 1: MILWAUKEE 119, Sixers 107
5/ 3: SIXERS 107, Milwaukee 103
5/ 5: Milwaukee 109, SIXERS 104
5/ 7: MILWAUKEE 113, Sixers 108
5/ 9: SIXERS 126, Milwaukee 108
5/11: MILWAUKEE 113, Sixers 112

1987

FIRST ROUND
Milwaukee 3, Sixers 2
4/24: MILWAUKEE 107, Sixers 104
4/26: Sixers 125, MILWAUKEE 122 (ot)
4/29: Milwaukee 121, SIXERS 120
5/ 1: SIXERS 124, Milwaukee 118
5/ 3: MILWAUKEE 102, Sixers 89

1989

FIRST ROUND
New York 3, Sixers 0
4/27: New York 102, Sixers 96
4/29: New York 107, Sixers 106
5/ 2: New York 116, Sixers 115 (ot)

Owner Harold Katz celebrates '83 NBA Title following Game 4 in Los Angeles

PROFILE

Wilt Chamberlain

Wilt.

Now that we have established who we are talking about ...

It is, of course, Wilton Norman Chamberlain. Wilt The Stilt, The Dipper. Probably the greatest basketball player who ever played, perhaps the greatest athlete who ever lived.

Even in 1989, as sports fans remember Kareem Abdul-Jabbar in his farewell season, Chamberlain won a Philadelphia *Daily News* poll of experts who were asked to name the greatest center of all time.

After all, it is hard to argue with the numbers. Actually, it is hard not to be overwhelmed by Chamberlain's numbers.

Let's take a look:

How about 100 points, by far the most ever scored in an NBA game? The Philadelphia Warriors' 7-1, 275-pound center set the mark against the New York Knicks in Hershey, Pa., on March 2, 1962.

Chamberlain holds NBA career records for free throw attempts (11,862), rebounds (23,924) and scoring average (30.1 points).

He holds single-game records for points (100) and rebounds in both the regular season (55 vs. Boston, Nov. 24, 1960) and playoffs (41 vs. Boston, April 5, 1967).

He led the NBA in scoring seven seasons, in rebounding 11 seasons and in field goal percentage nine seasons. In one remarkable year, 1967-68, he led the league in *assists*.

Chamberlain was born in Philadelphia on Aug. 21, 1936. He honed his skills and added inches while playing at Haddington Recreation Center at 57th St. and Haverford Ave.

At Overbrook High School, Chamberlain set city records for points in a game (90 vs. Roxborough, Feb. 17, 1955) and in a career (2,252).

From there, it was on to the University of Kansas, where he averaged 29.9 points for two seasons. Chamberlain passed on his senior season, 1958-59, so he could travel and play with the Harlem Globetrotters.

Chamberlain's NBA career began in 1959 after he was picked on the first round (territorial choice) by the Philadelphia Warriors. He played three seasons in Philadelphia, then 2½ in San Francisco when the franchise moved West.

Chamberlain returned home on Jan. 15, 1965, when he was traded from the Warriors to the 76ers for Connie Dierking, Paul Neumann, Lee Shaffer and cash. Wilt played 3½ seasons in Philadelphia before being traded to the Los Angeles Lakers on July 9, 1968 for Jerry Chambers, Archie Clark and Darrall Imhoff.

Chamberlain's 76ers won the 1966-67 NBA title, as did his '71-72 Lakers.

Julius Erving

Julius Erving's career spanned 16 years, two ABA championships, the jump to the NBA and the Sixers, 11 NBA All-Star appearances, a combined 30,026 points and, at last in 1983, a world championship.

Some say the reason the NBA went ahead with the ABA merger was to finally get his talents into the league.

But Erving is remembered, and will be remembered for far more than his statistics. Erving was the first player to gain superstar fame for flying.

This was the reaction of the Lakers' impressionable rookie Magic Johnson after a skywalking Erving effort in the 1980 NBA Finals:

"I swore he jumped out of bounds and glided on the other side of the hoop, spun it up off the glass and in," Johnson said. "Here I am, trying to win a championship, and my mouth just dropped open.

"We [Lakers] all just looked at each other like, 'What should we do? Should we take the ball out or should we ask him to do it again?'"

Erving, born in Roosevelt, N.Y., on Feb. 22, 1950, attended Roosevelt High School and the University of Massachusetts. He left college after his junior season as a none-too-highly regarded pro prospect. He went straight to the ABA, whose wide-open and wooly playing style fit him perfectly.

With the New York Nets, Erving was unquestionably the league's greatest star. In five ABA seasons, he averaged 28.7 points and 12.1 rebounds a game.

Then, when the merger came off in 1976, embroiled in a contract dispute with the Nets, it took $6 million — $3 million for his rights, $3 million to sign him — to get him into a Sixer uniform. And though his unbridled style had to be muted, he was still very much a superstar in the NBA. He averaged 21.6 points a game in his first Sixer season, well below his ABA mark.

Gradually, he got used to the Sixers and they got used to Erving, and the team made the Eastern Conference finals seven times in his career, getting to the championship finals four times, and winning the one title.

In 1979-80, his best year with the Sixers, Erving averaged 26.9 points a game, leading the team to a 59-23 record. The next year, with the Sixers on their way to a 62-20 record, Erving was named the league's MVP.

Two years later, the Sixers rolled to a 65-17 record and went on to sweep the Lakers in four straight to capture the NBA title.

With Erving, the Sixers never won less than 45 games, won more than 50 eight times, and more than 60 twice.

If you count his ABA stats, Erving is one of only three players (along with Wilt Chamberlain and Kareem Abdul-Jabbar) to score more than 30,000 points, and not counting the ABA, is ranked 21st among all-time NBA scorers.

In 1980, he was named to the NBA's 35th Anniversary All-Time team. He retired at the end of the 1986-87 season.

"He spawned a generation of NBA players who have worked to emulate him," said Detroit coach and former Sixer assistant Chuck Daly. "People look at him and say, 'He's the one.'"

FLYERS

YEAR-BY-YEAR RECORDS

Season	Head Coach	W	L	T	Pts.	Pos.
1967-68	Keith Allen	31	32	11	73	1
1968-69	Keith Allen	20	35	21	61	3
1969-70	Vic Stasiuk	17	35	24	58	5
1970-71	Vic Stasiuk	28	33	17	73	3
1971-72	Fred Shero	26	38	14	66	5
1972-73	Fred Shero	37	30	11	85	2
1973-74	Fred Shero	50	16	12	112	1
1974-75	Fred Shero	51	18	11	113	1
1975-76	Fred Shero	51	13	16	118	1
1976-77	Fred Shero	48	16	16	112	1
1977-78	Fred Shero	45	20	15	105	2
1978-79	Bob McCammon	22	17	11	55	4
	Pat Quinn	18	8	4	40	—
	Totals	40	25	15	95	2

Season	Head Coach	W	L	T	Pts.	Pos.
1979-80	Pat Quinn	48	12	20	116	1
1980-81	Pat Quinn	41	24	15	97	2
1981-82	Pat Quinn	34	29	9	77	3
	Bob McCammon	4	2	2	10	—
	Totals	38	31	11	87	3
1982-83	Bob McCammon	49	23	8	106	1
1983-84	Bob McCammon	44	26	10	98	3
1984-85	Mike Keenan	53	20	7	113	1
1985-86	Mike Keenan	53	23	4	110	1
1986-87	Mike Keenan	46	26	8	100	1
1987-88	Mike Keenan	38	33	9	85	3
1988-89	Paul Holmgren	36	36	8	80	4

POSTSEASON RESULTS

(Home team in CAPS)

1967-68

QUARTERFINALS
St. Louis 4, Flyers 3
4/ 4: St. Louis 1, FLYERS 0
4/ 6: FLYERS 4, St. Louis 3
4/10: ST. LOUIS 3, Flyers 2 (ot)
4/11: ST. LOUIS 5, Flyers 2
4/13: FLYERS 6, St. Louis 1
4/16: Flyers 2, ST. LOUIS 1 (ot)
4/18: St. Louis 3, FLYERS 1

1968-69

QUARTERFINALS
St. Louis 4, Flyers 0
4/ 2: ST. LOUIS 5, Flyers 2
4/ 3: ST. LOUIS 5, Flyers 0
4/ 5: St. Louis 4, FLYERS 0
4/ 6: St. Louis 4, FLYERS 1

1970-71

QUARTERFINALS
Chicago 4, Flyers 0
4/ 7: CHICAGO 5, Flyers 2
4/ 8: CHICAGO 6, Flyers 2
4/10: Chicago 3, FLYERS 2
4/11: Chicago 6, FLYERS 2

1972-73

QUARTERFINALS
Flyers 4, Minnesota 2
4/ 4: Minnesota 3, FLYERS 0
4/ 5: FLYERS 4, Minnesota 1
4/ 7: MINNESOTA 5, Flyers 0
4/ 8: Flyers 3, MINNESOTA 0
4/10: FLYERS 3, Minnesota 2 (ot)
4/12: Flyers 4, MINNESOTA 1

SEMIFINALS
Montreal 4, Flyers 1
4/14: Flyers 5, MONTREAL 4 (ot)
4/16: MONTREAL 4, Flyers 3 (ot)
4/19: Montreal 2, FLYERS 1
4/22: Montreal 4, FLYERS 1
4/24: MONTREAL 5, Flyers 3

1973-74

QUARTERFINALS
Flyers 4, Atlanta 0
4/ 9: FLYERS 4, Atlanta 1
4/11: FLYERS 5, Atlanta 1
4/12: Flyers 4, ATLANTA 1
4/14: Flyers 4, ATLANTA 3 (ot)
SEMIFINALS
Flyers 4, New York Rangers 3
4/20: FLYERS 4, New York 0
4/23: FLYERS 5, New York 2
4/25: NEW YORK 5, Flyers 3
4/28: NEW YORK 2, Flyers 1 (ot)
4/30: FLYERS 4, New York 1
5/ 2: NEW YORK 4, Flyers 1
5/ 5: FLYERS 4, New York 3
STANLEY CUP FINALS
Flyers 4, Boston 2
5/ 7: BOSTON 2, Flyers 1
5/ 9: Flyers 3, BOSTON 2 (ot)
5/12: FLYERS 4, Boston 1
5/14: FLYERS 4, Boston 2
5/16: BOSTON 5, Flyers 1
5/19: FLYERS 1, Boston 0

1974-75

QUARTERFINALS
Flyers 4, Toronto 0
4/13: FLYERS 6, Toronto 3
4/15: FLYERS 3, Toronto 0
4/17: Flyers 2, TORONTO 0
4/19: Flyers 4, TORONTO 3 (ot)

SEMIFINALS
Flyers 4, New York Islanders 3
4/29: FLYERS 4, New York 0
5/ 1: FLYERS 5, New York 4 (ot)
5/ 4: Flyers 1, NEW YORK 0
5/ 7: NEW YORK 4, Flyers 3 (ot)
5/ 8: New York 5, FLYERS 1
5/11: NEW YORK 2, Flyers 1
5/13: FLYERS 4, New York 1
STANLEY CUP FINALS
Flyers 4, Buffalo 2
5/15: FLYERS 4, Buffalo 1
5/18: FLYERS 2, Buffalo 1
5/20: BUFFALO 5, Flyers 4 (ot)
5/22: BUFFALO 4, Flyers 2
5/25: FLYERS 5, Buffalo 1
5/27: Flyers 2, BUFFALO 0

1975-76

QUARTERFINALS
Flyers 4, Toronto 3
4/12: FLYERS 4, Toronto 1
4/13: FLYERS 3, Toronto 1
4/15: TORONTO 5, Flyers 4
4/17: TORONTO 4, Flyers 3
4/20: FLYERS 7, Toronto 1
4/22: TORONTO 8, Flyers 5
4/25: FLYERS 7, Toronto 3
SEMIFINALS
Flyers 4, Boston 1
4/27: Boston 4, FLYERS 2
4/29: FLYERS 2, Boston 1
5/ 2: Flyers 5, BOSTON 2
5/ 4: Flyers 4, BOSTON 2
5/ 6: FLYERS 6, Boston 3
STANLEY CUP FINALS
Montreal 4, Flyers 0
5/ 9: MONTREAL 4, Flyers 3
5/11: MONTREAL 2, Flyers 1
5/13: Montreal 3, FLYERS 2
5/16: Montreal 5, FLYERS 3

POSTSEASON RESULTS

1976-77

QUARTERFINALS
Flyers 4, Toronto 2
4/11: Toronto 3, FLYERS 2
4/13: Toronto 4, FLYERS 1
4/15: Flyers 4, TORONTO 3 (ot)
4/17: Flyers 6, TORONTO 5 (ot)
4/19: FLYERS 2, Toronto 0
4/21: Flyers 4, TORONTO 3
SEMIFINALS
Boston 4, Flyers 0
4/24: Boston 4, FLYERS 3 (ot)
4/26: Boston 5, FLYERS 4 (ot)
4/28: BOSTON 2, Flyers 1
5/ 1: BOSTON 3, Flyers 0

1977-78

PRELIMINARY ROUND
Flyers 2, Colorado 0
4/11: FLYERS 3, Colorado 2 (ot)
4/13: Flyers 3, COLORADO 1

QUARTERFINALS
Flyers 4, Buffalo 1
4/17: FLYERS 4, Buffalo 1
4/19: FLYERS 3, Buffalo 2
4/22: BUFFALO 4, Flyers 1
4/23: Flyers 4, BUFFALO 2
4/25: FLYERS 4, Buffalo 2
SEMIFINALS
Boston 4, Flyers 1
5/ 2: BOSTON 3, Flyers 2 (ot)
5/ 4: BOSTON 7, Flyers 4
5/ 7: FLYERS 3, Boston 1
5/ 9: Boston 4, FLYERS 2
5/11: BOSTON 6, Flyers 3

1978-79

PRELIMINARY ROUND
Flyers 2, Vancouver 1
4/10: Vancouver 3, FLYERS 2
4/12: Flyers 6, VANCOUVER 4
4/14: FLYERS 7, Vancouver 2

QUARTERFINALS
New York Rangers 4, Flyers 1
4/16: FLYERS 3, New York 2 (ot)
4/18: New York 7, FLYERS 1
4/20: NEW YORK 5, Flyers 1
4/22: NEW YORK 6, Flyers 0
4/24: New York 8, FLYERS 3

1979-80

PRELIMINARY ROUND
Flyers 3, Edmonton 0
4/ 8: FLYERS 4, Edmonton 3 (ot)
4/ 9: FLYERS 5, Edmonton 1
4/11: Flyers 4, EDMONTON 2 (ot)
QUARTERFINALS
Flyers 4, New York Rangers 1
4/16: FLYERS 2, New York 1
4/17: FLYERS 4, New York 1
4/19: Flyers 3, NEW YORK 0
4/20: NEW YORK 4, Flyers 2
4/22: FLYERS 3, New York 1
SEMIFINALS
Flyers 4, Minnesota 1
4/29: Minnesota 6, FLYERS 5
5/ 1: FLYERS 7, Minnesota 0
5/ 4: Flyers 5, MINNESOTA 3
5/ 6: Flyers 3, MINNESOTA 2
5/ 8: FLYERS 7, Minnesota 3
STANLEY CUP FINALS
New York Islanders 4, Flyers 2
5/13: New York 4, Flyers 3 (ot)
5/15: FLYERS 8, New York 3
5/17: NEW YORK 6, Flyers 2
5/19: NEW YORK 5, Flyers 2
5/22: FLYERS 6, New York 3
5/24: NEW YORK 5, Flyers 4 (ot)

1980-81

PRELIMINARY ROUND
Flyers 3, Quebec 2
4/ 8: FLYERS 6, Quebec 4
4/ 9: FLYERS 8, Quebec 5
4/11: QUEBEC 2, Flyers 0
4/12: QUEBEC 4, Flyers 3 (ot)
4/14: FLYERS 5, Quebec 2
QUARTERFINALS
Calgary 4, Flyers 3
4/16: FLYERS 4, Calgary 0
4/17: Calgary 5, FLYERS 4
4/19: CALGARY 2, Flyers 1
4/20: CALGARY 5, Flyers 4
4/22: FLYERS 9, Calgary 4
4/24: Flyers 3, CALGARY 2
4/26: Calgary 4, FLYERS 1

1981-82

PATRICK DIVISION SEMIFINALS
New York Rangers 3, Flyers 1
4/ 7: Flyers 4, NEW YORK 1
4/ 8: NEW YORK 7, Flyers 3
4/10: New York 4, FLYERS 3
4/11: New York 7, FLYERS 5

1982-83

PATRICK DIVISION SEMIFINALS
New York Rangers 3, Flyers 0
4/ 5: New York 5, FLYERS 3
4/ 7: New York 4, FLYERS 3
4/ 9: NEW YORK 9, Flyers 3

1983-84

PATRICK DIVISION SEMIFINALS
Washington 3, Flyers 0
4/ 4: WASHINGTON 4, Flyers 2
4/ 5: WASHINGTON 6, Flyers 2
4/ 7: Washington 5, FLYERS 1

Quebec's Daniel Bouchard stops Ken Linseman's shot in 1981 playoffs

POSTSEASON RESULTS

1984-85

PATRICK DIVISION SEMIFINALS
Flyers 3, New York Rangers 0
4/10: FLYERS 5, New York 4 (ot)
4/11: FLYERS 3, New York 1
4/13: Flyers 6, New York 0
PATRICK DIVISION FINALS
Flyers 4, New York Islanders 1
4/18: FLYERS 3, New York 0
4/21: FLYERS 5, New York 2
4/23: Flyers 5, NEW YORK 3
4/25: NEW YORK 6, Flyers 2
4/28: FLYERS 1, New York 0
WALES CONFERENCE FINALS
Flyers 4, Quebec 2
5/ 5: QUEBEC 2, Flyers 1 (ot)
5/ 7: Flyers 4, QUEBEC 2
5/ 9: FLYERS 4, Quebec 2
5/12: Quebec 5, FLYERS 3
5/14: Flyers 2, QUEBEC 1
5/16: FLYERS 3, Quebec 0
STANLEY CUP FINALS
Edmonton 4, Flyers 1
5/21: FLYERS 4, Edmonton 1
5/23: Edmonton 3, FLYERS 1
5/25: EDMONTON 4, Flyers 3
5/28: EDMONTON 5, Flyers 3
5/30: Edmonton 8, FLYERS 3

1985-86

PATRICK DIVISION SEMIFINALS
New York Rangers 3, Flyers 2
4/ 9: New York 6, FLYERS 2
4/10: FLYERS 2, New York 1
4/12: NEW YORK 5, Flyers 2
4/14: Flyers 7, NEW YORK 1
4/15: New York 5, FLYERS 2

1986-87

PATRICK DIVISION SEMIFINALS
Flyers 4, New York Rangers 2
4/ 8: New York 3, FLYERS 0
4/ 9: FLYERS 8, New York 3
4/11: Flyers 3, NEW YORK 0
4/12: NEW YORK 6, Flyers 3
4/14: FLYERS 3, New York 1
4/16: Flyers 5, NEW YORK 0
PATRICK DIVISION FINALS
Flyers 4, New York Islanders 3
4/20: FLYERS 4, New York 2
4/22: New York 2, FLYERS 1
4/24: Flyers 4, NEW YORK 1
4/26: Flyers 6, NEW YORK 4
4/28: New York 2, FLYERS 1
4/30: NEW YORK 4, Flyers 2
5/ 2: FLYERS 5, New York 1
WALES CONFERENCE FINALS
Flyers 4, Montreal 2
5/ 4: FLYERS 4, Montreal 3 (ot)
5/ 6: Montreal 5, FLYERS 2
5/ 8: Flyers 4, MONTREAL 3
5/10: Flyers 6, MONTREAL 3
5/12: Montreal 5, FLYERS 2
5/14: Flyers 4, MONTREAL 3
STANLEY CUP FINALS
Edmonton 4, Flyers 3
5/17: EDMONTON 4, Flyers 2
5/20: EDMONTON 3, Flyers 2 (ot)
5/22: FLYERS 5, Edmonton 3
5/24: Edmonton 4, FLYERS 1
5/26: Flyers 4, EDMONTON 3
5/28: FLYERS 3, Edmonton 2
5/31: EDMONTON 3, Flyers 1

1987-88

PATRICK DIVISION SEMIFINALS
Washington 4, Flyers 3
4/ 6: Flyers 4, WASHINGTON 2
4/ 7: WASHINGTON 5, Flyers 4
4/ 9: FLYERS 4, Washington 3
4/10: FLYERS 5, Washington 4 (ot)
4:12: WASHINGTON 5, Flyers 2
4/14: Washington 7, FLYERS 2
4/16: WASHINGTON 5, Flyers 4 (ot)

1988-89

PATRICK DIVISION SEMIFINALS
Flyers 4, Washington 2
4/ 5: WASHINGTON 3, Flyers 2
4/ 6: Flyers 3, WASHINGTON 2
4/ 8: Washington 4, FLYERS 3 (ot)
4/ 9: FLYERS 5, Washington 2

4/11: Flyers 8, WASHINGTON 5
4/13: FLYERS 4, Washington 3
PATRICK DIVISION FINALS
Flyers 4, Pittsburgh 3
4/17: PITTSBURGH 4, Flyers 3
4/19: Flyers 4, PITTSBURGH 2
4/21: Pittsburgh 4, FLYERS 3 (ot)
4/23: FLYERS 4, Pittsburgh 1
4/25: PITTSBURGH 10, Flyers 7
4/27: FLYERS 6, Pittsburgh 2
4/29: Flyers 4, PITTSBURGH 1
WALES CONFERENCE FINALS
Montreal 4, Flyers 2
5/ 1: Flyers 3, MONTREAL 1
5/ 3: MONTREAL 3, Flyers 0
5/ 5: Montreal 5, FLYERS 1
5/ 7: Montreal 3, FLYERS 0
5/ 9: Flyers 2, MONTREAL 1 (ot)
5/11: MONTREAL 4, Flyers 2

Todd Bergen (left) and Tim Kerr celebrate Flyers' 1985 Division Final victory

COACHES' RECORDS

Seasons Head Coach	Regular Season				Playoffs		
	W-	L-	T	Pct.	W-	L	Pct.
1967-69 Keith Allen	51-	67-	32	.447	3-	8	.273
1969-71 Vic Stasiuk	45-	68-	41	.425	0-	4	.000
1971-78 Fred Shero	308-	151-	95	.642	48-	35	.578
1978-79 Bob McCammon	22-	17-	11	.550	0-	0	—
1982-84 Bob McCammon	97-	51-	20	.637	1-	9	.100
Totals	119-	68-	31	.617	1-	9	.100
1979-82 Pat Quinn	141-	73-	48	.630	22-	17	.564
1984-88 Mike Keenan	190-	102-	28	.638	32-	25	.561
1988-89 Paul Holmgren	36-	36-	8	.500	10-	9	.526

YEAR-BY-YEAR LEADERS

SEASON	GOALS		ASSISTS		POINTS	
1967-68	Leon Rochefort	21	Lou Angotti	37	Lou Angotti	49
1968-69	Andre Lacroix	24	Jean-Guy Gendron	35	Andre Lacroix	56
1969-70	Gary Dornhoefer	26	Andre Lacroix	36	Andre Lacroix	58
1970-71	Bob Clarke	27	Bob Clarke	36	Bob Clarke	63
1971-72	Bob Clarke	35	Bob Clarke	46	Bob Clarke	81
1972-73	Rick MacLeish	50	Bob Clarke	67	Bob Clarke	104
1973-74	Bob Clarke	35	Bob Clarke	52	Bob Clarke	87
1974-75	Reggie Leach	45	Bob Clarke	89	Bob Clarke	116
1975-76	Reggie Leach	61	Bob Clarke	89	Bob Clarke	119
1976-77	Rick MacLeish	49	Bob Clarke	62	Rick MacLeish	97
1977-78	Bill Barber	41	Bob Clarke	68	Bob Clarke	89
1978-79	Bill Barber Reggie Leach	34 34	Bob Clarke	57	Bill Barber	80
1979-80	Reggie Leach	50	Bob Clarke Ken Linseman	57 57	Ken Linseman	79
1980-81	Bill Barber	43	Behn Wilson	47	Bill Barber	85
1981-82	Bill Barber	45	Ken Linseman	68	Ken Linseman	92
1982-83	Darryl Sittler	43	Bob Clarke	62	Bob Clarke	85
1983-84	Tim Kerr	54	Brian Propp	53	Tim Kerr	93
1984-85	Tim Kerr	54	Brian Propp	54	Tim Kerr	98
1985-86	Tim Kerr	58	Mark Howe	58	Brian Propp	97
1986-87	Tim Kerr	58	Dave Poulin	45	Tim Kerr	95
1987-88	Rick Tocchet	31	Brian Propp	49	Murray Craven Brian Propp	76 76
1988-89	Tim Kerr	48	Pelle Eklund	51	Tim Kerr	88

SEASON	PENALTY MINUTES		GOALS AGAINST AVG.		WINS	
1967-68	Ed Van Impe	141	Doug Favell	2.27	Bernie Parent	16
1968-69	Forbes Kennedy	195	Bernie Parent	2.69	Bernie Parent	17
1969-70	Earl Heiskala	171	Bernie Parent	2.79	Bernie Parent	13
1970-71	Gary Dornhoefer	93	Doug Favell	2.66	Doug Favell	16
1971-72	Gary Dornhoefer	183	Doug Favell	2.80	Doug Favell	18
1972-73	Dave Schultz	259	Doug Favell	2.83	Doug Favell	20
1973-74	Dave Schultz	348	Bernie Parent	1.89	Bernie Parent	47
1974-75	Dave Schultz	472	Bernie Parent	2.03	Bernie Parent	44
1975-76	Dave Schultz	307	Wayne Stephenson	2.58	Wayne Stephenson	40
1976-77	Paul Holmgren	201	Wayne Stephenson	2.31	Bernie Parent	35
1977-78	Andre Dupont	225	Bernie Parent	2.22	Bernie Parent	29
1978-79	Behn Wilson	197	Bernie Parent	2.70	Wayne Stephenson	20
1979-80	Paul Holmgren	267	Pete Peeters	2.73	Pete Peeters	29
1980-81	Paul Holmgren	306	Rick St. Croix	2.49	Pete Peeters	22
1981-82	Glen Cochrane	329	Pete Peeters	3.71	Pete Peeters	23
1982-83	Glen Cochrane	237	Bob Froese	2.52	Pelle Lindbergh	23
1983-84	Glen Cochrane	225	Bob Froese	3.14	Bob Froese	28
1984-85	Rick Tocchet	181	Pelle Lindbergh	3.02	Pelle Lindbergh	40
1985-86	Rick Tocchet	284	Bob Froese	2.55	Bob Froese	31
1986-87	Rick Tocchet	286	Ron Hextall	3.00	Ron Hextall	37
1987-88	Rick Tocchet	301	Ron Hextall	3.51	Ron Hextall	30
1988-89	Jeff Chychrun	245	Ron Hextall	3.23	Ron Hextall	30

CAREER LEADERS

GOALS		ASSISTS		POINTS	
Bill Barber	420	Bob Clarke	852	Bob Clarke	1,210
Bob Clarke	358	Brian Propp	465	Bill Barber	883
Brian Propp	356	Bill Barber	463	Brian Propp	821
Tim Kerr	329	Rick MacLeish	369	Rick MacLeish	697
Rick MacLeish	328	Gary Dornhoefer	316	Tim Kerr	578
Reggie Leach	306	Mark Howe	293	Gary Dornhoefer	518
Gary Dornhoefer	202	Tim Kerr	249	Reggie Leach	514
Iikka Sinisalo	176	Dave Poulin	225	Mark Howe	417
Dave Poulin	152	Reggie Leach	208	Dave Poulin	377
Ross Lonsberry	144	Mel Bridgman	205	Ilkka Sinisalo	363

GAMES		PENALTY MINUTES	
Bob Clarke	1,144	Paul Holmgren	1,600
Bill Barber	903	Andre Dupont	1,505
Brian Propp	750	Bob Clarke	1,453
Joe Watson	746	Dave Schultz	1,386
Bob Kelly	741	Bob Kelly	1,285
Rick MacLeish	741	Gary Dornhoefer	1,256
Gary Dornhoefer	725	Rick Tocchet	1,235
Ed Van Impe	617	Glen Cochrane	1,110
Jim Watson	613	Dave Brown	1,031
Reggie Leach	606	Mel Bridgman	971

GOALTENDING

GAMES	
Bernie Parent	486
Doug Favell	215
Ron Hextall	192
Wayne Stephenson	165
Pelle Lindbergh	157
Bob Froese	144
Pete Peeters	129

SHUTOUTS	
Bernie Parent	50
Doug Favell	16
Bob Froese	12
Wayne Stephenson	10
Pelle Lindbergh	7
Pete Peeters	3
Ron Hextall	1

GOALS AGAINST AVG.	
Bernie Parent	2.42
Bob Froese	2.74
Wayne Stephenson	2.77
Doug Favell	2.78
Pete Peeters	3.16
Rick St. Croix	3.23
Ron Hextall	3.24

WINS	
Bernie Parent	232
Ron Hextall	97
Wayne Stephenson	93
Bob Froese	92
Pelle Lindbergh	87
Doug Favell	76
Pete Peeters	75

Goaltender Ron Hextall has 97 wins to place second on Flyers' all-time list

INDIVIDUAL RECORDS

	GAME
Goals	4: Rick MacLeish, vs. New York Islanders, 2/13/73 Rick MacLeish, vs. Toronto, 3/4/73 Tom Bladon, vs. Cleveland, 12/11/77 Tim Kerr, vs. St. Louis, 10/25/84 Tim Kerr, vs. Detroit, 1/17/85 Tim Kerr, vs. Washington, 2/9/85 Tim Kerr, vs. Chicago, 11/20/86 Brian Propp, vs. St. Louis, 12/2/86 Rick Tocchet, vs. Los Angeles, 2/27/88
Assists	5: Bob Clarke, vs. Washington, 4/1/76
Points	8: Tom Bladon, vs. Cleveland, 12/11/77
Penalty Minutes	55: Frank Bathe, vs. Los Angeles, 3/11/79

	SEASON	CAREER
Goals	61: Reggie Leach, 1975-76	420: Bill Barber, 1972-85
Power-play Goals	34: Tim Kerr, 1985-86	NA
Shorthanded Goals	7: Brian Propp, 1984-85 Mark Howe, 1985-86	NA
Assists	89: Bob Clarke, 1974-75, 1975-76	852: Bob Clarke, 1969-84
Points	119: Bob Clarke, 1975-76	1,210: Bob Clarke, 1969-84
Penalty Minutes	472: Dave Schultz, 1974-75	1,600: Paul Holmgren, 1975-84

TEAM RECORDS

GAME

	FLYERS	OPPONENT
Goals	13: vs. Pittsburgh, 3/22/84 vs. Vancouver, 10/18/84	12: Chicago, 1/30/69
Power-play Goals	6: vs. California, 1/9/72	6: Colorado, 2/19/80
Shorthanded Goals	3: vs. Washington, 12/15/84 vs. Calgary, 1/13/85	NA
Shots	62: vs. Washington, 4/1/76	55: Montreal, 1/3/77
Fewest Shots	14: vs. Detroit, 12/28/67 vs. Los Angeles, 12/4/68	7: Washington, 2/12/78
Assists	22: vs. Detroit, 2/2/74 vs. Pittsburgh, 3/22/84	NA
Points	35: vs. Pittsburgh, 3/22/84	NA
Penalties	27: vs. Los Angeles, 3/11/79	23: Los Angeles, 3/11/79
Penalty Minutes	194: vs. Los Angeles, 3/11/79	186: Los Angeles, 3/11/79
Fewest Penalty Minutes	0: vs. St. Louis, 3/18/79	0: Four times

SEASON

	MOST	FEWEST
Goals	350: 1983-84	173: 1967-68
Goals Against	313: 1981-82	164: 1973-74
Assists	632: 1985-86	290: 1967-68
Points	970: 1985-86	463: 1967-68
Penalty Minutes	2,621: 1980-81	964: 1968-69
Power-play Goals	98: 1988-89	31: 1967-68
Shorthanded Goals	22: 1986-87	3: 1970-71

Bobby Clarke

There are many who will say that there was no hockey in Philadelphia before a bespectacled, toothless kid from Flin Flon, Manitoba named Bobby Clarke came to town.

They may be right.

Bobby Clarke and his spirit, dedication and relentless style, was, is, and always will be synonymous with the Philadelphia Flyers.

Clarke was born in Flin Flon on Aug. 13, 1949. Within three years of his being drafted in the second round in 1969 (17th pick overall), Clarke's play and fiery leadership had the Flyers on a path to success that would lead to back-to-back Stanley Cups in 1974 and '75.

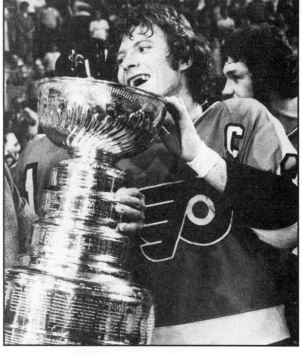

And it was Clarke's clutch goal-scoring that lifted them over the hump.

Few people around the NHL had given the Flyers much chance of beating the Boston Bruins in the 1974 Stanley Cup Finals. And the Flyers, having lost Game 1, found themselves down by a goal in the final minute of Game 2 before Andre Dupont gave them new life by scoring with just 52 seconds remaining.

Clarke then scored off a pass from Bill Flett in the overtime and all of a sudden — if they hadn't before — the Flyers believed they could go all the way.

And, indeed they did.

In his illustrious 15-year career, Clarke literally pinned the city's heart to his suspenders while becoming the club's all-time leading scorer (1,210 points on 358 goals and 852 assists) before he retired to become the Flyers general manager in 1984. He's 14th on the NHL's all-time scoring list.

Clarke, a three-time Hart Trophy winner as the league's Most Valuable Player, is regarded as one of the best defensive forwards ever to play the game. His No. 16 jersey was retired by the Flyers in a memorable Spectrum ceremony on Nov. 15, 1984.

"I counted on that number [16] so often," said Fred Shero, the legendary Flyers ex-coach. "Probably too much. He's the only man I ever coached who made me cry. He worked so hard night after night. I thought, 'No one should have to work that hard.'

"You can talk about players who were bigger and faster, with harder shots. But show me a player who accomplished more."

During his career, Clarke led the Flyers in scoring eight times and participated in nine All-Star games.

He also won each of the three major honors given by the Philadelphia Sports Writers Association, being named the Athlete of the Year in 1974, the Most Courageous Athlete in 1980 and winning the Good Guy Award in 1983.

Wrote the *Philadelphia Daily News's* Jay Greenberg, on the night of Clarke's induction into the Hockey Hall of Fame on June 15, 1987: "Lord, he was great. He was peerless as an inspiration and a leader, and so much more skilled as a player than the legend grew to allow.

"Until Wayne Gretzky, no player ever had a better grasp of the other 11 players on the ice."

Bernie Parent

"Only The Lord Saves More Than Bernie Parent."

It was the bumper sticker of the 1970's in Philadelphia, and you'd have a hard time convincing Flyers fans that it wasn't true.

Parent dominated the game with his acrobatics in front of the nets from 1974 until an eye injury forced his early retirement in 1979.

Now in his seventh season as the Flyers' goaltending instructor, Parent compiled an outstanding 2.42 goals-against average, with 50 shutouts, in his 10 seasons in Philadelphia. His 55 career shutouts in 13 NHL seasons ranks him 14th in NHL history. He won the Conn Smythe Trophy as the Most Valuable Player in the playoffs in the Flyers' two Stanley Cup-winning seasons, 1974 and '75.

Parent remains one of the most popular athletes ever to play in Philadelphia.

"I can't tell you the kind of impact that Bernie had on our game, on Philadelphia and on me personally," Flyers' owner Ed Snider said on Sept. 25, 1984, the night of Parent's induction into the Hockey Hall of Fame.

"Eighteen years ago [when the franchise was founded] I was a young businessman with a dream and Bernie Parent played a major part in helping that dream come true. Thank you, Bernie."

Parent will be remembered most in Philadelphia for his 1-0 shutout of Boston to win Stanley Cup I, and the 2-0 shutout of Buffalo to lock up the '75 Cup.

Everyone remembers Parent's highlights differently, but one save that will stand out forever in Flyers history was his robbery of the Bruins' Ken Hodge with less than three minutes remaining in Game 6 that protected the Flyers' 1-0 victory.

Hodge, the right wing on a powerful line with Phil Esposito and Wayne Cashman, unloaded a shot from the right circle.

Hodge's shot exploded off his stick, seemingly destined to find a corner and tie the game. Suddenly, an erect and perfectly balanced Parent thrust out his right skate, got a piece of it, with his arms parallel to the ice, steered the puck safely away as the Spectrum erupted.

"We were on the bench then, watching," said Bobby Clarke. "I don't know how Bernie made that save. It was unbelievable. We could have played all night after that and no one would have scored."

Parent, ironically, was traded, along with a No. 1 draft pick, to Toronto in 1971 in a three-way deal that also included Boston. The Flyers received Rick MacLeish, who would become a vital part of the Flyers' Cup teams three seasons later.

Two years later, the Flyers reaquired Parent, along with a No. 2 draft choice (Larry Goodenough) in exchange for the Flyers' No. 1 pick (Bob Neely). Doug Favell, the Flyers' starting goalie, was sent to the Leafs two months later to complete the deal.

It was the acquisition what would shape Flyers history.

DREXEL

YEAR-BY-YEAR RECORDS

Season	Head Coach	W- L	Pct.	Season	Head Coach	W- L	Pct.
1894-95	John Gray	7- 2	.778	1940-41	Lawrence Mains	5- 9	.357
1895-96	F. Knight	0- 1	.000	1941-42	Lawrence Mains	9- 5	.643
1904-05	None	3- 2	.667	1942-43	Lawrence Mains	12- 3	.800
1905-06	W.S. Brokaw	1- 1	.500	1943-44	Maury McMains	5- 6	.455
1906-07	W.S. Brokaw	11- 4	.733	1944-45	John Marino	2-11	.154
1907-08	F. Bennett	8- 9	.471	1945-46	Ralph Chase	2-13	.133
1908-09	G. Doughty	1- 2	.333	1946-47	Ralph Chase	10- 9	.526
1909-10	None	2- 7	.222	1947-48	Ralph Chase	4-14	.222
1910-11	Frank Griffin	4- 4	.500	1948-49	Ralph Chase	12- 4	.750
1911-12	Frank Griffin	7- 7	.500	1949-50	Hal Kollar	11- 5	.688
1912-13	Frank Griffin	4- 4	.500	1950-51	Hal Kollar	5-12	.294
1913-14	None	2- 0	1.000	1951-52	Hal Kollar	9-10	.474
1914-15	E.L. Lucas	7- 5	.583	1952-53	Sam Cozen	9- 8	.529
1915-16	E.L. Lucas	7- 5	.583	1953-54	Sam Cozen	15- 3	.833
1916-17	E.L. Lucas	0- 2	.000	1954-55	Sam Cozen	14- 5	.737
1917-18	None	0- 2	.000	1955-56	Sam Cozen	10- 8	.556
1918-19	James Barrett	7- 2	.778	1956-57	Sam Cozen	14- 3	.824
1919-20	James Barrett	4- 7	.364	1957-58	Sam Cozen	10- 8	.556
1920-21	William McAvoy	7- 8	.467	1958-59	Sam Cozen	10- 9	.526
1921-22	William McAvoy	4- 2	.667	1959-60	Sam Cozen	12- 7	.632
1922-23	H.J. O'Brien	4- 3	.571	1960-61	Sam Cozen	12- 5	.706
1923-24	H.J. O'Brien	8- 5	.615	1961-62	Sam Cozen	11- 8	.579
1924-25	H.J. O'Brien	1-15	.063	1962-63	Sam Cozen	18- 5	.783
1925-26	E.O. Lange	6-11	.353	1963-64	Sam Cozen	17- 5	.773
1926-27	E.O. Lange	6- 8	.429	1964-65	Sam Cozen	18- 4	.818
1927-28	Walter Halas	9-13	.409	1965-66	Sam Cozen	20- 4	.833
1928-29	Walter Halas	10- 9	.526	1966-67	Sam Cozen	13-10	.565
1929-30	Walter Halas	8-11	.421	1967-68	Bob Morgan	12- 9	.571
1930-31	Walter Halas	10-10	.500	1968-69	Frank Szymanski	8-11	.421
1931-32	Walter Halas	9- 7	.563	1969-70	Frank Szymanski	11-11	.500
1932-33	Walter Halas	2-16	.111	**MOVED UP TO DIVISION I:**			
1933-34	Walter Halas	4-12	.250	1970-71	Frank Szymanski	7-17	.292
1934-35	E.O. Lange	7-10	.412	1971-72	Ray Haesler	11-14	.440
1935-36	E.O. Lange	8- 9	.471	1972-73	Ray Haesler	14- 7	.667
1936-37	E.O. Lange	8- 8	.500	1973-74	Ray Haesler	15- 9	.625
1937-38	E.O. Lange	3-12	.200	1974-75	Ray Haesler	12-11	.522
1938-39	E.O. Lange	1-13	.071	1975-76	Ray Haesler	17- 6	.739
1939-40	E.O. Lange	3-13	.188	1976-77	Ray Haesler	11-13	.458

YEAR-BY-YEAR RECORDS

Season	Head Coach	W- L	Pct.
1977-78	Eddie Burke	13-13	.500
1978-79	Eddie Burke	18- 9	.667
1979-80	Eddie Burke	12-15	.462
1980-81	Eddie Burke	14-13	.519
1981-82	Eddie Burke	19-11	.633
1982-83	Eddie Burke	14-15	.483
1983-84	Eddie Burke	17-12	.586
1984-85	Eddie Burke	10-18	.357
1985-86	Eddie Burke	19-12	.613
1986-87	Eddie Burke	14-14	.500
1987-88	Eddie Burke	18-10	.643
1988-89	Eddie Burke	12-16	.429

1,000-POINT CLUB

Player	Games	Points
Michael Anderson	115	2,208
John Rankin	110	2,111
Bob Stephens	99	1,612
David Broadus	100	1,371
Len Hatzenbeller	107	1,364
Randy Burkert	111	1,265
Richard Congo	88	1,228
Walter Fuller	116	1,159
Casper Cooper	116	1,124
Ron Coley	65	1,098
Todd Lehmann	84	1,081
Mike Mitchell	115	1,069
Greg Newman	62	1,016

COACHES' RECORDS

Seasons	Coach	W- L	Pct.
1894-95	John Gray	7- 2	.778
1895-96	F. Knight	0- 1	.000
1905-07	W.S. Brokaw	12- 5	.706
1907-08	F. Bennett	8- 9	.471
1908-09	G. Doughty	1- 2	.333
1910-13	Frank Griffin	15- 15	.500
1914-17	E.L. Lucas	14- 12	.538
1918-20	James Barrett	11- 9	.550
1920-22	William McAvoy	11- 10	.524
1922-25	H.J. O'Brien	13- 23	.361
1925-27	E.O. Lange	12- 19	.387
1934-40	E.O. Lange	30- 65	.316
	Total	42- 84	.333
1927-34	Walter Halas	52- 78	.400
1940-43	Lawrence Mains	26- 17	.605
1943-44	Maury McMains	5- 6	.455
1944-45	John Marino	2- 11	.154
1945-49	Ralph Chase	28- 40	.412
1949-52	Hal Kollar	25- 27	.481
1952-68	Sam Cozen	213- 94	.694
1967-68	Bob Morgan	2- 7	.222
1968-71	Frank Szymanski	26- 39	.400
1971-77	Ray Haesler	80- 60	.571
1977-89	Eddie Burke	180-158	.533

POSTSEASON RESULTS

1986 NCAA TOURNAMENT: Lost to Louisville, 93-73 (Ogden, Utah)

Eddie Burke, who guided Drexel to its only NCAA Tournament appearance in 1986, speaks to the team in practice

LEADING SCORERS

Season Player	Pts.	Season Player	Pts.
1946-47 Hal Kollar	288	1964-65 Mike McCurdy	358
1947-48 Jules Schwab	235	1965-66 Dick Stanton	347
1948-49 Al MacCart	194	1966-67 Bill Murphy	301
1949-50 Don Breeder	211	1967-68 Jack Linderman	412
1950-51 Al MacCart	295	1968-69 Ron Coley	305
1951-52 Basil Berno	283	1969-70 Ron Coley	403
1952-53 Dick Valker	240	1970-71 Ron Coley	390
1953-54 Dan Promizio	308	1971-72 Steve Lilly	310
1954-55 Bob Buckley	372	1972-73 Greg Newman	319
1955-56 Bob Buckley	283	1973-74 Greg Newman	465
1956-57 Bob Buckley	344	1974-75 Doug Romanczuk	335
1957-58 Charles Morrow	274	1975-76 Bob Stephens	343
1958-59 Bob Morgan	354	1976-77 Bob Stephens	380
1959-60 Bob Morgan	325	1977-78 Bob Stephens	378
1960-61 Bob Morgan	265	1978-79 Bob Stephens	511
1961-62 Chuck King	273	1979-80 David Broadus	446
1962-63 Mike McCurdy	335	1980-81 Len Hatzenbeller	589
1963-64 Mike McCurdy	278	1981-82 Randy Burkert	374

Michael Anderson

Season Player	Pts.
1982-83 Richard Congo	401
1983-84 Richard Congo	480
1984-85 Michael Anderson	393
1985-86 Michael Anderson	582
1986-87 Michael Anderson	563
1987-88 Michael Anderson	670
1988-89 John Rankin	662

RECORDS

	INDIVIDUAL, GAME	TEAM, GAME
Points	44: John Rankin, vs. Rider, 1/6/88	115: vs. Siena, 2/20/78 (3 ot)
FG Made	16: Charles Morrow, vs. Haverford, 2/26/58 Greg Newman, vs. Franklin & Marshall, 2/16/74	51: vs. Siena, 2/20/78 (3 ot)
FG Att.	30: Michael Anderson, vs. Bucknell, 2/24/88	104: vs. Siena, 2/20/78 (3 ot)
FG Pct.	100: Michael Mitchell, vs. Hofstra, 2/15/84 (8-8)	70.8: vs. Long Island, 12/9/86 (34-48)
FT Made	18: Bob Buckley, vs. Swarthmore, 2/9/57 Michael Anderson, vs. NW Louisiana, 12/16/84	42: vs. NW Louisiana, 12/16/84
FT Att.	24: Michael Anderson, vs. Villanova, 11/22/85	55: vs. NW Louisiana, 12/16/84
FT Pct.	100: Randy Burkert, vs. S. Illinois, 12/28/79 (12-12) Michael Anderson, vs. Lafayette, 2/24/86 (12-12)	100: vs. Hofstra, 3/2/84 (17-17)
Rebounds	30: Steve Lilly, vs. Muhlenberg, 1/5/72	89: vs. Delaware Valley, 12/7/63
Assists	15: Michael Anderson, vs. Rider, 1/28/87	34: vs. Siena, 2/20/78 (3 ot)
Blocks	9: Bob Stephens, vs. Chicago, 12/15/77	20: vs. Chicago, 12/15/77
Steals	9: Chris O'Brien, vs. Hofstra, 2/11/85	25: vs. Hofstra, 2/11/85

	INDIVIDUAL, SEASON	INDIVIDUAL, CAREER
Points	670: Michael Anderson, 1987-88	2,208: Michael Anderson, 1984-88
FG Made	266: John Rankin, 1988-89	854: John Rankin, 1985-89
FG Att.	487: John Rankin, 1988-89	1,566: John Rankin, 1985-89
FG Pct.	56.3: John Rankin, 1985-86 (191-339)	54.5: John Rankin, 1985-89 (854-1,566)
FT Made	208: Michael Anderson, 1985-86	705: Michael Anderson, 1984-88
FT Att.	278: Michael Anderson, 1985-86	958: Michael Anderson, 1984-88
FT Pct.	87.7: John Siorek, 1981-82 (64-73)	84.0: John Siorek, 1979-83 (199-237)
Rebounds	360: Bob Stephens, 1978-79	1,316: Bob Stephens, 1975-79
Assists	225: Michael Anderson, 1985-86	724: Michael Anderson, 1984-88
Blocks	107: Bob Stephens, 1975-76	404: Bob Stephens, 1975-79
Steals	92: Michael Anderson, 1985-86	341: Michael Anderson, 1984-88

LA SALLE

YEAR-BY-YEAR RECORDS

Season	Head Coach	W- L	Pct.
1930-31	James J. Henry	15- 4	.789
1931-32	Thomas Conley	11- 9	.550
1932-33	Thomas Conley	13- 3	.813
1933-34	Len Tanseer	14- 3	.824
1934-35	Len Tanseer	15- 6	.714
1935-36	Len Tanseer	4-13	.235
1936-37	Len Tanseer	12- 7	.632
1937-38	Len Tanseer	9- 8	.529
1938-39	Len Tanseer	13- 6	.684
1939-40	Len Tanseer	12- 8	.600
1940-41	Len Tanseer	11- 8	.579
1941-42	Obie O'Brien	12-11	.522
1942-43	Obie O'Brien	13- 9	.591
1943-44	Joseph Meehan	7- 7	.500
1944-45	Joseph Meehan	11- 8	.579
1945-46	Joseph Meehan	9-14	.391
1946-47	Charley McGlone	20- 6	.769
1947-48	Charley McGlone	20- 4	.833
1948-49	Charley McGlone	21- 7	.750
1949-50	Ken Loeffler	21- 4	.840
1950-51	Ken Loeffler	22- 7	.759
1951-52	Ken Loeffler	25- 7	.781
1952-53	Ken Loeffler	25- 3	.893
1953-54	Ken Loeffler	26- 4	.867
1954-55	Ken Loeffler	26- 5	.839
1955-56	Jim Pollard	15-10	.600
1956-57	Jim Pollard	17- 9	.654
1957-58	Jim Pollard	16- 9	.640
1958-59	Dudey Moore	16- 7	.696
1959-60	Dudey Moore	16- 6	.727
1960-61	Dudey Moore	15- 7	.682
1961-62	Dudey Moore	19- 9	.679
1962-63	Dudey Moore	16- 8	.667
1963-64	Bob Walters	16- 9	.640
1964-65	Bob Walters	15- 8	.652
1965-66	Joe Heyer	10-15	.400
1966-67	Joe Heyer	14-12	.538
1967-68	Jim Harding	20- 8	.714
1968-69	Tom Gola	23- 1	.958
1969-70	Tom Gola	14-12	.538
1970-71	Paul Westhead	20- 7	.741
1971-72	Paul Westhead	6-19	.240
1972-73	Paul Westhead	15-10	.600
1973-74	Paul Westhead	18-10	.643
1974-75	Paul Westhead	22- 7	.759
1975-76	Paul Westhead	11-15	.423
1976-77	Paul Westhead	17-12	.586
1977-78	Paul Westhead	18-12	.600
1978-79	Paul Westhead	15-13	.536
1979-80	Lefty Ervin	22- 9	.710
1980-81	Lefty Ervin	14-13	.519
1981-82	Lefty Ervin	16-13	.552
1982-83	Lefty Ervin	18-14	.563
1983-84	Lefty Ervin	20-11	.645
1984-85	Lefty Ervin	15-13	.536
1985-86	Lefty Ervin	14-14	.500
1986-87	Speedy Morris	20-13	.606
1987-88	Speedy Morris	24-10	.706
1988-89	Speedy Morris	26- 6	.813

COACHES' RECORDS

Seasons	Coach	W- L	Pct.
1930-31	James J. Henry	15- 4	.789
1931-33	Thomas Conley	24- 12	.667
1933-41	Len Tanseer	90- 59	.604
1941-43	Obie O'Brien	25- 20	.556
1943-46	Joseph Meehan	27- 29	.482
1946-49	Charley McGlone	61- 17	.782
1949-55	Ken Loeffler	145- 30	.829
1955-58	Jim Pollard	48- 28	.632
1958-63	Dudey Moore	79- 37	.681
1963-65	Bob Walters	31- 17	.646
1965-67	Joe Heyer	24- 27	.471
1967-68	Jim Harding	20- 8	.714
1968-70	Tom Gola	37- 13	.740
1970-79	Paul Westhead	142-105	.575
1979-86	Lefty Ervin	119- 87	.578
1986-89	Speedy Morris	70- 29	.707

Steve Black goes into the stands to give his mother the ball with which he scored his 1,000th career point

POSTSEASON RESULTS

1948 NIT: Lost to Western Kentucky, 68-60 (New York).

1950 NIT: Defeated Arizona, 72-66; Lost to Duquesne, 49-47 (both games at New York).

1951 NIT: Lost to St. Louis, 73-61 (New York).

1952 NIT: Defeated Seton Hall, 80-76; Defeated St. John's, 51-45; Defeated Duquesne, 59-46, in semifinals; Defeated Dayton, 75-64, in championship game (all games at New York).

1953 NIT: Lost to St. John's, 75-74 (New York).

1954 NCAA TOURNAMENT: Defeated Fordham, 76-74 (ot) (Buffalo); Defeated North Carolina St., 88-81 (Palestra); Defeated Navy, 64-48, in East Regional final (Palestra); Defeated Penn St., 69-54, in the national semifinals (Kansas City); Defeated Bradley, 92-76, in national championship game (Kansas City).

1955 NCAA TOURNAMENT: Defeated West Virginia, 95-61 (New York); Defeated Princeton, 73-46 (Palestra); Defeated Canisius, 99-64, in East Regional final (Palestra); Defeated Iowa, 76-73, in national semifinals (Kansas City); Lost to San Francisco, 77-63, in national championship game (Kansas City).

1963 NIT: Lost to St. Louis, 62-61 (New York).

1965 NIT: Lost to Detroit, 93-86 (New York).

1968 NCAA TOURNAMENT: Lost to Columbia, 83-69 (College Park, Md.).

1971 NIT: Lost to Georgia Tech, 70-67 (New York).

1975 NCAA TOURNAMENT: Lost to Syracuse, 87-83 (ot) (Palestra).

1978 NCAA TOURNAMENT: Lost to Villanova, 103-97 (Palestra).

1980 NCAA TOURNAMENT: Lost to Purdue, 90-82 (West Lafayette, Ind.).

1983 NCAA TOURNAMENT: Defeated Boston University, 70-58 (Palestra); Lost to Virginia Commonwealth, 76-67 (Greensboro, N.C.).

1984 NIT: Lost to Pittsburgh, 95-91 (Palestra).

1987 NIT: Defeated Villanova, 86-84 (duPont Pavilion); Defeated Niagara, 89-81 (Buffalo, N.Y.); Defeated Illinois St., 70-50 (Palestra); Defeated Arkansas-Little Rock, 92-73, in semifinal (New York); Lost to Southern Mississippi, 84-80, in championship game (New York).

1988 NCAA TOURNAMENT: Lost to Kansas St., 66-54 (South Bend, Ind.).

1989 NCAA TOURNAMENT: Lost to Louisiana Tech, 83-74 (Nashville, Tenn.)

1,000-POINT CLUB

Player	Games	Points
Michael Brooks	114	2,628
Tom Gola	118	2,461
Lionel Simmons	99	2,370
Steve Black	102	2,012
Ralph Lewis	116	1,807
Tim Legler	121	1,699
Ken Durrett	71	1,679
Hubie Marshall	74	1,576
Bill Taylor	82	1,554
Larry Foust	103	1,464
Larry Cannon	75	1,430
Frank Corace	73	1,411
Larry Koretz	120	1,382
Kurt Kanaskie	105	1,356
Charlie Wise	97	1,245
Norm Grekin	88	1,243
Mo Connolly	108	1,232
Bernie Williams	74	1,230
Chip Greenberg	110	1,227
Jim Crawford	77	1,213
Fred Iehle	94	1,204
Bob Walters	80	1,193
Craig Conlin	119	1,159
Alonzo Lewis	82	1,137
Donn Wilber	90	1,127
Joe Bryant	54	1,118
Albert Butts	88	1,060
Bob McAteer	69	1,056
George Paull	74	1,016
Bob Fields	52	1,016
Rich Tarr	119	1,004

LEADING SCORERS

Season	Player	Pts.	Season	Player	Pts.	Season	Player	Pts.
1930-31	Mort Gratz	98	1951-52	Tom Gola	504	1970-71	Bob Fields	605
1931-32	Clem Meehan	158	1952-53	Tom Gola	517	1971-72	Jim Crawford	394
1933-34	Charles Mosicant	116	1953-54	Tom Gola	690	1972-73	Jim Crawford	489
1934-35	Clem Meehan	198	1954-55	Tom Gola	750	1973-74	Bill Taylor	551
1935-36	Frank Hoerst	105	1955-56	Al Lewis	326	1974-75	Joe Bryant	632
1936-37	Frank Hoerst	147	1956-57	Al Lewis	459	1975-76	Donn Wilber	446
1937-38	Frank Hoerst	133	1957-58	Bill Katheder	326	1976-77	Michael Brooks	579
1938-39	Frank Hoerst	174	1958-59	Joe Heyer	402	1977-78	Michael Brooks	696
1939-40	Tom Carroll	152	1959-60	Bob Alden	360	1978-79	Michael Brooks	606
1940-41	Charles McGlone	188	1960-61	Bill Raftery	392	1979-80	Michael Brooks	747
1941-42	Charles McGlone	182	1961-62	Bob McAteer	543	1980-81	Stan Williams	448
1943-44	Bob Walters	215	1962-63	Frank Corace	441	1981-82	Steve Black	561
1944-45	Bob Walters	263	1963-64	Frank Corace	601	1982-83	Ralph Lewis	418
1945-46	Bob Walters	367	1964-65	Curt Fromal	441	1983-84	Ralph Lewis	638
1946-47	Bob Walters	348	1965-66	Hubie Marshall	674	1984-85	Steve Black	552
1947-48	Larry Foust	401	1966-67	Hubie Marshall	549	1985-86	Chip Greenberg	471
1948-49	Larry Foust	453	1967-68	Larry Cannon	546	1986-87	Lionel Simmons	670
1949-50	Larry Foust	355	1968-69	Ken Durrett	480	1987-88	Lionel Simmons	792
1950-51	Jack George	469	1969-70	Ken Durrett	632	1988-89	Lionel Simmons	908

RECORDS

	INDIVIDUAL, GAME	TEAM, GAME
Points	51: Michael Brooks, vs. Brigham Young, 12/15/79	125: vs. Loyola (La.), 2/4/67
FG Made	24: Michael Brooks, vs. Brigham Young, 12/15/79	57: vs. American, 2/3/79
FG Att.	36: Michael Brooks, vs. Brigham Young, 12/15/79	112: vs. Furman, 2/6/54
FG Pct.	100: Craig Conlin, vs. Manhattan, 1/23/88 (7-7)	67.1: vs. American, 2/3/79 (57-85)
FT Made	18: Lionel Simmons, vs. American, 2/2/88	39: vs. Bucknell, 3/1/82
FT Att.	21: Bob Fields, vs. Rider, 3/1/71	51: vs. Duquesne, 2/16/54
FT Pct.	100: Lionel Simmons, vs. American, 2/2/88 (18-18)	93.8: vs. Army, 2/19/86 (15-16)
Rebounds	37: Tom Gola, vs. Lebanon Valley, 1/15/55	85: vs. Syracuse, 12/27/54 vs. Brandeis, 1/8/55
Assists	18: Doug Overton, vs. Holy Cross, 2/13/89	35: vs. Loyola (La.), 2/4/67
Blocks	7: Ron Barnes, vs. Bowling Green, 12/28/87 Lionel Simmons, vs. American, 2/2/88	9: vs. Pennsylvania, 1/24/84 vs. Manhattan, 1/23/88 vs. American, 2/2/88
Steals	8: Doug Overton, vs. Army, 2/3/89	21: vs. Army, 2/3/89

	INDIVIDUAL, SEASON	INDIVIDUAL, CAREER
Points	900: Lionel Simmons, 1988-89	2,628: Michael Brooks, 1976-80
FG Made	349: Lionel Simmons, 1988-89	1,064: Michael Brooks, 1976-80
FG Att.	716: Lionel Simmons, 1988-89	2,222: Tom Gola, 1951-55
FG Pct.	64.6: Craig Conlin, 1987-88 (144-223)	58.8: Craig Conlin, 1985-89 (470-800)
FT Made	202: Tom Gola, 1954-55	653: Tom Gola, 1951-55
FT Att.	267: Tom Gola, 1954-55	877: Tom Gola, 1951-55
FT Pct.	91.7: Kurt Kanaskie, 1978-79 (55-60)	86.3: Kevin Lynam, 1977-81 (157-182)
Rebounds	652: Tom Gola, 1953-54	2,201: Tom Gola, 1951-55
Assists	244: Doug Overton, 1988-89	461: Darryl Gladden, 1977-79 Chip Greenberg, 1982-86
Blocks	77: Lionel Simmons, 1987-88	183: Lionel Simmons, 1986-89
Steals	98: Doug Overton, 1988-89	200: Ralph Lewis, 1981-85

Tom Gola

From grade school to high school to college to the pros. Tom Gola was a rousing success at every level of basketball and virtually all of it was accomplished in Philadelphia.

Born in the city on Jan. 13, 1933, Gola's home court as a youth was the Incarnation Catholic Club at 4th St. and Lindley Ave. in Olney, where he played under the tutelage of Lefty Huber.

"All everyone in 'Inky' wanted to do was go to the club," Gola recalled. "We'd go over there and play pool, or baskets, instead of hanging out on the corner. Every kid at Incarnation knew how to play basketball."

No one played better than Gola, however. They knew it at Incarnation and soon found out at La Salle High School. Under coach Charles "Obie" O'Brien, Gola led La Salle to the Catholic League title in his junior year, 1949-50. The Explorers went on to win the City Title that year by defeating Overbrook, 55-31. Gola still holds the high school's career scoring record with 1,392 points

Gola stayed in the city and attended La Salle College (now La Salle University), where his reputation as a smart, gifted and fiercely competitive athlete became well known across the nation. Although Gola set his share of scoring records, he is best recognized for his versatility. He was an outstanding rebounder and passer.

A three-time All-American, Gola led La Salle in scoring in each of his four seasons (1951-52 through 1954-55), all with Ken Loeffler as coach.

As a freshman, the 6-6 Gola led La Salle to the NIT championship, defeating Dayton in the title game.

In his junior year, Gola's Explorers became the first Philadelphia team to win an NCAA Tournament title. La Salle knocked off Fordham, North Carolina State, Navy and Penn State before easily handling Bradley, 92-76, in the championship game. Gola was named MVP.

It took a guy named Bill Russell to keep Gola from carrying La Salle to a repeat performance the following season. Russell, who later would win five NBA MVP awards with the Boston Celtics, helped the University of San Francisco thwart La Salle's bid in the 1955 championship game by a score of 77-63.

Gola is La Salle's second-leading career scorer (2,461 points), behind only Michael Brooks (2,628). But Gola soon will have to make way for Lionel Simmons, who trailed Gola by only 91 points entering his senior season. Gola also is the University's leading career rebounder with 2,201. He once pulled down 37 rebounds in a 1955 game against Lebanon Valley.

Gola played six seasons for the Philadelphia Warriors in the NBA and played his first games for a team outside the city when the Warriors moved to San Francisco for the 1962-63 season. Gola was traded from San Francisco to the New York Knicks on Dec. 5, 1962 for Willie Naulls and Ken Sears. He played three full seasons with the Knicks, his last in 1965-66.

Shortly after his retirement, Gola served two seasons as La Salle's head coach. He compiled a 37-13 record overall, and his 1968-69 team finished the season ranked No. 2 in the nation after compiling a 23-1 mark.

Gola maintained a high profile during a distinguished political career in Philadelphia. He served as a state representative and Philadelphia's City Controller, then failed in a bid to win the Republican nomination for mayor in 1983.

PENN

YEAR-BY-YEAR RECORDS

Season	Head Coach	W- L	Pct.	Season	Head Coach	W- L	Pct.
1901-02	None	7- 2	.778	1940-41	Lon Jourdet	5-12	.294
1902-03	None	8- 6	.571	1941-42	Lon Jourdet	9- 9	.500
1903-04	None	10- 4	.714	1942-43	Lon Jourdet	14- 7	.667
1904-05	None	8-15	.348	1943-44	Donald Kellett	10- 4	.714
1905-06	R.B. Smith	16- 4	.800	1944-45	Donald Kellett	12- 5	.706
1906-07	R.B. Smith	15- 8	.652	1945-46	Bob Dougherty	7-10	.412
1907-08	R.B. Smith	23- 4	.852	1946-47	Donald Kellett	14- 8	.636
1908-09	R.B. Smith	19- 6	.760	1947-48	Donald Kellett	10-14	.417
1909-10	Charles Keinath	10-10	.500	1948-49	Howard Dallmar	15- 8	.652
1910-11	Charles Keinath	15- 8	.652	1949-50	Howard Dallmar	11-14	.440
1911-12	Charles Keinath	10- 7	.588	1950-51	Howard Dallmar	19- 8	.704
1912-13	Arthur Kiefaber	6-12	.333	1951-52	Howard Dallmar	21- 8	.724
1913-14	Arthur Kiefaber	4-12	.250	1952-53	Howard Dallmar	22- 5	.815
1914-15	Lon Jourdet	9-10	.474	1953-54	Howard Dallmar	17- 8	.680
1915-16	Lon Jourdet	11- 7	.611	1954-55	Ray Stanley	19- 6	.760
1916-17	Lon Jourdet	11- 7	.611	1955-56	Ray Stanley	12-13	.480
1917-18	Lon Jourdet	19- 2	.905	1956-57	Jack McCloskey	7-19	.269
1918-19	Lon Jourdet	15- 1	.938	1957-58	Jack McCloskey	13-12	.520
1919-20	Lon Jourdet	22- 1	.957	1958-59	Jack McCloskey	12-14	.462
1920-21	Edward McNichol	21- 2	.913	1959-60	Jack McCloskey	14-11	.560
1921-22	Edward McNichol	24- 3	.889	1960-61	Jack McCloskey	16- 9	.640
1922-23	Edward McNichol	14-11	.560	1961-62	Jack McCloskey	17- 8	.680
1923-24	Edward McNichol	18- 8	.692	1962-63	Jack McCloskey	19- 6	.760
1924-25	Edward McNichol	17- 5	.773	1963-64	Jack McCloskey	14-10	.583
1925-26	Edward McNichol	14- 7	.667	1964-65	Jack McCloskey	15-10	.600
1926-27	Edward McNichol	16-10	.615	1965-66	Jack McCloskey	19- 6	.760
1927-28	Edward McNichol	22- 5	.815	1966-67	Dick Harter	11-14	.440
1928-29	Edward McNichol	20- 6	.769	1967-68	Dick Harter	9-17	.346
1929-30	Edward McNichol	20- 6	.769	1968-69	Dick Harter	15-10	.600
1930-31	Lon Jourdet	9-17	.346	1969-70	Dick Harter	25- 2	.926
1931-32	Lon Jourdet	10-11	.476	1970-71	Dick Harter	28- 1	.966
1932-33	Lon Jourdet	12- 6	.667	1971-72	Chuck Daly	25- 3	.893
1933-34	Lon Jourdet	16- 3	.842	1972-73	Chuck Daly	21- 7	.750
1934-35	Lon Jourdet	16- 4	.800	1973-74	Chuck Daly	21- 6	.778
1935-36	Lon Jourdet	13- 8	.619	1974-75	Chuck Daly	23- 5	.821
1936-37	Lon Jourdet	17- 3	.850	1975-76	Chuck Daly	17- 9	.654
1937-38	Lon Jourdet	8-10	.444	1976-77	Chuck Daly	18- 8	.692
1938-39	Lon Jourdet	7-11	.389	1977-78	Bob Weinhauer	20- 8	.714
1939-40	Lon Jourdet	5-13	.278	1978-79	Bob Weinhauer	25- 7	.781

YEAR-BY-YEAR RECORDS

Season	Head Coach	W- L	Pct.
1979-80	Bob Weinhauer	17-12	.586
1980-81	Bob Weinhauer	20- 8	.714
1981-82	Craig Littlepage	17-10	.630
1982-83	Craig Littlepage	17- 9	.654
1983-84	Craig Littlepage	10-16	.385
1984-85	Craig Littlepage	13-14	.481
1985-86	Tom Schneider	15-11	.577
1986-87	Tom Schneider	13-14	.481
1987-88	Tom Schneider	10-16	.385
1988-89	Tom Schneider	13-13	.500

1,000-POINT CLUB

Player	Games	Points
Ernie Beck	82	1,827
Perry Bromwell	80	1,670
Keven McDonald	79	1,644
Ron Haigler	83	1,552
Stan Pawlak	74	1,501
Bruce Lefkowitz	104	1,443
Bob Morse	84	1,381
Herbert Lyon	86	1,333
Tony Price	85	1,322
Tyrone Pitts	106	1,301
Joe Sturgis	74	1,292
Phil Hankinson	85	1,236
Dave Wohl	81	1,226
Dick Censits	NA	1,220
Jeff Neuman	NA	1,187
Paul Little	NA	1,116
Steve Bilsky	NA	1,108
Corky Calhoun	NA	1,066
Dick Heylmun	NA	1,058
John Engles	NA	1,038
Bart Leach	NA	1,033

Bruce Lefkowitz

Perry Bromwell

COACHES' RECORDS

Seasons	Coach	W- L	Pct.
1905-09	R.B. Smith	73- 22	.768
1909-12	Charles Keinath	35- 25	.583
1912-14	Arthur Kiefaber	10- 24	.294
1914-20	Lon Jourdet	87- 28	.757
1930-43	Lon Jourdet	141-114	.553
	Totals	228-142	.616
1920-30	Edward McNichol	186- 63	.747
1943-45	Donald Kellett	22- 9	.710
1946-48	Donald Kellett	24- 22	.522
	Totals	46- 31	.597
1945-46	Bob Dougherty	7- 10	.412
1948-54	Howard Dallmar	105- 51	.673
1954-56	Ray Stanley	31- 19	.620
1956-66	Jack McCloskey	146-105	.582
1966-71	Dick Harter	88- 44	.667
1971-77	Chuck Daly	125- 38	.767
1977-81	Bob Weinhauer	99- 45	.688
1981-85	Craig Littlepage	40- 39	.506
1985-89	Tom Schneider	41- 38	.518

POSTSEASON RESULTS

1953 NCAA TOURNAMENT: Lost to Notre Dame, 69-57; Defeated De Paul, 90-70, in regional third place game (both games at Chicago).

1970 NCAA TOURNAMENT: Lost to Niagara, 79-69 (Princeton, N.J.).

1971 NCAA TOURNAMENT: Defeated Duquesne, 70-65 (Morgantown, W. Va.); Defeated South Carolina, 79-64 (Raleigh, N.C.); Lost to Villanova, 90-47, in East Regional final (Raleigh, N.C.).

1972 NCAA TOURNAMENT: Defeated Providence, 76-60 (Jamaica, N.Y.); Defeated Villanova, 78-67 (Morgantown, W. Va.); Lost to North Carolina, 73-59, in East Regional final (Morgantown, W. Va.).

1973 NCAA TOURNAMENT: Defeated St. John's, 62-61 (Williamsburg, Va.); Lost to Providence, 87-65 (Charlotte, N.C.); Lost to Syracuse, 69-68 (Charlotte, N.C.).

1974 NCAA TOURNAMENT: Lost to Providence, 84-69 (Jamaica, N.Y.).

1975 NCAA TOURNAMENT: Lost to Kansas St., 69-62 (Palestra).

1978 NCAA TOURNAMENT: Defeated St. Bonaventure, 92-83 (Palestra); Lost to Duke, 84-80 (Providence, R.I.).

1979 NCAA TOURNAMENT: Defeated Iona, 73-69 (Raleigh, N.C.); Defeated North Carolina, 72-71 (Raleigh, N.C.); Defeated Syracuse, 84-76 (Greensboro, N.C.); Defeated St. John's, 64-62, in East Regional final (Greensboro, N.C.); Lost to Michigan St., 101-67, in national semifinals (Salt Lake City, Utah); Lost to De Paul, 96-93, (ot), in third place game (Salt Lake City, Utah).

1980 NCAA TOURNAMENT: Defeated Washington St., 62-55 (West Lafayette, Ind.); Lost to Duke, 52-42 (West Lafayette, Ind.).

1981 NIT: Lost to Virginia, 67-64 (Morgantown, W. Va.).

1982 NCAA TOURNAMENT: Lost to St. John's, 66-56 (Uniondale, N.Y.).

1985 NCAA TOURNAMENT: Lost to Memphis St., 67-55 (Houston).

1987 NCAA TOURNAMENT: Lost to North Carolina, 113-82 (Charlotte, N.C.).

LEADING SCORERS

Season	Player	Pts.	Season	Player	Pts.	Season	Player	Pts.
1924-25	Jim Carmack	148	1946-47	Frank Crossin	333	1967-68	Tòm Northrup	297
1925-26	Franklin Lindsey	104	1947-48	Herbert Lyon	344	1968-69	Dave Wohl	402
1926-27	Paul Davenport	163	1948-49	Herbert Lyon	395	1969-70	Bob Morse	429
1927-28	Joe Schaaf	327	1949-50	Herbert Lyon	421	1970-71	Bob Morse	446
1928-29	Joe Schaaf	273	1950-51	Ernie Beck	558	1971-72	Bob Morse	506
1929-30	Len Tanseer	150	1951-52	Ernie Beck	596	1972-73	Phil Hankinson	512
1930-31	Harold Sander	134	1952-53	Ernie Beck	673	1973-74	Ron Haigler	471
1931-32	Len Tanseer	111	1953-54	Joe Sturgis	395	1974-75	Ron Haigler	606
1932-33	Robert Freeman	139	1954-55	Bart Leach	452	1975-76	Keven McDonald	492
1933-34	Robert Freeman	126	1955-56	Joe Sturgis	466	1976-77	Keven McDonald	529
1934-35	Robert Freeman	145	1956-57	Dick Censits	460	1977-78	Keven McDonald	623
1935-36	Roger Hanger	122	1957-58	Dick Censits	377	1978-79	Tony Price	633
1936-37	Roy Menzel	138	1958-59	George Schmidt	342	1979-80	"Booney" Salters	422
1937-38	Bob Dougherty	165	1959-60	Bob Mlkvy	472	1980-81	Ken Hall	316
1938-39	Anton Mischo	180	1960-61	Bob Mlkvy	358	1981-82	Paul Little	313
1939-40	Henry Soleliac	129	1961-62	Bob Purdy	330	1982-83	Michael Brown	355
1940-41	Sidney Levinson	126		John Wideman	330	1983-84	Karl Racine	340
1941-42	Charles Viguers	182	1962-63	John Wideman	346	1984-85	Perry Bromwell	412
1942-43	Frank Crossin	237	1963-64	Stan Pawlak	384	1985-86	Bruce Lefkowitz	355
1943-44	Frank Crossin	190	1964-65	Stan Pawlak	538	1986-87	Bruce Lefkowitz	506
1944-45	Howard Dallmar	175	1965-66	Stan Pawlak	579	1987-88	Tyrone Pitts	451
1945-46	Herbert Lyon	173	1966-67	Tom Northrup	302	1988-89	Walt Frazier	462

RECORDS

	INDIVIDUAL, GAME	TEAM, GAME
Points	47: Ernie Beck, vs. Duke, 12/30/53	115: vs. Muhlenberg, 12/1/69
FG Made	18: Ernie Beck, vs. Dartmouth, 1/27/51	48: vs. Swarthmore, 12/12/62
FG Att.	23: Karl Racine, vs. Harvard, 1/12/85	101: vs. Navy, 1/28/50
FG Pct.	Not Available	71.9: vs. Cornell, 2/6/76 (41-57)
FT Made	17: Ernie Beck, vs. Harvard, 2/6/52 Joe Sturgis, vs. Iowa, 12/17/54 Dick Censits, vs. Havard, 2/22/56 Steve Bilsky, vs. Columbia, 1/5/70 Steve Bilsky, vs. Princeton, 2/8/69	40: vs. Brown, 1/15/55 vs. Rutgers, 12/3/70
FT Att.	20: Dick Censits, vs. Harvard, 2/22/56 Steve Bilsky, vs. Columbia, 2/8/69 Bruce Lefkowitz, vs. Dartmouth, 1/11/86	60: vs. Brown, 1/15/55
FT Pct.	100: By several	95.0: vs. Notre Dame, 2/26/52 (19-20)
Rebounds	32: Bart Leach, vs. Harvard, 2/8/55	78: vs. Army, 1/21/55
Assists	13: Dave Wohl, vs. Brown, 2/14/70	31: vs. Columbia, 2/7/75

	INDIVIDUAL, SEASON	INDIVIDUAL, CAREER
Points	673: Ernie Beck, 1952-53	1,827: Ernie Beck, 1951-53
FG Made	259: Ron Haigler, 1974-75	704: Ernie Beck, 1951-53
FG Att.	500: Ron Haigler, 1974-75	NA
FG Pct.	63.3: Matt White, 1979 (157-248)	59.1: Matt White, 1977-79 (304-514)
FT Made	183: Ernie Beck, 1952-53	469: Bruce Lefkowitz, 1984-87
FT Att.	229: Ernie Beck, 1952-53	NA
FT Pct.	94.0: Chris Elzey, 1984-85 (47-50)	84.8: Chris Elzey, 1984-87 (195-230)
Rebounds	556: Ernie Beck, 1950-51	1,557: Ernie Beck, 1951-53
Assists	151: Dave Wohl, 1970-71	345: Dave Wohl, 1969-71

PENN

YEAR-BY-YEAR RECORDS

Year	Head Coach	W- L- T	Pct.	Season	Head Coach	W- L	Pct.
1876	None	1- 2- 0	.333	1916	Robert Folwell	7- 3- 1	.682
1878	None	1- 2- 1	.375	1917	Robert Folwell	9- 2- 0	.818
1879	None	2- 2- 0	.500	1918	Robert Folwell	5- 3- 0	.625
1880	None	2- 2- 0	.500	1919	Robert Folwell	6- 2- 1	.722
1881	None	0- 5- 0	.000	1920	John Heisman	6- 4- 0	.600
1882	None	2- 4- 0	.333	1921	John Heisman	4- 3- 2	.556
1883	None	6- 2- 1	.722	1922	John Heisman	6- 3- 0	.667
1884	None	5- 1- 1	.786	1923	Louis Young	5- 4- 0	.556
1885	Frank Dole	8- 5- 0	.615	1924	Louis Young	9- 1- 1	.864
1886	Frank Dole	9- 7- 1	.559	1925	Louis Young	7- 2- 0	.778
1887	Frank Dole	6- 7- 0	.462	1926	Louis Young	7- 1- 1	.833
1888	E.O. Wagenhurst	9- 7- 0	.563	1927	Louis Young	6- 4- 0	.600
1889	E.O. Wagenhurst	7- 6- 0	.538	1928	Louis Young	8- 1- 0	.889
1890	E.O. Wagenhurst	11- 3- 0	.786	1929	Louis Young	7- 2- 0	.778
1891	E.O. Wagenhurst	11- 2- 0	.846	1930	Ludlow Wray	5- 4- 0	.556
1892	George Woodruff	15- 1- 0	.938	1931	Harvey Harman	6- 3- 0	.667
1893	George Woodruff	12- 3- 0	.800	1932	Harvey Harman	6- 2- 0	.750
1894	George Woodruff	12- 0- 0	1.000	1933	Harvey Harman	2- 4- 1	.357
1895	George Woodruff	14- 0- 0	1.000	1934	Harvey Harman	4- 4- 0	.500
1896	George Woodruff	14- 1- 0	.933	1935	Harvey Harman	4- 4- 0	.500
1897	George Woodruff	15- 0- 0	1.000	1936	Harvey Harman	7- 1- 0	.875
1898	George Woodruff	12- 1- 0	.923	1937	Harvey Harman	2- 5- 1	.313
1899	George Woodruff	8- 3- 2	.692	1938	George Munger	3- 2- 3	.563
1900	George Woodruff	12- 1- 0	.923	1939	George Munger	4- 4- 0	.500
1901	George Woodruff	10- 5- 0	.667	1940	George Munger	6- 1- 1	.813
1902	Carl Williams	9- 4- 0	.692	1941	George Munger	7- 1- 0	.875
1903	Carl Williams	9- 3- 0	.750	1942	George Munger	5- 3- 1	.611
1904	Carl Williams	12- 0- 0	1.000	1943	George Munger	6- 2- 1	.722
1905	Carl Williams	12- 0- 1	.962	1944	George Munger	5- 3- 0	.625
1906	Carl Williams	7- 2- 3	.708	1945	George Munger	6- 2- 0	.750
1907	Carl Williams	11- 1- 0	.917	1946	George Munger	6- 2- 0	.750
1908	Sol Metzger	11- 0- 1	.958	1947	George Munger	7- 0- 1	.938
1909	Andrew Smith	7- 1- 2	.800	1948	George Munger	5- 3- 0	.625
1910	Andrew Smith	9- 1- 1	.864	1949	George Munger	4- 4- 0	.500
1911	Andrew Smith	7- 4- 0	.636	1950	George Munger	6- 3- 0	.667
1912	Andrew Smith	7- 4- 0	.636	1951	George Munger	5- 4- 0	.556
1913	George Brooke	6- 3- 1	.650	1952	George Munger	4- 3- 2	.556
1914	George Brooke	4- 4- 1	.500	1953	George Munger	3- 5- 1	.389
1915	George Brooke	3- 5- 2	.400	1954	Steve Sebo	0- 9- 0	.000

YEAR-BY-YEAR RECORDS

Year	Head Coach	W- L- T	Pct.	Season	Head Coach	W- L	Pct.
1955	Steve Sebo	0- 9- 0	.000	1972	Harry Gamble	6- 3- 0	.667
1956	Steve Sebo	4- 5- 0	.444	1973	Harry Gamble	6- 3- 0	.667
1957	Steve Sebo	3- 6- 0	.333	1974	Harry Gamble	6- 2- 1	.722
1958	Steve Sebo	4- 5- 0	.444	1975	Harry Gamble	3- 6- 0	.333
1959	Steve Sebo	7- 1- 1	.833	1976	Harry Gamble	3- 6- 0	.333
1960	John Stiegman	3- 6- 0	.333	1977	Harry Gamble	5- 4- 0	.556
1961	John Stiegman	2- 7- 0	.286	1978	Harry Gamble	2- 6- 1	.278
1962	John Stiegman	3- 6- 0	.333	1979	Harry Gamble	0- 9- 0	.000
1963	John Stiegman	3- 6- 0	.333	1980	Harry Gamble	1- 9- 0	.100
1964	John Stiegman	1- 8- 0	.111	1981	Jerry Berndt	1- 9- 0	.100
1965	Bob Odell	4- 4- 1	.500	1982	Jerry Berndt	7- 3- 0	.700
1966	Bob Odell	2- 7- 0	.286	1983	Jerry Berndt	6- 3- 1	.650
1967	Bob Odell	3- 6- 0	.333	1984	Jerry Berndt	8- 1- 0	.889
1968	Bob Odell	7- 2- 0	.778	1985	Jerry Berndt	7- 2- 1	.750
1969	Bob Odell	4- 5- 0	.444	1986	Ed Zubrow	10- 0- 0	1.000
1970	Bob Odell	4- 5- 0	.444	1987	Ed Zubrow	4- 6- 0	.400
1971	Harry Gamble	2- 7- 0	.286	1988	Ed Zubrow	9- 1- 0	.900

Head coach Ed Zubrow and Penn players celebrate their 10-3 homecoming victory over Yale on Oct. 22, 1988

COACHES' RECORDS

Seasons Head Coach	W- L- T	Pct.
1876-84 None	19-20- 3	—
1885-87 Frank Dole	23-19- 1	.547
1888-91 E.O. Wagenhurst	38-18- 0	.679
1892-01 George Woodruff	124-15- 2	.887
1902-07 Carl Williams	60-10- 4	.838
1908 Sol Metzger	11- 0- 1	.958
1909-12 Andrew Smith	30-10- 3	.733
1913-15 George Brooke	13-12- 4	.517
1916-19 Robert Folwell	27-10- 2	.718
1920-22 John Heisman	16-10- 2	.607
1923-29 Louis Young	49-15- 2	.758
1930 Ludlow Wray	5- 4- 0	.556
1931-37 Harvey Harman	31-23- 2	.571
1938-53 George Munger	82-42-10	.649
1954-59 Steve Sebo	18-35- 1	.343
1960-64 John Stiegman	12-33- 0	.267
1965-70 Bob Odell	24-29- 1	.454
1971-80 Harry Gamble	34-55- 2	.385
1981-85 Jerry Berndt	29-18- 2	.612
1986-88 Ed Zubrow	23- 7- 0	.767

CAREER LEADERS

RUSHING YARDS	
Rich Comizio	2,479
Chris Flynn	2,181
Adolph Bellizeare	2,155
Denis Grosvenor	1,805
Jack Wixted	1,713

PASSING YARDS	
Marty Vaughn	3,429
Bill Creeden	3,213
Jim Crocicchia	2,890
Gary Vura	2,859

RECEPTIONS	
Don Clune	121
Rick Owens	95
Bob Bucola	80

BOWL GAME

1916 ROSE BOWL (Pasadena, Calif.)
Lost to Oregon, 14-0

RECORDS

	INDIVIDUAL, GAME	INDIVIDUAL, SEASON
Rushing Yardage	214: Reds Bagnell, vs. Dartmouth, 10/14/50 Adolph Bellizeare, vs. Lehigh, 10/21/72	1,165: Bryan Keys, 1988
Rushing Attempts	37: Bruce Molloy, vs. Brown, 10/2/65	248: Bryan Keys, 1988
Rushing TDs	5: Frank Reagan, vs. Princeton, 10/19/40 Ed Allen, vs. Lafayette, 10/5/46 Chris Flynn, vs. Dartmouth, 11/21/87	18: Robert Folwell, 1907
Passing Yardage	326: Marty Vaughn, vs. Dartmouth, 11/23/74	1,926: Marty Vaughn, 1973
Passes Attempted	48: Bill Creeden, vs. Yale, 11/5/66	275: Gary Vura, 1982
Passes Completed	28: Gary Vura, vs. Lafayette, 10/16/82	148: Gary Vura, 1982
Passing TDs	4: Bob Evans, vs. Columbia, 11/10/45 Glenn Adams, vs. Dartmouth, 10/6/51 Marty Vaughn, vs. Columbia, 11/17/73; Marty Vaughn, vs. Lafayette, 10/19/74 Jim Crocicchia, vs. Navy, 10/18/86	17: Marty Vaughn, 1973
Receiving Yardage	284: Don Clune, vs. Harvard, 10/30/71	891: Don Clune, 1971
Receptions	12: Rick Owens, vs. Cornell, 11/25/65 Karl Hall, vs. Brown, 10/10/81	53: Don Clune, 1973
Receiving TDs	3: Frank Jenkins, vs. Columbia, 11/10/45 Don Clune, vs. Harvard, 10/30/71 Karl Hall, vs. Cornell, 9/19/81 Brent Novoselsky, vs. Navy, 10/18/86	7: Don Clune, 1973 Bob Bucola, 1974
Points Scored	33: Rex Wray, vs. Delaware, 1921	109: Howard Berry, 1917
Touchdowns	5: Frank Reagan, vs. Princeton, 10/19/40 Ed Allen, vs. Lafayette, 10/5/46 Chris Flynn, vs. Dartmouth, 11/21/87	18: Robert Folwell, 1907
PATs Made	7: Bob Evans, vs. North Carolina, 10/13/45 Tom Murphy, vs. Dartmouth, 9/22/84 Jim Grass, vs. Dartmouth, 11/21/87	34: Jim Grass, 1986
Field Goals Made	4: Rich Friedenberg, vs. Colgate, 10/15/88	15: Rich Friedenberg, 1988
Interceptions By	4: Jack Welsh, vs. Princeton, 10/19/40	9: Jack Welsh, 1940
Punts	13: Harry Edenborn, vs. Navy, 10/28/44	69: Ed Gramigna, 1981

Rich Comizio holds the University of Pennsylvania career records for rushing attempts and rushing yardage

RECORDS

	INDIVIDUAL, CAREER	TEAM, GAME
Rushing Yardage	2,479: Rich Comizio, 1984-86	440: vs. Lafayette, 10/14/77
Rushing Attempts	484: Rich Comizio, 1984-86	79: vs. Lafayette, 10/14/77
Rushing TDs	30: Adolph Bellizeare, 1972-74 Leroy Mercer, 1910-12	9: vs. Lafayette, 10/5/46
Passing Yardage	3,429: Marty Vaughn, 1973-74	352: vs. Harvard, 10/30/71
Passes Attempted	520: Bill Creeden, 1965-67	51: vs. Brown, 10/10/81
Passes Completed	236: Bill Creeden, 1965-67	28: vs. Brown, 10/10/81 vs. Lafayette, 10/16/82
Passing TDs	29: Marty Vaughn, 1973-74	4: vs. North Carolina, 10/13/45 vs. Columbia, 11/10/45 vs. Virginia, 10/19/46 vs. Columbia, 11/17/73 vs. Lafayette, 10/19/74 vs. Cornell, 9/19/81 vs. Columbia, 9/30/83 vs. Navy, 10/18/86
Receiving Yardage	2,419: Don Clune, 1971-73	352: vs. Harvard, 10/30/71
Receptions	121: Don Clune, 1971-73	28: vs. Brown, 10/10/81 vs. Lafayette, 10/16/82
Receiving TDs	17: Don Clune, 1971-73	4: See Passing TDs
Points Scored	185: Paul Scull, 1926-28	96: vs. Vineland College, 1886
Touchdowns	30: LeRoy Mercer, 1910-12 Adolph Bellizeare, 1972-74	10: vs. Lafayette, 10/5/46
PATs Made	75: Tim Martin, 1972-74	Not Available
Field Goals Made	22: Eliot Berry, 1968-70	4: vs. Colgate, 10/15/88
Interceptions By	15: Tim Chambers, 1982-84	NA
Punts	125: Rich Serino, 1976-77	NA

PROFILE

Chuck Bednarik

Chuck Bednarik played hard, mean, ferocious football. He was the last of the great two-way players, a powerful center and a crunching, smashing linebacker.

And he, complete down to his dirty No. 60 uniform, more than any player in the history of this city, is the one man who defines Philadelphia football.

At Penn, he was the greatest player that program has ever had. He made the All-America team twice as a center and in 1948 became the first lineman ever to win the Maxwell Award.

With the Eagles, he was the only man to play on both the Eagles' 1949 and '60 championship teams. He made the Pro Bowl eight times.

No Eagle has played more years with the team or been named All-Pro more.

And Bednarik, the center on the NFL's First 50-Year Team, is one of only three players (Jim Thorpe and Don Hudson are the others) elected to both the college and pro football halls of fame.

Born in Bethlehem, Pa., on May 1, 1925, Bednarik attended the University of Pennsylvania, where he was a dominant force as a center and on defense. He led the Quakers to a combined 24-7-1 record from 1945-48.

Because of his wartime service before playing at Penn, Bednarik entered the NFL as a 24-year-old rookie. He was the Eagles' first pick in the 1949 college draft.

Soon enough, he was playing every down for the team at a time when the offensive-defensive platoon system was overtaking the league for good.

In 1960, when he was 35 years old, Bednarik capped his legendary career off by playing 58½ minutes, everything but two kickoffs, in the Eagles' 17-13 NFL Championship Game victory over the Green Bay Packers.

And beyond all his accomplishments, his longevity, his status as the NFL's last two-way player, Bednarik is best remembered for two plays made during the magic 1960 championship season.

The first came during the regular season, when Bednarik knocked Frank Gifford of the New York Giants out and caused him to miss the entire 1961 season.

The second won a championship.

It came in the championship game, on a cold Franklin Field day, as Jim Taylor was about to scamper in for a fourth-quarter, game-winning touchdown. Instead, Bednarik and a pack of Eagle defenders stopped Taylor, at the eight-yard line.

"I held him down and watched the last five seconds run off the clock," Bednarik recalled. "I said, 'You can get up now, you bleeper. This game is over.' "

Bednarik ended his 14-year career two seasons later, at age 37.

All told, he played in a total of 255 exhibition, regular season and playoff games with the Eagles. He missed just three, two of those in his rookie year.

And that, more than anything, says all you need to know about Chuck Bednarik.

PENN STATE

YEAR-BY-YEAR RECORDS

Year	Head Coach	W- L-T	Pct.	Season	Head Coach	W- L	Pct.
1887	None	2- 0-0	1.000	1926	Hugo Bezdek	5- 4-0	.556
1888	None	0- 2-1	.167	1927	Hugo Bezdek	6- 2-1	.722
1889	None	2- 2-0	.500	1928	Hugo Bezdek	3- 5-1	.389
1890	None	2- 2-0	.500	1929	Hugo Bezdek	6- 3-0	.667
1891	None	6- 2-0	.750	1930	Bob Higgins	3- 4-2	.444
1892	George Hoskins	5- 1-0	.833	1931	Bob Higgins	2- 8-0	.200
1893	George Hoskins	4- 1-0	.800	1932	Bob Higgins	2- 5-0	.286
1894	George Hoskins	6- 0-1	.923	1933	Bob Higgins	3- 3-1	.500
1895	George Hoskins	2- 2-3	.500	1934	Bob Higgins	4- 4-0	.500
1896	Dr. Samuel Newton	3- 4-0	.429	1935	Bob Higgins	4- 4-0	.500
1897	Dr. Samuel Newton	3- 6-0	.333	1936	Bob Higgins	3- 5-0	.375
1898	Dr. Samuel Newton	6- 4-0	.600	1937	Bob Higgins	5- 3-0	.625
1899	Sam Boyle	4- 6-0	.400	1938	Bob Higgins	3- 4-1	.438
1900	Pop Golden	4- 6-1	.409	1939	Bob Higgins	5- 1-2	.750
1901	Pop Golden	5- 3-0	.625	1940	Bob Higgins	6- 1-1	.813
1902	Pop Golden	7- 3-0	.700	1941	Bob Higgins	7- 2-0	.778
1903	Dan Reed	5- 3-0	.625	1942	Bob Higgins	6- 1-1	.813
1904	Tom Fennell	6- 4-0	.600	1943	Bob Higgins	5- 3-1	.611
1905	Tom Fennell	8- 3-0	.727	1944	Bob Higgins	6- 3-0	.667
1906	Tom Fennell	8- 1-1	.850	1945	Bob Higgins	5- 3-0	.625
1907	Tom Fennell	6- 4-0	.600	1946	Bob Higgins	6- 2-0	.750
1908	Tom Fennell	5- 5-0	.500	1947	Bob Higgins	9- 0-1	.950
1909	Bill Hollenback	5- 0-2	.857	1948	Bob Higgins	7- 1-1	.833
1910	Jack Hollenback	5- 2-1	.688	1949	Joe Bedenk	5- 4-0	.556
1911	Bill Hollenback	8- 0-1	.944	1950	Rip Engle	5- 3-1	.611
1912	Bill Hollenback	8- 0-0	1.000	1951	Rip Engle	5- 4-0	.556
1913	Bill Hollenback	2- 6-0	.250	1952	Rip Engle	7- 2-1	.750
1914	Bill Hollenback	5- 3-1	.611	1953	Rip Engle	6- 3-0	.667
1915	Dick Harlow	7- 2-0	.875	1954	Rip Engle	7- 2-0	.778
1916	Dick Harlow	8- 2-0	.800	1955	Rip Engle	5- 4-0	.556
1917	Dick Harlow	5- 4-0	.556	1956	Rip Engle	6- 2-1	.722
1918	Hugo Bezdek	1- 2-1	.375	1957	Rip Engle	6- 3-0	.667
1919	Hugo Bezdek	7- 1-0	.875	1958	Rip Engle	6- 3-1	.650
1920	Hugo Bezdek	7- 0-2	.889	1959	Rip Engle	9- 2-0	.818
1921	Hugo Bezdek	8- 0-2	.900	1960	Rip Engle	7- 3-0	.700
1922	Hugo Bezdek	6- 4-1	.591	1961	Rip Engle	8- 3-0	.727
1923	Hugo Bezdek	6- 2-1	.722	1962	Rip Engle	9- 2-0	.818
1924	Hugo Bezdek	6- 3-1	.650	1963	Rip Engle	7- 3-0	.700
1925	Hugo Bezdek	4- 4-1	.500	1964	Rip Engle	6- 4-0	.600

YEAR-BY-YEAR RECORDS

Year	Head Coach	W- L-T	Pct.
1965	Rip Engle	5- 5-0	.500
1966	Joe Paterno	5- 5-0	.500
1967	Joe Paterno	8- 2-1	.773
1968	Joe Paterno	11- 0-0	1.000
1969	Joe Paterno	11- 0-0	1.000
1970	Joe Paterno	7- 3-0	.700
1971	Joe Paterno	11- 1-0	.917
1972	Joe Paterno	10- 2-0	.833
1973	Joe Paterno	12- 0-0	1.000
1974	Joe Paterno	10- 2-0	.833
1975	Joe Paterno	9- 3-0	.750
1976	Joe Paterno	7- 5-0	.583
1977	Joe Paterno	11- 1-0	.917
1978	Joe Paterno	11- 1-0	.917
1979	Joe Paterno	8- 4-0	.667
1980	Joe Paterno	10- 2-0	.833
1981	Joe Paterno	10- 2-0	.833
1982	Joe Paterno	11- 1-0	.917
1983	Joe Paterno	8- 4-1	.654
1984	Joe Paterno	6- 5-0	.545
1985	Joe Paterno	11- 1-0	.917
1986	Joe Paterno	12- 0-0	1.000
1987	Joe Paterno	8- 4-0	.667
1988	Joe Paterno	5- 6-0	.455

Bob Higgins: 1930-48   Rip Engle: 1950-65

COACHES' RECORDS

Seasons	Head Coach	W- L- T	Pct.
1892-95	George Hoskins	17- 4- 4	.826
1896-98	Samuel Newton	12-14- 0	.462
1899	Sam Boyle	4- 6- 0	.400
1900-02	Pop Golden	16-12- 1	.569
1903	Dan Reed	5- 3- 0	.625
1904-08	Tom Fennell	33-17- 1	.657
1909	Bill Hollenback	5- 0- 2	.788
1911-14	Bill Hollenback	23- 9- 2	.706
	Total	28- 9- 4	.732
1910	Jack Hollenback	5- 2- 1	.688
1915-17	Dick Harlow	20- 8- 0	.714
1918-29	Hugo Bezdek	65-30-11	.665
1930-48	Bob Higgins	91-57-10	.608
1949	Joe Bedenk	5- 4- 0	.556
1950-65	Rip Engle	104-48- 4	.679
1966-88	Joe Paterno	212-54- 2	.795

BOWL GAMES

1/ 1/23 Rose Bowl (Pasadena, Calif.)
Southern California 14, Penn St. 3

1/ 1/48 Cotton Bowl (Dallas)
Penn St. 13, Southern Methodist 13

12/19/59 Liberty Bowl (Philadelphia)
Penn St. 7, Alabama 0

12/17/60 Liberty Bowl (Philadelphia)
Penn St. 41, Oregon 12

12/30/61 Gator Bowl (Jacksonville, Fla.)
Penn St. 30, Georgia Tech 15

12/29/62 Gator Bowl (Jacksonville, Fla.)
Florida 17, Penn St. 7

12/30/67 Gator Bowl (Jacksonville, Fla.)
Penn St. 17, Florida St. 17

1/ 1/69 Orange Bowl (Miami)
Penn St. 15, Kansas 14

1/ 1/70 Orange Bowl (Miami) Penn St. 10, Missouri 3

1/ 1/72 Orange Bowl (Miami) Penn St. 30, Texas 6

12/31/72 Sugar Bowl (New Orleans)
Oklahoma 14, Penn St. 0

1/ 1/74 Orange Bowl (Miami)
Penn St. 16, Louisiana St. 9

1/ 1/75 Cotton Bowl (Dallas)
Penn St. 41, Baylor 20

12/31/75 Sugar Bowl (New Orleans)
Alabama 13, Penn St. 6

12/27/76 Gator Bowl (Jacksonville, Fla.)
Notre Dame 20, Penn St. 9

12/25/77 Fiesta Bowl (Tempe, Ariz.)
Penn St. 42, Arizona St. 30

1/ 1/79 Sugar Bowl (New Orleans)
Alabama 14, Penn St. 7

12/22/79 Liberty Bowl (Memphis, Tenn.)
Penn St. 9, Tulane 6

12/26/80 Fiesta Bowl (Tempe, Ariz.)
Penn St. 31, Ohio St. 19

1/ 1/82 Fiesta Bowl (Tempe, Ariz.)
Penn St. 26, Southern California 10

1/ 1/83 Sugar Bowl (New Orleans)
Penn St. 27, Georgia 23

12/26/83 Aloha Bowl (Honolulu)
Penn St. 13, Washington 10

1/ 1/86 Orange Bowl (Miami)
Oklahoma 25, Penn St. 10

1/ 2/87 Fiesta Bowl (Tempe, Ariz.)
Penn St. 14, Miami (Fla.) 10

1/ 1/88 Florida Citrus Bowl (Orlando, Fla.)
Clemson 35, Penn St. 10

CAREER LEADERS

RUSHING YARDS		PASSING YARDS		RECEPTIONS	
Curt Warner	3,398	Chuck Fusina	5,382	Jack Curry	117
D.J. Dozier	3,227	Todd Blackledge	4,812	Kenny Jackson	109
Lydell Mitchell	2,934	John Hufnagel	3,545	Ted Kwalick	86
Matt Suhey	2,818	John Shaffer	3,470	Dan Natale	67
John Cappelletti	2,639	Doug Strang	2,966	Mickey Shuler	66
Lenny Moore	2,380	Tom Shuman	2,886	D.J. Dozier	66
Charlie Pittman	2,236	Tom Sherman	2,588	Junior Powell	65
Booker Moore	2,072	Tony Rados	2,437	Scott Fitzkee	65
Jon Williams	2,042	Pete Liske	2,370	Kevin Baugh	60
Franco Harris	2,002	Chuck Burkhart	2,076	Gregg Garrity	58
Blair Thomas	1,960	Matt Knizner	1,873	Brad Scovill	58
Fran Rogel	1,496	Rich Lucas	1,822	Jesse Arnelle	58

RECORDS

	INDIVIDUAL, GAME	INDIVIDUAL, SEASON
Rushing Yardage	256: Curt Warner, vs. Syracuse, 10/17/81	1,527: Lydell Mitchell, 1971
Rushing Attempts	45: Harry Wilson, vs. Pennsylvania, 11/17/23	286: John Cappelletti, 1973
Rushing TDs	6: Harry Robb, vs. Gettysburg, 10/6/17	26: Lydell Mitchell, 1971
Passing Yardage	358: Todd Blackledge, vs. Miami (Fla.), 10/31/81	2,221: Chuck Fusina, 1977
Passes Attempted	41: Todd Blackledge, vs. Miami (Fla.), 10/31/81	292: Todd Blackledge, 1982
Passes Completed	26: Todd Blackledge, vs. Miami (Fla.), 10/31/81	161: Todd Blackledge, 1982
Passing TDs	4: Tom Sherman, vs. Pittsburgh, 11/25/67 Chuck Fusina, vs. Syracuse, 10/21/78 Todd Blackledge, vs. Temple, 9/4/82; vs. Maryland, 9/11/82; vs. Rutgers, 9/18/82	22: Todd Blackledge, 1982
Interceptions	4: Rich Lucas, vs. Illinois, 10/24/59 Bob Parsons, vs. Syracuse, 10/17/70 Chuck Fusina, vs. Alabama, 1/1/79 Todd Blackledge, vs. Alabama, 10/9/82	15: Vince O'Bara, 1950
Receiving Yardage	158: Kenny Jackson, vs. Pittsburgh, 11/28/81	697: Kenny Jackson, 1982
Receptions	10: Jack Curry, vs. Syracuse, 10/16/65 vs. California, 10/30/65	42: Jack Curry, 1965
Receiving TDs	2: 21 times; Last done by Ray Roundtree, vs. Alabama, 9/12/87	7: Kenny Jackson, 1982 Kenny Jackson, 1983
Points Scored	36: Harry Robb, vs. Gettysburg, 10/6/17	174: Lydell Mitchell, 1971
Touchdowns	6: Harry Robb, vs. Gettysburg, 10/6/17	29: Lydell Mitchell, 1971
PATs Made	10: Charles Atherton, vs. Gettysburg, 10/13/94	59: Alberto Vitiello, 1971
Field Goals Made	5: Brian Franco, vs. Nebraska, 9/26/81 Massimo Manca, vs. Notre Dame, 11/16/85	22: Matt Bahr, 1978
Interceptions By	4: Mike Smith, vs. Ohio U., 11/14/70	10: Neal Smith, 1969 Pete Harris, 1978
Punts	12: Six times; Last done by Ralph Giacomarro, vs. Pittsburgh, 12/1/79	79: John Bruno, 1984
Punt Returns	7: Elwood Petchell, vs. West Virginia, 10/25/47 Joe Vargo, vs. Ohio St., 11/7/64 Kevin Baugh, vs. Rutgers, 9/18/82 Jim Coates, vs. East Carolina, 9/27/86	36: Jim Coates, 1986
Punt Return Yardage	145: Matt Suhey, vs. North Carolina St., 11/11/78	596: Shorty Miller, 1912
Kickoff Returns	6: Mike Irwin, vs. Michigan St., 9/25/65	26: Kevin Baugh, 1983
Kickoff Ret. Yardage	152: Bob Campbell, vs. Navy, 9/23/67	503: Kevin Baugh, 1983

Todd Blackledge celebrates one of 41 career TD passes

Curt Warner is Penn State's all-time leading rusher

RECORDS

	INDIVIDUAL, CAREER	TEAM, GAME
Rushing Yardage	3,398: Curt Warner, 1979-82	622: vs. Lebanon Valley, 9/27/24
Rushing Attempts	649: Curt Warner, 1979-82	83: vs. West Virginia, 10/11/75
Rushing TDs	39: Lydell Mitchell, 1969-71	Not Available
Passing Yardage	5,382: Chuck Fusina, 1975-78	358: vs. Miami (Fla.), 10/31/81
Passes Attempted	665: Chuck Fusina, 1975-78	41: vs. Miami (Fla.), 10/31/81 vs. Alabama, 10/9/82
Passes Completed	371: Chuck Fusina, 1975-78	26: vs. Miami (Fla.), 10/31/81
Passing TDs	41: Todd Blackledge, 1980-82	NA
Interceptions	41: Todd Blackledge, 1980-82	NA
Receiving Yardage	2,006: Kenny Jackson, 1980-83	358: vs. Miami (Fla.), 10/31/81
Receptions	117: Jack Curry, 1965-67	26: vs. Miami (Fla.), 10/31/81
Receiving TDs	25: Kenny Jackson, 1980-83	NA
Points Scored	246: Lydell Mitchell, 1969-71	109: vs. Lebanon Valley, 10/23/20
Touchdowns	41: Lydell Mitchell, 1969-71	NA
PATs Made	98: Alberto Vitiello, 1971-72	NA
Field Goals Made	40: Massimo Manca, 1982, '84-86	NA
Interceptions By	19: Neal Smith, 1967-69	7: vs. Missouri, 1/1/70 vs. Boston College, 10/10/70
Punts	225: Ralph Giacomarro, 1979-82	NA
Punt Returns	62: Kevin Baugh, 1980-83	12: vs. Rutgers, 9/18/82
Punt Ret. Yardage	717: Gary Hayman, 1972-73	256: vs. Rutgers, 9/18/82
Kickoff Returns	62: Kevin Baugh, 1980-83	NA
Kickoff Ret. Yardage	1,216: Kevin Baugh, 1980-83	NA

Joe Paterno

In some ways, it took a losing season to point out the incredible history of Penn State football.

By dropping their final two games, the Nittany Lions finished 5-6, their first losing season in 50 years. It also was the first losing season in the amazing 23-year tenure of Penn State coach Joe Paterno.

Paterno's career head coaching record, all at Penn State, is 212-54-2. His record in bowls is 12-6-1. Paterno teams have won the mythical national championship twice.

In 1982, the Lions went 11-1 and beat the University of Georgia and Herschel Walker, 27-23, in the Sugar Bowl on Jan. 1, 1983.

In 1986, Penn State went 12-0 and beat Miami (Fla.), led by quarterback Vinnie Testeverde, 14-10, in the Fiesta Bowl.

But Paterno is quick to point out that "our 1968, 1969 and 1973 teams were as good as the ones that were named No. 1."

The Nittany Lions also have finished in the top 20 postseason *Associated Press* poll in 17 of Paterno's 23 seasons.

Of course, the program's success is not entirely due to its coach. Paterno has coached 40 All-Americas. Some of the more renowned of that group are running back John Cappelletti, the Monsignor Bonner product who won the Heisman Trophy in 1973; defensive tackle Mike Reid (class of 1969); linebacker Jack Ham ('70), now in the Pro Football Hall of Fame; running backs Lydell Mitchell ('71), Curt Warner ('82) and D.J. Dozier ('86) and quarterback Chuck Fusina ('78).

However, Paterno is more proud of the numerous academic All-Americas who have played in Happy Valley. Academics take a high priority with Paterno-coached teams.

"You don't see many athletes from Penn State who struggle the rest of their lives," said Eagles receiver Gregg Garrity, a 1983 Penn State grad.

Paterno was born in Brooklyn on Dec. 21, 1926. He attended Brooklyn Prep and Brown University, where he played quarterback for coach Rip Engle, his predecessor as Penn State coach.

In a Penn State publication, sports writer Stanley Woodward is quoted on Paterno's days as a quarterback at Brown. "He can't run and can't pass," Woodward wrote. "All he can do is think and win." Paterno led Brown to records of 7-2 in 1948 and 8-1 in 1949.

Upon graduation from Brown, Paterno joined the coaching staff at Penn State, when Engle was named head coach in 1950. Paterno remained an assistant for 16 seasons under Engle, who compiled a record of 104-48-4. Paterno was rewarded for his loyalty when he was named head coach before the 1966 season.

ST. JOSEPH'S

BASKETBALL

YEAR-BY-YEAR RECORDS

Season	Head Coach	W- L	Pct.	Season	Head Coach	W- L	Pct.
1909-10	John Dever	10- 6	.625	1949-50	Bill Ferguson	10-15	.400
1910-11	Edward Bennis	6- 6	.500	1950-51	Bill Ferguson	13-14	.481
1911-12	John Donahue	6-22	.214	1951-52	Bill Ferguson	20- 7	.741
1912-13	John Donahue	11- 5	.688	1952-53	Bill Ferguson	14-11	.560
1913-14	John Donahue	10- 5	.667	1953-54	John McMenamin	14- 9	.609
1914-15	John Donahue	14- 1	.933	1954-55	John McMenamin	12-14	.462
1915-16	John Donahue	11- 9	.550	1955-56	Jack Ramsay	23- 6	.793
1916-17	John Donahue	18- 5	.783	1956-57	Jack Ramsay	17- 7	.708
1917-18	John Donahue	5- 2	.714	1957-58	Jack Ramsay	18- 9	.667
1918-19	John Donahue	3- 3	.500	1958-59	Jack Ramsay	22- 5	.815
1919-20	John Lavin	9- 6	.600	1959-60	Jack Ramsay	20- 7	.741
1920-21	John Lavin	4-10	.286	1960-61	Jack Ramsay	25- 5	.833
1921-22	John Lavin	8- 9	.471	1961-62	Jack Ramsay	18-10	.643
1922-23	John Lavin	7- 8	.467	1962-63	Jack Ramsay	23- 5	.821
1923-24	John Lavin	9- 9	.500	1963-64	Jack Ramsay	18-10	.643
1924-25	John Lavin	9- 9	.500	1964-65	Jack Ramsay	26- 3	.897
1925-26	John Lavin	4-11	.267	1965-66	Jack Ramsay	24- 5	.828
1926-27	Tom Temple	6-11	.353	1966-67	Jack McKinney	16-10	.615
1927-28	Tom Temple	6-11	.353	1967-68	Jack McKinney	17- 9	.654
1928-29	Bill Ferguson	8-10	.444	1968-69	Jack McKinney	17-11	.607
1929-30	Bill Ferguson	12- 9	.571	1969-70	Jack McKinney	15-12	.556
1930-31	Bill Ferguson	16- 5	.762	1970-71	Jack McKinney	19- 9	.679
1931-32	Bill Ferguson	8-10	.444	1971-72	Jack McKinney	19- 9	.679
1932-33	Bill Ferguson	7- 9	.438	1972-73	Jack McKinney	22- 6	.786
1933-34	Bill Ferguson	6-11	.353	1973-74	Jack McKinney	19-11	.633
1934-35	Bill Ferguson	12- 3	.800	1974-75	Harry Booth	8-17	.320
1935-36	Bill Ferguson	14- 5	.737	1975-76	Harry Booth	10-16	.385
1936-37	Bill Ferguson	15- 4	.789	1976-77	Harry Booth	13-13	.500
1937-38	Bill Ferguson	13- 5	.722	1977-78	Harry Booth	13-15	.464
1938-39	Bill Ferguson	9-12	.429	1978-79	Jim Lynam	19-11	.633
1939-40	Bill Ferguson	10- 5	.667	1979-80	Jim Lynam	21- 9	.700
1940-41	Bill Ferguson	12- 6	.667	1980-81	Jim Lynam	25- 8	.758
1941-42	Bill Ferguson	12- 6	.667	1981-82	Jim Boyle	25- 5	.833
1942-43	Bill Ferguson	18- 4	.818	1982-83	Jim Boyle	15-13	.536
1943-44	Bill Ferguson	18- 7	.720	1983-84	Jim Boyle	20- 9	.690
1944-45	Bill Ferguson	12-11	.522	1984-85	Jim Boyle	19-12	.613
1945-46	Bill Ferguson	9-11	.450	1985-86	Jim Boyle	26- 6	.813
1946-47	Bill Ferguson	16- 6	.727	1986-87	Jim Boyle	16-13	.552
1947-48	Bill Ferguson	13-11	.542	1987-88	Jim Boyle	15-14	.517
1948-49	Bill Ferguson	12-11	.522	1988-89	Jim Boyle	8-21	.276

John Smith shoots over two defenders in St. Joe's 49-48 win over top-ranked De Paul in the 1981 NCAA Tournament

POSTSEASON RESULTS

1956 NIT: Defeated Seton Hall, 74-65; Lost to Louisville, 89-79, in semifinals; Defeated St. Francis (N.Y.), 93-82, in third place game (all games at Madison Square Garden).

1958 NIT: Defeated St. Peter's, 83-72; Lost to St. Bonaventure, 79-75 (both games at Madison Square Garden).

1959 NCAA TOURNAMENT: Lost to West Virginia, 95-92 (Charlotte, N.C.); Lost to Navy, 70-56, in East Regional third place game (Charlotte, N.C.).

1960 NCAA TOURNAMENT: Lost to Duke, 58-56, in East Regional semifinal (Charlotte, N.C.); Lost to West Virginia, 106-100, in regional third place game (Charlotte, N.C.).

1961 NCAA TOURNAMENT: Defeated Princeton, 72-67 (Charlotte, N.C.); Defeated Wake Forest, 96-86, in East Regional final (Charlotte, N.C.); Lost to Ohio St., 95-69, in national semifinal (Kansas City, Mo.); Defeated Utah, 127-120 (4 ot), in third place game (Kansas City, Mo.). Vacated.

1962 NCAA TOURNAMENT: Lost to Wake Forest, 96-85 (ot) (College Park, Md.); Lost to New York U., 94-85, in East Regional third place game (College Park, Md.).

1963 NCAA TOURNAMENT: Defeated Princeton, 82-81 (ot) (Palestra); Defeated West Virginia, 97-88 (College Park, Md.); Lost to Duke, 73-59, in East Regional final (College Park, Md.).

1964 NIT: Defeated Miami (Fla.), 86-76; Lost to Bradley, 83-81 (both games at Madison Square Garden).

1965 NCAA TOURNAMENT: Defeated Connecticut, 67-61 (Palestra); Lost to Providence, 81-73 (ot) (College Park, Md.); Lost to North Carolina St., 103-81, in East Regional third place game (College Park, Md.).

1966 NCAA TOURNAMENT: Defeated Providence, 65-48 (Blacksburg, Va.); Lost to Duke, 76-74 (Raleigh, N.C.); Defeated Davidson, 92-76, in East Regional third place game (Raleigh, N.C.).

1969 NCAA TOURNAMENT: Lost to Duquesne, 74-52 (Kingston, R.I.).

1971 NCAA TOURNAMENT: Lost to Villanova, 93-75 (Palestra).

1972 NIT: Lost to Maryland, 67-55 (Madison Square Garden).

1973 NCAA TOURNAMENT: Lost to Providence, 89-76 (Jamaica, N.Y.).

1974 NCAA TOURNAMENT: Lost to Pittsburgh, 54-42 (Morgantown, W. Va.).

1979 NIT: Lost to Ohio St., 80-66 (Columbus, O.).

1980 NIT: Lost to Texas, 70-61 (Austin, Texas).

1981 NCAA TOURNAMENT: Defeated Creighton, 59-57 (Dayton, O.); Defeated De Paul, 49-48 (Dayton, O.); Defeated Boston College, 42-41 (Bloomington, Ind.); Lost to Indiana, 78-46, in Mideast Regional final (Bloomington, Ind.).

1982 NCAA TOURNAMENT: Lost to Northeastern, 63-62 (Uniondale, N.Y.).

1984 NIT: Lost to Boston College, 76-63 (Palestra).

1985 NIT: Defeated Missouri, 68-67 (Columbia, Mo.); Lost to Virginia, 68-61 (Charlottesville, Va.).

1986 NCAA TOURNAMENT: Defeated Richmond, 60-59 (Syracuse, N.Y.); Lost to Cleveland St., 75-69 (Syracuse, N.Y.).

COACHES' RECORDS

Seasons	Coach	W- L	Pct.
1909-10	John Dever	10- 6	.625
1910-11	Edward Bennis	6- 6	.500
1911-19	John Donahue	78- 52	.557
1919-26	John Lavin	50- 62	.446
1926-28	Tom Temple	12- 22	.353
1928-52	Bill Ferguson	309-208	.598
1953-55	John McMenamin	26- 23	.531
1955-66	Jack Ramsay	234- 72	.765
1966-74	Jack McKinney	144- 77	.652
1974-78	Harry Booth	44- 61	.419
1978-81	Jim Lynam	65- 28	.699
1981-89	Jim Boyle	144- 93	.608

1,000-POINT CLUB

Player	Games	Points
Tony Costner	120	1,729
Cliff Anderson	84	1,728
Maurice Martin	114	1,726
Norman Black	104	1,726
Mike Bantom	84	1,684
Bob Lojewski	116	1,682
Rodney Blake	116	1,679
Boo Williams	115	1,554
Pat McFarland	84	1,545
Dan Kelly	80	1,524
Mike Hauer	78	1,496
Paul Senesky	71	1,471
Bob McNeill	81	1,393
Jack Egan	83	1,363
Tom Wynne	85	1,321
Bryan Warrick	113	1,273
Kurt Engelbert	76	1,243
Lonnie McFarlan	86	1,152
Billy Oakes	84	1,129
Tom Duff	86	1,103
Bill Lynch	94	1,079
Steve Courtin	82	1,060
Joe Gallo	78	1,053
Wayne Williams	106	1,048
Mike Thomas	99	1,029
Jim Lynam	83	1,012
Zane Major	89	1,001

Wayne Williams rises for two of his 1,048 points

Maurice Martin fell shy of all-time leader Tony Costner

Bob Lojewski's intensity carried him to 1,682 points

84

LEADING SCORERS

Season	Player	Pts.	Season	Player	Pts.	Season	Player	Pts.
1927-28	Billy Oakes	NA	1948-49	Paul Senesky	482	1968-69	Dan Kelly	527
1928-29	Jim Osborne	NA	1949-50	Paul Senesky	570	1969-70	Dan Kelly	538
1929-30	Jim Osborne	NA	1950-51	Mike Fallon	334	1970-71	Mike Bantom	507
1930-31	Phil Zuber	139	1951-52	John Hughes	412	1971-72	Mike Bantom	609
1931-32	Phil Zuber	195	1952-53	Ed Garrity	403	1972-73	Pat McFarland	569
1932-33	Not Available	NA	1953-54	Tom Lynch	359	1973-74	Ron Righter	363
1933-34	John Kane	68	1954-55	Mike Fallon	374	1974-75	Ron Righter	402
1934-35	Matt Guokas	145	1955-56	Kurt Engelbert	458	1975-76	Norman Black	440
1935-36	Jim Smale	149	1956-57	Kurt Engelbert	486	1976-77	Norman Black	434
1936-37	NA	NA	1957-58	Bob McNeill	501	1977-78	Boo Williams	481
1937-38	NA	NA	1958-59	Bob McNeill	442	1978-79	Norman Black	464
1938-39	Larry Kenney	249	1959-60	Bob McNeill	450	1979-80	Boo Williams	417
1939-40	NA	NA	1960-61	Jack Egan	636	1980-81	Boo Williams	409
1940-41	Larry Kenney	277	1961-62	Tom Wynne	527	1981-82	Bryan Warrick	447
1941-42	NA	NA	1962-63	Tom Wynne	464	1982-83	Bob Lojewski	473
1942-43	George Senesky	515	1963-64	Steve Courtin	579	1983-84	Tony Costner	540
1943-44	Jack Flannery	292	1964-65	Cliff Anderson	519	1984-85	Bob Lojewski	481
1944-45	Bob O'Neill	348	1965-66	Cliff Anderson	519	1985-86	Maurice Martin	534
1945-46	Bob O'Neill	159	1966-67	Cliff Anderson	690	1986-87	Rodney Blake	423
1946-47	Norm Butz	177	1967-68	Mike Hauer	462	1987-88	Rodney Blake	529
1947-48	Paul Senesky	419				1988-89	Brian Leahy	479

RECORDS

	INDIVIDUAL, GAME	TEAM, GAME
Points	47: Jack Egan, vs. Gettysburg, 1/21/61 Tony Costner, vs. Alaska-Anchorage, 12/30/83	128: vs. Nevada-Reno, 12/15/71
FG Made	19: George Senesky, vs. Rutgers-Newark, 2/3/43	53: vs. Nevada-Reno, 12/15/71
FG Att.	38: Tom Wynne, vs. Gettysburg, 2/13/62	114: vs. King's, 12/15/61
FG Pct.	100: Bryan Warrick, vs. N.C.-Char., 1/16/82 (12-12)	68.3: vs. Northeastern, 12/18/82 (41-60)
FT Made	18: Bob McNeill, vs. La Salle, 2/26/58	37: vs. Virginia, 2/22/58 vs. Utah, 3/25/61
FT Att.	22: Bob McNeill, vs. La Salle, 2/26/58	52: vs. Temple, 3/10/56
FT Pct.	100: Mike Hauer, vs. Seton Hall, 2/21/70 (15-15)	100: vs. W. Virginia, 12/21/87 (13-13)
Rebounds	34: John Doogan, vs. West Chester St., 2/18/53	83: vs. St. Peter's, 2/28/62
Assists	14: Tom Haggerty, vs. Fairfield, 2/21/76	30: vs. Alaska-Anchorage, 12/30/83
Blocks	12: Rodney Blake, vs. Cleveland St., 12/2/87	13: vs. Cleveland St., 12/2/87
Steals	10: Billy DeAngelis, vs. Bowling Green, 12/9/67	18: vs. Penn St., 1/26/85

	INDIVIDUAL, SEASON	INDIVIDUAL, CAREER
Points	690: Cliff Anderson, 1966-67	1,729: Tony Costner, 1980-84
FG Made	256: Pat McFarland, 1972-73	712: Norman Black, 1975-79
FG Att.	605: Cliff Anderson, 1966-67	1,528: Norman Black, 1975-79
FG Pct.	57.7: Maurice Martin, 1983-84 (190-329)	54.5: Rodney Blake, 1984-88 (662-1,214)
FT Made	204: Cliff Anderson, 1966-67	483: Mike Hauer, 1967-70
FT Att.	279: Cliff Anderson, 1966-67	701: Cliff Anderson, 1964-67
FT Pct.	86.1: Jeffery Clark, 1980-81 (62-72)	83.7: Jeffery Clark, 1977-82 (226-270)
Rebounds	450: Cliff Anderson, 1964-65	1,228: Cliff Anderson, 1964-67
Assists	176: Matt Guokas Jr., 1965-66	523: Luke Griffin, 1976-80
Blocks	121: Rodney Blake, 1985-86	419: Rodney Blake, 1984-88
Steals	104: Billy DeAngelis, 1966-67	250: Jeffery Clark, 1977-82

Jack Ramsay

Philadelphia Big 5 fans will always be able to close their eyes and picture Jack Ramsay in front of the St. Joseph's bench, on one knee, coaxing greatness from any of his 11 Hawk teams that dominated the Big 5 from 1955-66.

The man they reverently call "Dr. Jack" was the soul of the Big 5 in its early days, an emotional, inspirational firebrand who turned the tiny school on Hawk Hill into one of the basketball capitals of America.

Before moving on to the NBA, as general manager of the Philadelphia 76ers, Ramsay's teams posted an astonishing 234-72 record and 10 post-season tournaments.

It always was little St. Joe's against the rest of the world back then, and the Hawks built a dragon-slayer reputation during his era.

Who can forget the chills that Jimmy Boyle's one-hander at the buzzer sent up their spines that night in 1962, when the Hawks stunned highly ranked Bowling Green, 58-57, in the opening round of the Quaker City tournament?

And remember the night Ramsay's Hawks bounced Temple and Guy Rodgers and Hal Lear in a City Series shocker, in 1956? Or the victory over powerful Wake Forest to reach the 1961 Final Four? And who doesn't remember the Sunday afternoon when Steve Donches's 30-footer at the buzzer gave Ramsay a 71-69 victory over arch-rival Villanova?

Born in Philadelphia on Feb. 21, 1925, Ramsay attended Upper Darby High School and spent three years in the Navy before attending St. Joseph's. He played with an AAU team and in the Eastern League before returning to Hawk Hill as a coach in 1955.

Ramsay's first team finished 23-6 and finished third in the NIT, and there would be six more 20-win seasons, that sadly, includes the scandal-plagued Final Four team of 1961.

The Hawk team regarded as Ramsay's best was the 1964-65 squad — featuring Cliff Anderson and Matt Guokas, Jr. — that finished 26-3 and ranked third in both wire service polls. The Hawks — who did not have a senior nor a starter over 6-6 — reached the NCAA Eastern Regional semifinals before losing to Providence, 81-73, in overtime. It is believed to be Ramsay's greatest coaching job ever.

Although he never won an NCAA Championship, a title did not escape Ramsay in the NBA. His Portland Trail Blazers team — led by center Bill Walton — captured the 1976-77 NBA crown by defeating the 76ers in six games.

In 1989, at age 63, Ramsay ended a 21-year coaching career in the NBA, when he resigned as head coach of the Indiana Pacers seven games into the season.

Ramsay's resume also includes two seasons as Philadelphia's GM, four seasons as 76ers head coach, four more with Buffalo, and 10 years with Portland before he took over the Pacers.

Ramsay retired as the second-winningest coach in league history, with 864 career victories, which are topped only by the 938 accumulated by Red Auerbach.

"His career speaks for itself," said Jim Lynam, coach of the 76ers and a product of Ramsay's teachings at St. Joe's. "Look at his college success, his NBA record, his longevity, accomplishing what he has over a long period of time . . . In the college game, he repopularized the zone press in the East. He brought the concept of [offensive] motion to the pro game. In the two-year span in Portland with Bill Walton [as the center in 1976-77 and most of 1977-78], to me, was basketball at its best."

TEMPLE

YEAR-BY-YEAR RECORDS

Season	Head Coach	W- L	Pct.	Season	Head Coach	W- L	Pct.
1894-95	Charles Williams	8- 3	.727	1933-34	Jimmy Usilton	9-12	.429
1895-96	Charles Williams	15- 7	.682	1934-35	Jimmy Usilton	17- 7	.708
1896-97	Charles Williams	10-11	.476	1935-36	Jimmy Usilton	18- 8	.692
1897-98	Charles Williams	22- 5	.815	1936-37	Jimmy Usilton	17- 6	.739
1898-99	Charles Williams	18- 6	.750	1937-38	Jimmy Usilton	23- 2	.920
1899-00	John Rogers	14- 8	.636	1938-39	Jimmy Usilton	10-12	.455
(1900-01: No varsity team)				1939-40	Ernie Messikomer	13-10	.565
1901-02	H. Shindle Wingert	8- 3	.727	1940-41	Ernie Messikomer	12- 9	.571
1902-03	H. Shindle Wingert	5- 6	.455	1941-42	Ernie Messikomer	10- 8	.556
1903-04	H. Shindle Wingert	4- 4	.500	1942-43	Josh Cody	11-11	.500
1904-05	H. Shindle Wingert	3- 3	.500	1943-44	Josh Cody	14- 9	.609
1905-06	John Crescenzo	3- 4	.429	1944-45	Josh Cody	16- 7	.696
1906-07	John Crescenzo	5- 4	.556	1945-46	Josh Cody	12- 7	.632
1907-08	John Crescenzo	6- 2	.750	1946-47	Josh Cody	8-12	.400
1908-09	Edward McCone	8- 3	.727	1947-48	Josh Cody	12-11	.522
1909-10	Frederick Prosch Jr.	4- 6	.400	1948-49	Josh Cody	14- 9	.609
1910-11	Frederick Prosch Jr.	3- 5	.375	1949-50	Josh Cody	14-10	.583
1911-12	Frederick Prosch Jr.	4- 4	.500	1950-51	Josh Cody	12-13	.480
1912-13	Frederick Prosch Jr.	6- 5	.545	1951-52	Josh Cody	9-15	.375
1913-14	William Nicolai	5- 7	.417	1952-53	Harry Litwack	16-10	.615
1914-15	William Nicolai	9- 4	.692	1953-54	Harry Litwack	15-12	.556
1915-16	William Nicolai	7- 6	.538	1954-55	Harry Litwack	11-10	.524
1916-17	William Nicolai	10- 9	.526	1955-56	Harry Litwack	27- 4	.871
1917-18	Elwood Geiges	8- 7	.533	1956-57	Harry Litwack	20- 9	.690
(1918-19: No varsity team)				1957-58	Harry Litwack	27- 3	.900
1919-20	Francois D'Eliscu	9- 7	.563	1958-59	Harry Litwack	6-19	.240
1920-21	Francois D'Eliscu	7- 4	.636	1959-60	Harry Litwack	17- 9	.654
1921-22	Francois D'Eliscu	4- 7	.364	1960-61	Harry Litwack	20- 8	.714
1922-23	Francois D'Eliscu	10- 4	.714	1961-62	Harry Litwack	18- 9	.667
1923-24	Samuel Dienes	15- 5	.750	1962-63	Harry Litwack	15- 7	.682
1924-25	Samuel Dienes	12-10	.545	1963-64	Harry Litwack	17- 8	.680
1925-26	Samuel Dienes	12- 6	.667	1964-65	Harry Litwack	14-10	.583
1926-27	Jimmy Usilton	14- 5	.737	1965-66	Harry Litwack	21- 7	.750
1927-28	Jimmy Usilton	17- 5	.773	1966-67	Harry Litwack	20- 8	.714
1928-29	Jimmy Usilton	17- 4	.810	1967-68	Harry Litwack	19- 9	.679
1929-30	Jimmy Usilton	18- 3	.857	1968-69	Harry Litwack	22- 8	.733
1930-31	Jimmy Usilton	17- 4	.810	1969-70	Harry Litwack	15-13	.536
1931-32	Jimmy Usilton	13- 7	.650	1970-71	Harry Litwack	13-12	.520
1932-33	Jimmy Usilton	15- 6	.714	1971-72	Harry Litwack	23- 8	.742

YEAR-BY-YEAR RECORDS

Season	Head Coach	W- L	Pct.
1972-73	Harry Litwack	17-10	.630
1973-74	Don Casey	16- 9	.640
1974-75	Don Casey	7-19	.269
1975-76	Don Casey	9-18	.333
1976-77	Don Casey	17-11	.607
1977-78	Don Casey	24- 5	.828
1978-79	Don Casey	25- 4	.862
1979-80	Don Casey	14-12	.538
1980-81	Don Casey	20- 8	.714
1981-82	Don Casey	19- 8	.704
1982-83	John Chaney	14-15	.483
1983-84	John Chaney	26- 5	.897
1984-85	John Chaney	25- 6	.806
1985-86	John Chaney	25- 6	.806
1986-87	John Chaney	32- 4	.889
1987-88	John Chaney	32- 2	.941
1988-89	John Chaney	18-12	.600

COACHES' RECORDS

Seasons	Coach	W- L	Pct.
1894-99	Charles Williams	73- 32	.695
1899-00	John Rogers	14- 8	.636
1901-05	H. Shindle Wingert	20- 18	.526
1905-08	John Crescenzo	14- 10	.583
1908-09	Edward McCone	8- 20	.286
1909-13	Frederick Prosch Jr.	17- 20	.459
1913-17	William Nicolai	31- 26	.544
1917-18	Elwood Geiges	8- 7	.533
1919-23	Francois D'Eliscu	30- 22	.577
1923-26	Samuel Dienes	39- 21	.650
1926-40	Jimmy Usilton	205- 79	.722
1939-42	Ernie Messikomer	35- 27	.565
1942-52	Josh Cody	122-104	.540
1952-73	Harry Litwack	373-193	.659
1973-82	Don Casey	151- 94	.616
1982-89	John Chaney	172- 50	.774

1,000-POINT CLUB

Player	Games	Points
Terence Stansbury	115	1,811
Guy Rodgers	90	1,767
Nate Blackwell	129	1,708
Granger Hall	115	1,652
Mike Vreeswyk	119	1,650
John Baum	86	1,544
Bill Mlkvy	73	1,539
Marty Stahurski	109	1,499
Hal Lear	79	1,499
"Pickles" Kennedy	81	1,468
Howard Evans	132	1,459
Bruce Drysdale	81	1,444
Tim Claxton	109	1,418
Clarence Brookins	83	1,386
Tim Perry	130	1,368
Jim Williams	77	1,306
Mark Macon	64	1,247
Ed Coe	120	1,177
Charles Rayne	107	1,131
Joe Cromer	85	1,118
Jim McLoughlin	104	1,112
Harry Silcox	84	1,111
Keith Parham	98	1,092
Walt Montford	107	1,067
Ollie Johnson	83	1,063
Alton McCullough	107	1,051
Rick Reed	110	1,031
Jay Norman	89	1,024

Terence Stansbury soars for two of his 1,811 points

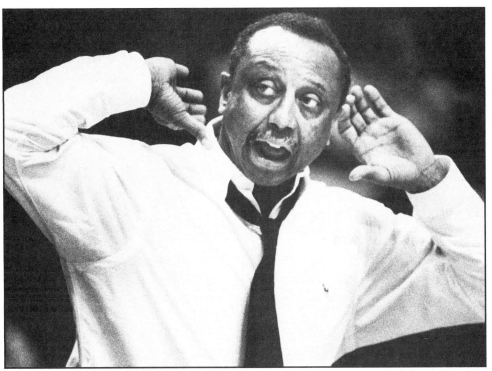

John Chaney disagrees with a call made in Temple's 74-53 victory over Georgetown in 1988 NCAA Tournament

POSTSEASON RESULTS

1938 NIT: Defeated Colorado, 60-36; Defeated Oklahoma A&M, 56-44; Defeated Bradley, 53-40, in championship game (all games at New York).

1944 NCAA TOURNAMENT: Defeated Catholic U., 55-35 (New York); Lost to Ohio St., 57-47 (New York).

1956 NCAA TOURNAMENT: Defeated Holy Cross, 74-72 (New York); Defeated Connecticut, 65-59 (New York); Defeated Canisius, 60-58, in East Regional final (New York); Lost to Iowa, 83-76, in national semifinals (Evanston, Ill.); Defeated Southern Methodist, 90-81, in third place game (Evanston, Ill.).

1957 NIT: Defeated Dayton, 77-66; Lost to Bradley, 94-66, in semifinals; Defeated St. Bonaventure, 57-50, in third place game (all games at New York).

1958 NCAA TOURNAMENT: Defeated Maryland, 71-67 (Charlotte, N.C.); Defeated Dartmouth, 69-50, in East Regional final (Charlotte, N.C.); Lost to Kentucky, 61-60, in national semifinals (Louisville, Ky.); Defeated Kansas St., 67-57, in third place game (Louisville, Ky.).

1960 NIT: Lost to Dayton, 72-51 (New York).

1961 NIT: Defeated Army, 80-78; Lost to Dayton, 62-60 (both games at New York).

1962 NIT: Defeated Providence, 80-78; Lost to Loyola (Ill.), 75-64 (both games at New York).

1964 NCAA TOURNAMENT: Lost to Connecticut, 53-48 (Palestra).

1966 NIT: Defeated Virginia Tech, 88-73; Lost to Brigham Young, 90-78 (both games at New York).

1967 NCAA TOURNAMENT: Lost to St. John's, 57-53 (Blacksburg, Va.).

1968 NIT: Lost to Kansas, 82-76 (New York).

1969 NIT: Defeated Florida, 82-66; Defeated St. Peter's, 94-78; Defeated Tennessee, 63-58, in semifinals; Defeated Boston College, 89-76, in championship game (all games at New York).

1970 NCAA TOURNAMENT: Lost to Villanova, 77-69 (Palestra).

1972 NCAA TOURNAMENT: Lost to South Carolina, 53-51 (Williamsburg, Va.).

1978 NIT: Lost to Texas, 72-58 (Austin, Texas).

1979 NCAA TOURNAMENT: Lost to St. John's, 75-70 (Raleigh, N.C.).

1981 NIT: Defeated Clemson, 90-82 (Clemson, S.C.); Lost to West Virginia, 77-76 (Morgantown, W. Va.).

1982 NIT: Lost to Georgia, 73-60 (Athens, Ga.).

1984 NCAA TOURNAMENT: Defeated St. John's, 65-63 (Charlotte, N.C.); Lost to North Carolina, 77-66 (Charlotte, N.C.).

1985 NCAA TOURNAMENT: Defeated Virginia Tech, 60-57 (Hartford, Conn.); Lost to Georgetown, 63-46 (Hartford, Conn.).

1986 NCAA TOURNAMENT: Defeated Jacksonville, 61-50 (Dayton, Ohio); Lost to Kansas, 65-43 (Dayton, Ohio).

1987 NCAA TOURNAMENT: Defeated Southern U., 75-56 (Rosemont, Ill.); Lost to Louisiana St., 72-62 (Rosemont, Ill.).

1988 NCAA TOURNAMENT: Defeated Lehigh, 87-73 (Hartford, Conn.); Defeated Georgetown, 74-53 (Hartford, Conn.); Defeated Richmond, 69-47 (East Rutherford, N.J.); Lost to Duke, 63-53, in East Regional final (East Rutherford, N.J.).

1989 NIT: Lost to Richmond, 70-56 (Richmond, Va.).

LEADING SCORERS

Season	Player	Pts.	Season	Player	Pts.
1949-50	Ike Borsavage	160	1967-68	John Baum	508
1950-51	Bill Mlkvy	731	1968-69	John Baum	579
1951-52	Bill Mlkvy	418	1969-70	Tom Wieczerak	443
1952-53	John Kane	537	1970-71	Ollie Johnson	341
1953-54	Harry Silcox	426	1971-72	Ollie Johnson	523
1954-55	Hal Lear	467	1972-73	John Kneib	312
1955-56	Hal Lear	745	1973-74	John Kneib	320
1956-57	Guy Rodgers	591	1974-75	Marty Stahurski	333
1957-58	Guy Rodgers	603	1975-76	Bruce Burnett	377
1958-59	Bill "Pickles" Kennedy	488	1976-77	Bruce Burnett	393
1959-60	Bill "Pickles" Kennedy	576	1977-78	Tim Claxton	540
1960-61	Bruce Drysdale	595	1978-79	Rick Reed	455
1961-62	Bruce Drysdale	468	1979-80	Keith Parham	316
1962-63	Dan Fitzgerald	262	1980-81	Neal Robinson	434
1963-64	Jim Williams	452	1981-82	Granger Hall	401
1964-65	Jim Williams	357	1982-83	Terence Stansbury	713
1965-66	Clarence Brookins	468	1983-84	Terence Stansbury	577
1966-67	Clarence Brookins	508	1984-85	Granger Hall	559

Nate Blackwell

Season	Player	Pts.
1985-86	Ed Coe	482
1986-87	Nate Blackwell	714
1987-88	Mark Macon	699
1988-89	Mark Macon	548

RECORDS

	INDIVIDUAL, GAME	TEAM, GAME
Points	73: Bill Mlkvy, vs. Wilkes, 3/3/51	114: vs. Glassboro, 12/19/51
FG Made	32: Bill Mlkvy, vs. Wilkes, 3/3/51	47: vs. Gettysburg, 1/31/67
FG Att.	69: Bill Mlkvy, vs. Wilkes, 3/3/51	90: vs. American, 12/14/63
FG Pct.	100: Alton McCullough, vs. Bucknell, 1/6/82 (8-8)	68.4: vs. Rhode Island, 2/21/73 (39-57)
FT Made	16: Hal Lear, vs. Albright, 12/14/54	45: vs. Rider, 2/27/70
FT Att.	20: Jim Williams, vs. Manhattan, 12/18/63	54: vs. St. Joseph's, 3/10/56
FT Pct.	100: Paul Collins, vs. St. Joseph's, 2/28/70 (14-14)	100: vs. Miami (Fla.), 12/27/68 (19-19)
Rebounds	34: Fred Cohen, vs. Connecticut, 3/16/56	74: vs. St. Joseph's, 1/25/58
Assists	20: Howard Evans, vs. Villanova, 2/10/88	27: vs. Pittsburgh, 2/16/72 vs. American, 1/1/78, 2/16/79
Blocks	10: Duane Causwell, vs. Penn St., 12/26/88 Duane Causwell, vs. Penn St., 1/19/89	13: vs. Penn St., 12/26/88
Steals	11: Mark Macon, vs. Notre Dame, 1/29/89	17: vs. George Washington, 2/9/89

	INDIVIDUAL, SEASON	INDIVIDUAL, CAREER
Points	745: Hal Lear, 1955-56	1,811: Terence Stansbury, 1980-84
FG Made	303: Bill Mlkvy, 1950-51	708: Guy Rodgers, 1955-58
FG Att.	601: Terence Stansbury, 1982-83	1,466: Terence Stansbury, 1980-84
FG Pct.	58.1: Jim Williams, 1965-66 (182-313)	54.4: Granger Hall, 1980-85 (585-1,075)
FT Made	189: Hal Lear, 1955-56	482: Granger Hall, 1980-85
FT Att.	236: Granger Hall, 1984-85	688: Granger Hall, 1980-85
FT Pct.	90.4: Nate Blackwell, 1986-87 (123-136)	84.1: Howard Evans, 1984-87 (360-428)
Rebounds	472: Bill Mlkvy, 1950-51	1,042: John Baum, 1966-69
Assists	294: Howard Evans, 1987-88	748: Howard Evans, 1984-88
Blocks	124: Duane Causwell, 1988-89	392: Tim Perry, 1984-88
Steals	91: Howard Evans, 1986-87	268: Howard Evans, 1984-88

Guy Rodgers

Every night, it seemed there was a different name tacked onto the legend of Guy Rodgers. Some called him the Wiz, as in wizard. Some media members referred to him as "the tan terror," for his skin color. Others simply called him Magic, almost 30 years before a Los Angeles Laker from Michigan State named Earvin Johnson would make it big.

"He was the best ever," said Rodgers' backcourt partner at Temple University, Hal Lear. "No question about that. He was the greatest.

"When you have a man who is as fast as Guy was with the ball, you can't help but get more than an average number of fastbreaks. The first pass is always half of the fastbreak. But after Guy got it, it was just poetry in motion. If you've ever seen any pictures of it, you won't believe it. In movies, he's faster than the camera."

There are those who rate Rodgers and Lear the greatest collegiate backcourt ever assembled, when the two led Temple to the NCAA Final Four in 1955-56.

Lear was a senior; Rodgers just a sophomore. But for one shining season, they painted masterpieces together, making Temple the most exciting team in the country, as well as its best.

Rodgers — who would star for 12 years in the NBA — was the catalyst for the Owls' devastating fastbreak, with Lear, the best pure shooter of his era at the trigger.

Rodgers, together with Lear, helped Temple establish a standard of excellence that only has been duplicated once, in 1958, when the Owls again reached the Final Four and again finished third.

Rodgers was born on Sept. 1, 1935, and attended Northeast High before making his way to Temple.

He was a three-time All-America, who in his first varsity season turned an 11-10 team into a fastbreaking, 27-4 powerhouse coached by Harry Litwack.

The Rodgers legend was born in the third game of his sophomore season, when the Owls traveled to Kentucky and shocked Adolph Rupp's perennial champions, 73-61, in their own building.

Rodgers' 708 career field goals remains a Temple University record, and his 1,767 points ranks him second on the Owls all-time list, in just three seasons of varsity action.

TEMPLE

YEAR-BY-YEAR RECORDS

Year	Head Coach	W- L-T	Pct.
1894	Charles Williams	4- 1-0	.800
1895	Charles Williams	1- 4-1	.250
1896	Charles Williams	3- 2-0	.600
1897	Charles Williams	3- 3-0	.500
1898	Charles Williams	2- 5-0	.286
1899	John Rogers	1- 4-1	.250
1900	John Rogers	3- 4-1	.438
1901	H. Shindle Wingert	3- 2-0	.600
1902	H. Shindle Wingert	1- 4-1	.250
1903	H. Shindle Wingert	4- 1-0	.800
1904	H. Shindle Wingert	3- 2-0	.600
1905	H. Shindle Wingert	2- 0-1	.833
(1906: No varsity team)			
1907	Horace Butterworth	4- 0-2	.833
1908	Dr. Frank White	3- 2-1	.583
1909	William Schatz	0- 4-1	.100
1910	William Schatz	3- 3-0	.500
1911	William Schatz	6- 1-0	.857
1912	William Schatz	3- 2-0	.600
1913	William Schatz	1- 3-2	.333
1914	William Nicolai	3- 3-0	.500
1915	William Nicolai	3- 1-1	.700
1916	William Nicolai	3- 1-2	.667
1917	Elwood Geiges	0- 6-1	.071
(1918-21: No varsity team, World War I)			
1922	Francois D'Eliscu	1- 4-1	.250
1923	Francois D'Eliscu	0- 5-0	.000
1924	Albert Barron	1- 4-0	.200
1925	Henry Miller	5- 2-2	.667
1926	Henry Miller	5- 3-0	.625
1927	Henry Miller	7- 1-0	.875
1928	Henry Miller	7- 1-2	.800
1929	Henry Miller	6- 3-1	.650
1930	Henry Miller	7- 3-0	.700
1931	Henry Miller	8- 1-1	.850
1932	Henry Miller	5- 1-2	.750
1933	Glenn "Pop" Warner	5- 3-0	.625
1934	Glenn "Pop" Warner	7- 1-2	.800
1935	Glenn "Pop" Warner	7- 3-0	.700

Season	Head Coach	W- L-T	Pct.
1936	Glenn "Pop" Warner	6- 3-2	.636
1937	Glenn "Pop" Warner	3- 2-4	.556
1938	Glenn "Pop" Warner	3- 6-1	.350
1939	Fred Swan	2- 7-0	.222
1940	Ray Morrison	4- 4-1	.500
1941	Ray Morrison	7- 2-0	.778
1942	Ray Morrison	2- 5-3	.350
1943	Ray Morrison	2- 6-0	.250
1944	Ray Morrison	2- 4-2	.375
1945	Ray Morrison	7- 1-0	.875
1946	Ray Morrison	2- 4-2	.375
1947	Ray Morrison	3- 6-0	.333
1948	Ray Morrison	2- 6-1	.278
1949	Albert Kawai	5- 4-0	.556
1950	Albert Kawai	4- 4-1	.500
1951	Albert Kawai	6- 4-0	.600
1952	Albert Kawai	2- 7-1	.250
1953	Albert Kawai	4- 4-1	.500
1954	Albert Kawai	3- 5-0	.375
1955	Josh Cody	0- 8-0	.000
1956	Pete Stevens	3- 5-0	.375
1957	Pete Stevens	1- 6-0	.143
1958	Pete Stevens	0- 8-0	.000
1959	Pete Stevens	0- 9-0	.000
1960	George Makris	2- 7-0	.222
1961	George Makris	2- 5-2	.333
1962	George Makris	3- 6-0	.333
1963	George Makris	5- 3-1	.611
1964	George Makris	7- 2-0	.778
1965	George Makris	5- 5-0	.500
1966	George Makris	6- 3-0	.667
1967	George Makris	7- 2-0	.778
1968	George Makris	4- 6-0	.400
1969	George Makris	4- 5-1	.450
1970	Wayne Hardin	7- 3-0	.700
1971	Wayne Hardin	6- 2-1	.722
1972	Wayne Hardin	5- 4-0	.556
1973	Wayne Hardin	9- 1-0	.900
1974	Wayne Hardin	8- 2-0	.800

YEAR-BY-YEAR RECORDS

Year Head Coach	W- L-T	Pct.	Season Head Coach	W- L	Pct.
1975 Wayne Hardin	6- 5-0	.545	1982 Wayne Hardin	4- 7-0	.364
1976 Wayne Hardin	4- 6-0	.400	1983 Bruce Arians	4- 7-0	.364
1977 Wayne Hardin	5- 5-1	.500	1984 Bruce Arians	6- 5-0	.545
1978 Wayne Hardin	7- 3-1	.682	1985 Bruce Arians	4- 7-0	.364
1979 Wayne Hardin	10- 2-0	.833	1986 Bruce Arians	0-11-0	.000
1980 Wayne Hardin	4- 7-0	.364	1987 Bruce Arians	4- 7-0	.364
1981 Wayne Hardin	5- 5-0	.500	1988 Bruce Arians	4- 7-0	.364

COACHES' RECORDS

Seasons Head Coach	W- L-T	Pct.	Seasons Head Coach	W- L-T	Pct.
1894-98 Charles Williams	13-15-1	.466	1925-32 Henry Miller	50-15-8	.740
1899-00 John Rogers	4- 8-2	.357	1933-38 Glenn "Pop" Warner	31-18-9	.612
1901-05 H. Shindle Wingert	13- 9-3	.580	1939 Fred Swan	2- 7-0	.222
1907 Horace Butterworth	4- 0-2	.833	1940-48 Ray Morrison	31-38-9	.455
1908 Dr. Frank White	3- 2-1	.583	1949-54 Albert Kawal	24-28-3	.464
1909-13 William Schatz	13-13-3	.500	1955 Josh Cody	0- 8-0	.000
1914-16 William Nicolai	9- 5-3	.618	1956-59 Pete Stevens	4-28-0	.125
1917 Elwood Geiges	0- 6-1	.071	1960-69 George Makris	45-44-4	.505
1922-23 Francois D'Eliscu	1- 9-1	.136	1970-82 Wayne Hardin	80-52-3	.604
1924 Albert Barron	1- 4-0	.200	1983-88 Bruce Arians	22-44-0	.333

Head coach Wayne Hardin goes over game plan with quarterback Brian Broomell during practice

CAREER LEADERS

RUSHING YARDS		PASSING YARDS		RECEPTIONS	
Paul Palmer	3,029	Lee Saltz	5,371	Gerald Lucear	126
Anthony Anderson	2,610	Doug Shobert	3,913	Clint Graves	120
Todd McNair	2,383	Brian Broomell	3,902	Willie Marshall	111
Henry Hynoski	2,218	Tim Riordan	3,679	Steve Watson	98
Mark Bright	1,943	Steve Joachim	3,262	Wiley Pitts	92
Harold Harmon	1,730	Pat Carey	3,217	Randy Grossman	79
Zachary Dixon	1,522	Tink Murphy	2,802	Paul Palmer	75
Bob Harris	1,487	Matt Baker	2,038	Pete Righi	72
Tom Sloan	1,485	James Thompson	1,237	Jeff Stempel	66
Kevin Duckett	1,259	Terry Gregory	931	Russell Carter	63

BOWL GAMES

1/ 1/35 Sugar Bowl (New Orleans)
Tulane 20, Temple 14

12/11/77 Mirage Bowl (Tokyo)
Grambling 35, Temple 32

12/10/78 Mirage Bowl (Tokyo)
Temple 28, Boston College 24

12/15/79 Garden State Bowl (Meadowlands)
Temple 28, California 17

RECORDS

	INDIVIDUAL, GAME	INDIVIDUAL, SEASON
Rushing Yardage	281: Paul Palmer, vs. Wm. & Mary, 10/19/85	1,516: Paul Palmer, 1985
Rushing Attempts	39: Paul Palmer, vs. East Carolina, 9/28/85	275: Paul Palmer, 1985
Rushing TDs	4: Sherman Myers, vs. Syracuse, 10/13/79 Paul Palmer, vs. Cincinnati, 11/3/84	11: Anthony Anderson, 1977
Passing Yardage	313: Brian Broomell, vs. Cincinnati, 10/20/79 Matt Baker, vs. Rutgers, 10/29/88	2,103: Brian Broomell, 1979
Passes Attempted	48: Tim Riordan, vs. East Carolina, 10/15/83	277: Tim Riordan, 1983
Passes Completed	24: Tim Riordan, vs. East Carolina, 10/15/83	143: Tim Riordan, 1983
Passing TDs	5: Steve Joachim, vs. Holy Cross, 10/19/74 Brian Broomell, vs. Cincinnati, 10/20/79	22: Brian Broomell, 1979
Interceptions	4: Doug Shobert, vs. Delaware, 10/28/72 Steve Joachim, vs. Cincinnati, 11/2/74 Brian Broomell, vs. Rutgers, 11/11/78	20: Doug Shobert, 1970
Receiving Yardage	184: Rich Drayton, vs. Rutgers, 10/29/88	964: Gerald Lucear, 1979
Receptions	15: Clint Graves, vs. Rhode Island, 11/11/72	63: Clint Graves, 1972
Receiving TDs	3: Gerald Lucear, vs. Cincinnati, 10/20/79 Gerald Lucear, vs. Villanova, 11/24/79 Willie Marshall, vs. Wm. & Mary, 10/19/85 Mike Palys, vs. Boston College, 11/26/88	13: Gerald Lucear, 1979
Points Scored	30: Sherman Myers, vs. Syracuse, 10/13/79	95: Don Bitterlich, 1975
Touchdowns	5: Sherman Myers, vs. Syracuse, 10/13/79	13: Gerald Lucear, 1979
PATs Made	8: Don Bitterlich, vs. Holy Cross, 10/19/74	48: Ron Fiorvanti, 1979
Field Goals Made	5: Bob Clauser, vs. Delaware, 9/18/82	21: Don Bitterlich, 1975
Interceptions By	3: Mark McCants, vs. Akron, 10/18/80	9: Sam Shaffer, 1981
Punts	11: Casey Murphy, vs. Penn St., 9/1/78 Ed Liberati, vs. Pittsburgh, 10/15/88	65: Kip Shenefelt, 1983
Punt Returns	6: Bob Mizia, vs. Holy Cross, 9/29/73	26: Anthony Young, 1982, '84
Punt Return Yardage	98: Todd McNair, vs. Brigham Young, 9/21/85	305: Anthony Young, 1982
Kickoff Returns	8: Mike Palys, vs. Houston, 11/14/87	37: Mike Palys, 1987
Kickoff Ret. Yardage	123: Mike Palys, vs. Penn St., 10/1/88	738: Mike Palys, 1988

Quarterback Lee Saltz holds Temple's career passing records for attempts (655) and yardage gained (5,371)

RECORDS

	INDIVIDUAL, CAREER	TEAM, GAME
Rushing Yardage	3,029: Paul Palmer, 1983-85	477: vs. Drake, 9/17/77
Rushing Attempts	589: Paul Palmer, 1983-85	70: vs. Boston College, 9/15/73 at Holy Cross, 9/29/73
Rushing TDs	24: Paul Palmer, 1983-85	5: vs. Cincinnati, 11/3/84
Passing Yardage	5,371: Lee Saltz, 1983-86	330: vs. Villanova, 11/24/79
Passes Attempted	655: Lee Saltz, 1983-86	48: vs. East Carolina, 10/15/83
Passes Completed	341: Doug Shobert, 1970-72	24: vs. East Carolina, 10/15/83
Passing TDs	35: Brian Broomell, 1976-79	6: vs. Holy Cross, 10/19/74
Interceptions	43: Doug Shobert, 1970-72	4: vs. Delaware, 10/28/72 vs. Cincinnati, 11/2/74 vs. West Virginia, 10/9/76 vs. Villanova, 11/20/76 vs. Rutgers, 11/11/78
Receiving Yardage	2,272: Willie Marshall, 1983-86	330: vs. Villanova, 11/24/79
Receptions	126: Gerald Lucear, 1978-81	24: vs. East Carolina, 10/15/83
Receiving TDs	18: Gerald Lucear, 1978-81	6: vs. Holy Cross, 10/19/74
Points Scored	227: Bill Wright, 1985-88	59: vs. Southern Illinois, 10/12/74
Touchdowns	28: Paul Palmer, 1983-85	8: vs. Southern Illinois, 10/12/74
PATs Made	115: Don Bitterlich, 1973-75	8: vs. Holy Cross, 10/19/74
Field Goals Made	46: Bill Wright, 1985-88	5: vs. Delaware, 9/18/82
Interceptions By	20: Anthony Young, 1981-84	6: vs. Villanova, 11/24/73
Punts	197: Casey Murphy, 1976-79	11: vs. Penn St., 9/1/78 vs. Pittsburgh, 10/15/88
Punt Returns	75: Anthony Young, 1981-84	7: vs. Cincinnati, 10/20/79
Punt Return Yardage	715: Anthony Young, 1981-84	107: vs. Villanova, 11/27/75
Kickoff Returns	76: Mike Palys, 1985-88	8: vs. Houston, 11/14/87 8 vs. Penn St., 10/1/88
Kickoff Ret. Yardage	1,590: Mike Palys, 1985-88	177: vs. Penn St., 9/6/86

VILLANOVA

BASKETBALL

YEAR-BY-YEAR RECORDS

Season	Head Coach	W- L	Pct.	Season	Head Coach	W- L	Pct.
1920-21	Michael Saxe	8- 7	.533	1959-60	Al Severance	20- 6	.769
1921-22	Michael Saxe	11- 4	.733	1960-61	Al Severance	11-13	.458
1922-23	Michael Saxe	10- 6	.625	1961-62	Jack Kraft	21- 7	.750
1923-24	Michael Saxe	14- 7	.667	1962-63	Jack Kraft	19-10	.655
1924-25	Michael Saxe	10- 1	.909	1963-64	Jack Kraft	24- 4	.857
1925-26	Michael Saxe	11- 5	.688	1964-65	Jack Kraft	23- 5	.821
1926-27	John Cashman	11- 7	.611	1965-66	Jack Kraft	18-11	.621
1927-28	John Cashman	4-11	.267	1966-67	Jack Kraft	17- 9	.654
1928-29	John Cashman	6- 8	.429	1967-68	Jack Kraft	19- 9	.679
1929-30	George Jacobs	11- 6	.647	1968-69	Jack Kraft	21- 5	.808
1930-31	George Jacobs	7-13	.350	1969-70	Jack Kraft	22- 7	.759
1931-32	George Jacobs	7-11	.389	1970-71	Jack Kraft	23- 6	.793
1932-33	George Jacobs	9- 4	.692	1971-72	Jack Kraft	20- 8	.714
1933-34	George Jacobs	9- 3	.750	1972-73	Jack Kraft	11-14	.440
1934-35	George Jacobs	13- 7	.650	1973-74	Rollie Massimino	7-19	.269
1935-36	George Jacobs	6-12	.333	1974-75	Rollie Massimino	9-18	.333
1936-37	Al Severance	15- 8	.652	1975-76	Rollie Massimino	16-11	.593
1937-38	Al Severance	25- 5	.833	1976-77	Rollie Massimino	23-10	.697
1938-39	Al Severance	20- 5	.800	1977-78	Rollie Massimino	23- 9	.719
1939-40	Al Severance	17- 2	.895	1978-79	Rollie Massimino	15-13	.536
1940-41	Al Severance	13- 3	.813	1979-80	Rollie Massimino	23- 8	.742
1941-42	Al Severance	13- 9	.591	1980-81	Rollie Massimino	20-11	.645
1942-43	Al Severance	19- 2	.905	1981-82	Rollie Massimino	24- 8	.750
1943-44	Al Severance	9-11	.450	1982-83	Rollie Massimino	24- 8	.750
1944-45	Al Severance	6-11	.353	1983-84	Rollie Massimino	19-12	.613
1945-46	Al Severance	10-13	.435	1984-85	Rollie Massimino	25-10	.714
1946-47	Al Severance	17- 7	.708	1985-86	Rollie Massimino	23-14	.622
1947-48	Al Severance	15- 9	.625	1986-87	Rollie Massimino	15-16	.484
1948-49	Al Severance	23- 4	.852	1987-88	Rollie Massimino	24-13	.649
1949-50	Al Severance	25- 4	.862	1988-89	Rollie Massimino	18-16	.529
1950-51	Al Severance	25- 7	.781				
1951-52	Al Severance	19- 8	.704				

COACHES' RECORDS

Season	Head Coach	W- L	Pct.	Seasons	Coach	W- L	Pct.
1952-53	Al Severance	19- 8	.704	1920-26	Michael Saxe	64- 30	.681
1953-54	Al Severance	20-11	.645	1926-29	John Cashman	21- 26	.447
1954-55	Al Severance	18-10	.643	1929-36	George Jacobs	62- 56	.525
1955-56	Al Severance	14-12	.538	1936-61	Al Severance	413-201	.673
1956-57	Al Severance	10-15	.400	1961-73	Jack Kraft	238- 95	.715
1957-58	Al Severance	12-11	.522	1973-89	Rollie Massimino	308-196	.611
1958-59	Al Severance	18- 7	.720				

POSTSEASON RESULTS

1939 NCAA TOURNAMENT: Defeated Brown, 42-30 (Palestra); Lost to Ohio St., 53-36, in national semifinals (Palestra).

1949 NCAA TOURNAMENT: Lost to Kentucky, 85-72 (New York); Defeated Yale, 78-67, in East Regional third place (New York).

1951 NCAA TOURNAMENT: Lost to North Carolina St., 67-62 (Raleigh, N.C.).

1955 NCAA TOURNAMENT: Defeated Duke, 74-73 (New York); Lost to Canisius, 73-71 (Palestra); Defeated Princeton, 64-57, in East Regional third place game (Palestra).

1959 NIT: Lost to St. John's, 75-67 (New York).

1960 NIT: Defeated Detroit, 88-86; Lost to Utah St., 73-72 (ot) (both games at New York).

1962 NCAA TOURNAMENT: Defeated West Virginia, 90-75 (Palestra); Defeated New York U., 79-70 (College Park, Md.); Lost to Wake Forest, 79-69, in East Regional final (College Park, Md.).

1963 NIT: Defeated De Paul, 63-51; Defeated Wichita St., 54-53; Lost to Canisius, 61-46, in semifinals; Lost to Marquette, 66-58, in third place game (all games at New York).

1964 NCAA TOURNAMENT: Defeated Providence, 77-66 (Palestra); Lost to Duke, 87-73 (Raleigh, N.C.); Defeated Princeton, 74-62, in East Regional third place game (Raleigh, N.C.).

Rollie Massimino in 1985 NCAA Championship game

1965 NIT: Defeated Manhattan, 73-71; Defeated New York U., 91-69, in semifinals; Lost to St. John's, 55-51, in championship game (all games at New York).

1966 NIT: Defeated St. John's, 63-61; Defeated Boston College, 86-85; Lost to New York U., 69-63, in semifinals; Defeated Army, 76-65, in third place game (all games at New York).

1967 NIT: Lost to Marshall, 70-68 (ot) (New York).

1968 NIT: Defeated Wyoming, 77-66; Lost to Kansas, 55-49 (both games at New York).

1969 NCAA TOURNAMENT: Lost to Davidson, 75-61 (Raleigh, N.C.)

1970 NCAA TOURNAMENT: Defeated Temple, 77-69 (Palestra); Defeated Niagara, 98-73 (Columbia, S.C.); Lost to St. Bonaventure, 94-74, in East Regional final (Columbia, S.C.).

1971 NCAA TOURNAMENT: Defeated St. Joseph's, 93-75 (Palestra); Defeated Fordham, 85-75 (Raleigh, N.C.); Defeated Penn, 90-47, in East Regional final (Raleigh, N.C.); Defeated Western Kentucky, 92-89 (2 ot), in national semifinal (Houston); Lost to UCLA, 68-62, in national final (Houston). Vacated.

1972 NCAA TOURNAMENT: Defeated East Carolina, 85-70 (Princeton, N.J.); Lost to Penn, 78-67, in East Regional semifinal (Morgantown, W. Va.); Lost to South Carolina, 90-78, in East Regional consolation (Morgantown, W. Va.).

1977 NIT: Defeated Old Dominion, 71-68 (ot) (Norfolk, Va.); Defeated Massachusetts, 81-71; Lost to St. Bonaventure, 86-82, in semifinals; Defeated Alabama, 102-89, in third place game (all games at New York).

1978 NCAA TOURNAMENT: Defeated La Salle, 103-97 (Palestra); Defeated Indiana, 61-60 (Providence, R.I.); Lost to Duke, 90-72, in East Regional final (Providence, R.I.).

1980 NCAA TOURNAMENT: Defeated Marquette, 77-59 (Providence, R.I.); Lost to Syracuse, 97-83 (Providence, R.I.)

1981 NCAA TOURNAMENT: Defeated Houston, 90-72 (Charlotte, N.C.); Lost to Virginia, 54-50 (Charlotte, N.C.).

1982 NCAA TOURNAMENT: Defeated Northeastern, 76-72 (3 ot) (Uniondale, N.Y.); Defeated Memphis St., 70-66 (ot) (Raleigh, N.C.); Lost to North Carolina, 70-60, in East Regional final (Raleigh, N.C.).

1983 NCAA TOURNAMENT: Defeated Lamar, 60-58 (Houston); Defeated Iowa, 55-54 (Kasnas City, Mo.); Lost to Houston, 89-71, in Midwest Regional final (Kansas City, Mo.).

1984 NCAA TOURNAMENT: Defeated Marshall, 84-72 (Milwaukee); Lost to Illinois, 64-56 (Milwaukee).

1985 NCAA TOURNAMENT: Defeated Dayton, 51-49 (Dayton, Ohio); Defeated Michigan, 59-55 (Dayton, Ohio); Defeated Maryland, 46-43 (Birmingham, Ala.); Defeated North Carolina, 56-44, in Southeast Regional final (Birmingham, Ala.); Defeated Memphis St., 52-45, in national semifinals (Lexington, Ky.); Defeated Georgetown, 66-64, in national championship game (Lexington, Ky.).

1986 NCAA TOURNAMENT: Defeated Virginia Tech, 71-62 (Baton Rouge, La.); Lost to Georgia Tech, 66-61 (Baton Rouge, La.).

1987 NIT: Lost to La Salle, 86-84 (duPont Pavilion).

1988 NCAA TOURNAMENT: Defeated Arkansas, 82-74 (Cincinnati); Defeated Illinois, 66-63 (Cincinnati); Defeated Kentucky, 80-74 (Birmingham, Ala.); Lost to Oklahoma, 78-59, in Southeast Regional final (Birmingham, Ala.).

1989 NIT: Defeated St. Peter's, 76-56 (duPont Pavilion); Defeated Penn State, 76-67 (duPont Pavilion); Lost to Michigan St., 70-63 (duPont Pavilion).

1,000-POINT CLUB

Player	Games	Points
Keith Herron	117	2,170
Bob Schafer	111	2,094
Doug West	138	2,037
Howard Porter	89	2,026
John Pinone	126	2,024
Ed Pinckney	129	1,865
Larry Hennessy	75	1,737
Paul Arizin	82	1,648
Alex Bradley	111	1,634
Tom Ingelsby	87	1,616
Bill Melchionni	84	1,612
Hubie White	78	1,608
Harold Pressley	135	1,572
Johnny Jones	80	1,568
Larry Herron	104	1,553
Dwayne McClain	125	1,544
Chris Ford	91	1,433
Wally Jones	85	1,428
Kenny Wilson	137	1,390
Reggie Robinson	119	1,309
Stewart Granger	125	1,307
Tom Sienkiewicz	115	1,271
Jack Devine	113	1,263
Hank Siemiontkowski	90	1,224
Mark Plansky	134	1,217
Rory Sparrow	124	1,183
Jim Huggard	75	1,184
Harold Jensen	130	1,155
Jim Washington	85	1,146
Joe Lord	71	1,125
Tom Greis	101	1,062
Jimmy Smith	80	1,014

Ed Pinckney left all but five Villanova scorers behind him

Rory Sparrow

Harold Pressley

Tom Greis

LEADING SCORERS

Season	Player	Pts.	Season	Player	Pts.	Season	Player	Pts.
1929-30	John Birmingham	136	1949-50	Paul Arizin	735	1969-70	Howard Porter	645
1930-31	Joseph Czescik	126	1950-51	Larry Hennessy	703	1970-71	Howard Porter	799
1931-32	Joseph Czescik	123	1951-52	Larry Hennessy	567	1971-72	Hank Siemiontkowski	534
1932-33	Arthur Lynch	75	1952-53	Bob Schafer	537	1972-73	Tom Ingelsby	638
1933-34	Ben Geraghty	114	1953-54	Bob Schafer	836	1973-74	Chubby Cox	306
1934-35	Mike O'Meara	136	1954-55	Bob Schafer	592	1974-75	Larry Herron	449
1935-36	Mike O'Meara	131	1955-56	Jim Smith	357	1975-76	Keith Herron	465
1936-37	Jim Montgomery	145	1956-57	Al Griffith	205	1976-77	Keith Herron	652
1937-38	George Duzminski	296	1957-58	Jack Kelly	342	1977-78	Keith Herron	618
1938-39	Jim Montgomery	190	1958-59	Joe Ryan	384	1978-79	Alex Bradley	485
1939-40	George Duzminski	213	1959-60	Hubie White	495	1979-80	John Pinone	450
1940-41	Paul Nugent	128	1960-61	Hubie White	509	1980-81	John Pinone	490
1941-42	Billy Wood	230	1961-62	Hubie White	604	1981-82	John Pinone	550
1942-43	Billy Wood	221	1962-63	Wally Jones	487	1982-83	John Pinone	434
1943-44	Frank Frascella	203	1963-64	Wally Jones	461	1983-84	Ed Pinckney	478
1944-45	Lee Carter	149	1964-65	Bill Melchionni	542	1984-85	Ed Pinckney	546
1945-46	Joe Lord	303	1965-66	Bill Melchionni	801	1985-86	Harold Pressley	620
1946-47	Joe Lord	438	1966-67	Johnny Jones	492	1986-87	Harold Jensen	492
1947-48	Paul Arizin	267	1967-68	Johnny Jones	565	1987-88	Doug West	565
1948-49	Paul Arizin	646	1968-69	Howard Porter	582	1988-89	Doug West	608

RECORDS

	INDIVIDUAL, GAME	TEAM, GAME
Points	85: Paul Arizin, vs. Naval Air Mat. Center, 2/12/49	126: vs. Seton Hall, 3/2/70
FG Made	35: Paul Arizin, vs. Naval Air Mat. Center, 2/12/49	52: vs. St. Peter's, 1/9/71
FG Att.	63: Paul Arizin, vs. Naval Air Mat. Center, 2/12/49	112: vs. Merrimack, 12/11/73
FG Pct.	100: Ed Pinckney, vs. Towson St., 12/14/81 (11-11)	78.6: vs. Georgetown, 4/1/85 (22-28)
FT Made	21: Tom Sienkiewicz, vs. Pennsylvania, 2/13/79	39: vs. Pennsylvania, 2/13/79
FT Att.	23: Tom Sienkiewicz, vs. Penn, 2/13/79	53: vs. Louisiana St., 12/29/52
FT Pct.	100: Alex Bradley, vs. Penn St., 2/4/79 (12-12) John Pinone, vs. St. Joseph's, 2/28/81 (12-12)	100: vs. Kentucky, 3/24/88 (17-17)
Rebounds	30: Howard Porter, vs. St. Peter's, 1/9/71	86: vs. Scranton, 1/31/52
Assists	16: Jim Huggard, vs. Scranton, 12/4/59 Fran O'Hanlon, vs. Toledo, 2/24/70	32: vs. Pace, 12/22/81
Blocks	10: Harold Pressley, vs. Providence, 1/11/86	12: vs. Georgetown, 2/1/88
Steals	9: Gary Massey, vs. Providence, 2/20/88	24: vs. Wagner, 1/27/77

	INDIVIDUAL, SEASON	INDIVIDUAL, CAREER
Points	836: Bob Schafer, 1953-54	2,170: Keith Herron, 1974-78
FG Made	336: Howard Porter, 1970-71	918: Keith Herron, 1974-78
FG Att.	780: Larry Hennessy, 1950-51	1,911: Keith Herron, 1974-78
FG Pct.	64.0: Ed Pinckney, 1981-82 (169-264)	60.4: Ed Pinckney, 1981-85 (637-1,054)
FT Made	262: Bob Schafer, 1953-54	642: Bob Schafer, 1951-55
FT Att.	377: Bob Schafer, 1953-54	948: Bob Schafer, 1951-55
FT Pct.	90.2: Tom Sienkiewicz, 1979-80 (74-82)	89.1: Tom Sienkiewicz, 1977-81 (221-248)
Rebounds	503: Howard Porter, 1970-71	1,325: Howard Porter, 1968-71
Assists	238: Chris Ford, 1970-71	627: Kenny Wilson, 1985-89
Blocks	88: Tom Greis, 1987-88	253: Ed Pinckney, 1981-85
Steals	83: Harold Pressley, 1985-86	216: Harold Pressley, 1982-86

Paul Arizin

It was 1947, and Al Severance, the basketball coach at Villanova, was watching a skinny kid shoot basketballs from 15, 18, 20 feet in the Field House Severance's team called home.

Severance, the story goes, watched for 20 minutes and could count the number of misses on one hand. Rarely did the makes skim the rim on the way in.

The sound of the net's *swoosh* continually disturbed the silence.

"I walked down there and asked him where he went to school," Severance once said. "He said, 'I go to Villanova.' I almost fell down. So I asked him if he'd like to come out for basketball, and he said, 'Sure.'"

It was Paul Arizin's first invitation to begin writing a portion of Philadelphia basketball history.

Over the next three seasons, Arizin led Severance's Villanova teams to a 63-17 record and twice was named All-America.

A member of the Basketball Hall of Fame, Arizin is regarded as the greatest player the Philadelphia Big 5 — formed in 1955 — could never call its own. But that has not kept Arizin's name from inclusion among the greatest players ever to play in Philadelphia, or anywhere else on the planet, for that matter.

Born in Philadelphia on April 9, 1928, Arizin went to La Salle High but did not play varsity basketball there.

As a senior at Villanova in 1949-50, he led the nation in scoring with 735 points in 29 games, a 25.3 average. From there, it was on to the NBA, where he averaged 22.8 points in 713 games stretched over 10 years with the Philadelphia Warriors from 1950-51 to 1961-62, with two seasons off for military duty.

He beat out legendary George Mikan for the 1951-52 scoring title with a 25.4 average, and led the league again in 1956-57 with a 25.6 average. In addition, he finished second twice.

When owner Eddie Gottlieb sold the Warriors franchise to San Francisco, Paul didn't want to make the move, so he stayed around home, and played for a while with the Camden Bullets of the Eastern League (the forerunner of the Continental Basketball Association) before formally retiring.

Along with Stanford's Hank Luisetti, Arizin is credited with popularizing the jump shot during an era when the two-handed set shot was in vogue.

"After Paul played here, [the jump shot] took off like wildfire," Severance said. "All of a sudden the kids in the schoolyard began practicing it. Before Luisetti and Paul, it was heresy to try a shot like that. It just wasn't done."

VILLANOVA

FOOTBALL

Year	Head Coach	W- L- T	Pct.	Season	Head Coach	W- L	Pct.
1894	Michael Murphy	1- 0- 0	1.000	1932	Harry Stuhldreher	7- 2- 0	.778
1895	James McDonald	4- 2- 0	.667	1933	Harry Stuhldreher	7- 2- 1	.750
1896	James McDonald	10- 4- 0	.714	1934	Harry Stuhldreher	3- 4- 2	.444
1897	John Bagley	3- 5- 1	.389	1935	Harry Stuhldreher	7- 2- 0	.778
1898	John Bagley	2- 4- 1	.357	1936	Clipper Smith	7- 2- 1	.750
1899	Richard Nallin	7- 2- 1	.750	1937	Clipper Smith	8- 0- 1	.944
1900	John Powers	5- 1- 3	.722	1938	Clipper Smith	8- 0- 1	.944
1901	John Egan	2- 3- 0	.400	1939	Clipper Smith	6- 2- 0	.750
1902	Timothy O'Rourke	4- 3- 0	.571	1940	Clipper Smith	4- 5- 0	.444
1903	Martin Caine	2- 2- 0	.500	1941	Clipper Smith	4- 4- 0	.500
1904	Fred Crolius	4- 2- 1	.643	1942	Clipper Smith	4- 4- 0	.500
1905	Fred Crolius	3- 7- 0	.300	1943	Jordan Oliver	5- 3- 0	.625
1906	Fred Crolius	3- 7- 0	.300	1944	Jordan Oliver	4- 4- 0	.500
1907	Fred Crolius	1- 5- 1	.214	1945	Jordan Oliver	4- 4- 0	.500
1908	Fred Crolius	1- 6- 0	.143	1946	Jordan Oliver	6- 4- 0	.600
1909	Fred Crolius	3- 2- 0	.600	1947	Jordan Oliver	6- 3- 1	.650
1910	Fred Crolius	0- 4- 2	.167	1948	Jordan Oliver	8- 2- 1	.773
1911	Fred Crolius	0- 5- 1	.083	1949	Jim Leonard	8- 1- 0	.889
1912	Charley McGeehan	3- 3- 0	.500	1950	Jim Leonard	4- 5- 0	.444
1913	Tom St. Germaine	4- 2- 1	.643	1951	Art Raimo	5- 3- 0	.625
1914	Frank Sommer	4- 3- 1	.563	1952	Art Raimo	7- 1- 1	.833
1915	Frank Sommer	6- 1- 0	.857	1953	Art Raimo	4- 6- 0	.400
1916	Edward Bennis	1- 8- 0	.111	1954	Frank Reagan	1- 9- 0	.100
1917	Thomas Reap	0- 3- 2	.200	1955	Frank Reagan	1- 9- 0	.100
1918	Thomas Reap	3- 2- 0	.600	1956	Frank Reagan	5- 4- 0	.556
1919	Thomas Reap	5- 3- 1	.611	1957	Frank Reagan	3- 6- 0	.333
1920	Thomas Reap	1- 4- 2	.286	1958	Frank Reagan	6- 4- 0	.600
1921	Allie Miller	6- 1- 2	.722	1959	Frank Reagan	0- 4- 0	.000
1922	Allie Miller	5- 3- 1	.611		Joe Rogers	1- 5- 0	.167
1923	Hugh McGeehan	0- 7- 1	.063		Total	1- 9- 0	.100
1924	Frank Sommer	2- 5- 1	.313	1960	Alex Bell	2- 8- 0	.200
1925	Harry Stuhldreher	6- 2- 1	.722	1961	Alex Bell	8- 2- 0	.800
1926	Harry Stuhldreher	6- 2- 1	.722	1962	Alex Bell	7- 3- 0	.700
1927	Harry Stuhldreher	6- 1- 0	.857	1963	Alex Bell	5- 4- 0	.556
1928	Harry Stuhldreher	7- 0- 1	.938	1964	Alex Bell	6- 2- 0	.750
1929	Harry Stuhldreher	7- 2- 1	.750	1965	Alex Bell	1- 8- 0	.111
1930	Harry Stuhldreher	5- 5- 0	.500	1966	Alex Bell	6- 3- 0	.667
1931	Harry Stuhldreher	4- 3- 2	.556	1967	Jack Gregory	4- 6- 0	.400
				1968	Jack Gregory	6- 4- 0	.600

YEAR-BY-YEAR RECORDS

Year Head Coach	W- L- T	Pct.	Year Head Coach	W- L- T	Pct.
1969 Jack Gregory	6- 3- 0	.667	1977 Dick Bedesem	4- 7- 0	.364
1970 Lou Ferry	9- 2- 0	.818	1978 Dick Bedesem	5- 6- 0	.455
1971 Lou Ferry	6- 4- 1	.591	1979 Dick Bedesem	5- 6- 0	.455
1972 Lou Ferry	2- 9- 0	.182	1980 Dick Bedesem	6- 5- 0	.545
1973 Lou Ferry	3- 8- 0	.273	(1981-84: No varsity team)		
1974 Jim Weaver	3- 5- 0	.375	1985 Andy Talley	5- 0- 0	1.000
Lou Ferry	0- 3- 0	.000	1986 Andy Talley	8- 1- 0	.889
Total	3- 8- 0	.273	1987 Andy Talley	6- 4- 0	.600
1975 Dick Bedesem	4- 7- 0	.364	1988 Andy Talley	5- 5- 1	.500
1976 Dick Bedesem	6- 4- 1	.591			

CAREER LEADERS

RUSHING YARDS		PASSING YARDS		RECEPTIONS	
Vince Thompson	2,522	Kirk Schulz	6,832	Mike Siani	148
Ralph Pasquariello	1,815	Daryl Woodring	3,171	John Mastronardo	140
Pat O'Brien	1,792	Bill Hatty	2,647	Robert Brady	134
Gene Filipski	1,594	Pat O'Brien	2,444	Tom Boyd	115
Peter Lombardi	1,568	Drew Gordon	2,370	Jim Cashman	94
Pete D'Alonzo	1,560	Brian Sikorski	2,099	Ron Sency	81
Ron Sency	1,491	Bill Andrejko	1,912	Peter Lombardi	77
Billy Walik	1,428	Bill Brannau	1,674	Chuck Driesbach	73
Don Ziesel	1,337	Steve Romanik	1,619	Ed Farmer	65
Joe Rogers	1,211	John Sodaski	1,420	Greg Downs	57

Dick Bedesem coached Villanova football for six seasons before the sport was dropped following the 1980 season

COACHES' RECORDS

Seasons	Head Coach	W- L- T	Pct.
1894	Michael Murphy	1- 0- 0	1.000
1895-96	James McDonald	14- 6- 0	.700
1897-98	John Bagley	5- 9- 2	.375
1899	Richard Nallin	7- 2- 1	.750
1900	John Powers	5- 1- 3	.722
1900-01	John Egan	2- 3- 0	.400
1902	Timothy O'Rourke	4- 3- 0	.571
1903	Martin Caine	2- 2- 0	.500
1904-11	Fred Crolius	15-38- 5	.302
1912	Charley McGeehan	3- 3- 0	.500
1913	Tom St. Germaine	4- 2- 1	.643
1914-15	Frank Sommer	10- 4- 1	.700
1924	Frank Sommer	2- 5- 1	.313
	Total	12- 9- 2	.565
1916	Edward Bennis	1- 8- 0	.111
1917-20	Thomas Reap	9-12- 5	.442
1921-22	Allie Miller	11- 4- 3	.694
1923	Hugh McGeehan	0- 7- 1	.063
1925-35	Harry Stuhldreher	65-25- 9	.702
1936-42	Clipper Smith	41-17- 3	.697
1943-48	Jordan Oliver	33-20- 2	.618
1949-50	Jim Leonard	12- 6- 0	.667

Seasons	Head Coach	W- L- T	Pct.
1951-53	Art Raimo	16-10- 1	.611
1953-59	Frank Reagan	16-36- 0	.308
1959	Joe Rogers	1- 5- 0	.167
1960-66	Alex Bell	35-30- 0	.538
1967-69	Jack Gregory	16-13- 0	.551
1970-73	Lou Ferry	20-23- 1	.466
1974	Lou Ferry	0- 3- 0	.000
	Total	20-26- 1	.436
1974	Jim Weaver	3- 5- 0	.375
1975-80	Dick Bedesem	30-35- 1	.462
1985-86	Andy Talley	24-10- 1	.700

BOWL GAMES

1/ 1/37 Bacardi Bowl (Havana, Cuba)
Villanova 7, Auburn 7

12/ 6/47 Great Lakes Bowl (Cleveland)
Kentucky 24, Villanova 14

1/ 1/49 Harbor Bowl (San Diego)
Villanova 27, Nevada 7

12/30/61 Sun Bowl (El Paso, Texas)
Villanova 17, Wichita 9

12/15/62 Liberty Bowl (Philadelphia)
Oregon St. 6, Villanova 0

RECORDS

	INDIVIDUAL, CAREER	TEAM, GAME
Rushing Yardage	2,522: Vince Thompson, 1975-78	627: vs. North Carolina St., 11/17/49
Rushing Attempts	628: Vince Thompson, 1975-78	74: vs. North Carolina St., 11/17/49
Rushing TDs	28: Ralph Pasquariello, 1946-49	8: vs. Holy Cross, 11/13/76
Passing Yardage	6,832: Kirk Schulz, 1986-88	417: vs. Xavier, 10/30/71
Passes Attempted	943: Kirk Schulz, 1986-88	56: vs. Boston College, 9/19/70
Passes Completed	563: Kirk Schulz, 1986-88	29: vs. West Chester, 11/10/73
Passing TDs	54: Kirk Schulz, 1986-88	6: vs. Buffalo, 11/11/67
Interceptions	51: Kirk Schulz, 1986-88	8: vs. Lousiana St., 11/24/51
Receiving Yardage	2,776: Mike Siani, 1969-71	417: vs. Xavier, 10/30/71
Receptions	148: Mike Siani, 1969-71	29: vs. West Chester, 11/10/73
Receiving TDs	33: Mike Siani, 1969-71	6: vs. Buffalo, 11/11/67
Points Scored	208: Mike Siani, 1969-71	63: vs. West Chester, 11/23/68
Touchdowns	34: Mike Siani, 1969-71	9: vs. Kings Point, 9/20/47 vs. West Chester, 11/23/68
PATs Made	64: Gus Fernandez, 1975-77	8: vs. Holy Cross, 11/13/76
Field Goals Made	28: Gus Fernandez, 1975-77	4: vs. Swarthmore, 11/13/15
Interceptions By	18: Frank Polito, 1971-73	7: vs. Manhattan, 11/16/40
Punts	179: Joe Borajkiewicz, 1978-80	14: vs. Detroit, 10/15/54
Punt Returns	58: Frank Polito, 1971-73	10: vs. Georgetown, 10/20/46 vs. Virginia Military, 9/22/62
Punt Ret. Yardage	649: Frank Boal, 1966-68	122: vs. Delaware, 11/3/73
Kickoff Returns	55: Ken Diminick, 1974-76	12: vs. Lehigh, 10/24/03 vs. Army, 11/4/44
Kickoff Ret. Yardage	1,088: Ken Dimincik, 1974-76	180: vs. Holy Cross, 11/2/71

Quarterback Kirk Schulz holds or shares six Villanova single-game and single-season passing records

RECORDS

	INDIVIDUAL, GAME	INDIVIDUAL, SEASON
Rushing Yardage	201: Pete D'Alonzo, vs. Duquesne, 9/23/50	977: Vince Thompson, 1977
Rushing Attempts	36: Vince Thompson, vs. West Virginia, 10/29/77 Vince Thompson, vs. Holy Cross, 11/12/77	233: Vince Thompson, 1977
Rushing TDs	4: Tony Serge, vs. Holy Cross, 11/13/76	12: Bob Haner, 1952
Passing Yardage	395: Drew Gordon, vs. Temple, 11/26/70	2,530: Kirk Schulz, 1988
Passes Attempted	53: Daryl Woodring, vs. Boston College, 9/19/70	367: Kirk Schulz, 1988
Passes Completed	28: Kirk Schulz, vs. Central Connecticut St., 10/10/87	214: Kirk Schulz, 1988
Passing TDs	6: Billy Andrejko, vs. Buffalo, 11/11/67	23: Kirk Schulz, 1987
Interceptions	6: Bill Bruno, vs. Louisiana St., 11/24/51 Bill Hatty, vs. Temple, 11/24/73	21: Bill Brannau, 1951 Kirk Schulz, 1988
Receiving Yardage	288: Mike Siani, vs. Xavier, 10/30/71	1,358: Mike Siani, 1970
Receptions	12: Tom Boyd, vs. Toledo, 9/21/68 Mike Siani, vs. Boston College, 9/19/70 Mike Siani, vs. Xavier, 10/30/71	74: Mike Siani, 1970
Receiving TDs	5: Mike Siani, vs. Xavier, 10/30/71	14: Mike Siani, 1971
Points Scored	30: Mike Siani, vs. Xavier, 10/30/71	99: Bob Haner, 1952
Touchdowns	5: Mike Siani, vs. Xavier, 10/30/71	15: Mike Siani, 1971
PATs Made	8: Gus Fernandez, vs. Holy Cross, 11/23/76	34: Tom Withka, 1987
Field Goals Made	4: Charles McGuckin, vs. Swarthmore, 11/13/15	11: Gus Fernandez, 1977
Interceptions By	4: Nick Basca, vs. Muhlenberg, 9/30/39	12: Frank Polito, 1971
Punts	16: John Brice, vs. Detroit, 11/14/31	83: Bob Schaeffer, 1971
Punt Returns	8: Romeo Capriotti, vs. Georgetown, 10/20/46	26: Charlie Gross, 1976
Punt Ret. Yardage	122: Frank Polito, vs. Delaware, 11/3/73	365: Bill Doherty, 1948
Kickoff Returns	6: Bob Carpenter, vs. Holy Cross, 10/28/72	29: Ken Diminick, 1974
Kickoff Ret. Yardage	141: Bob Dunn, vs. Holy Cross, 11/2/63	584: Ken Diminick, 1974

HIGH SCHOOL

BASKETBALL

SINGLE-GAME SCORING RECORDS

PUBLIC LEAGUE

Abraham Lincoln	51: Joe Hindelang, vs. Northeast, 1/15/63
Benjamin Franklin	48: Ira Miles, vs. Southern, 1/26/67
Central	47: Albie Ingerman, vs. Roxborough, 2/19/43
Edward Bok Tech	43: Jim Wilson, vs. Central, 2/9/65
Engineering and Science	66: Michael Anderson, vs. Edison, 2/9/84
Frankford	48: Harry Daut, vs. Franklin, 2/14/56
Franklin Learning Center	44: Antoine Jefferson, vs. Lamberton, 1/5/89
George Washington	49: Ellis McKennie, vs. Lincoln, 2/20/86
Germantown	46: Donnell Greene, vs. Washington, 1/18/66
John Bartram	84: Reggie Isaac, vs. Bodine, 2/20/86
Jules Mastbaum Tech	43: Warren Hawthorne, vs. Lincoln, 2/21/85
Kensington	32: Ron Jones, vs. Parkway, 12/11/86
Martin Luther King	40: Greg Jacobs, vs. Frankford, 1/13/83
Murrell Dobbins	49: Sherwin "Shy" Raiken, vs. Mastbaum, 2/14/46
Northeast (New Location)	47: Mike Kamen, vs. Franklin, 2/21/67
Northeast (Old Location)	44: Guy Rodgers, vs. Bok, 2/6/53
Olney	63: Willie Taylor, vs. Bok, 2/17/72
Overbrook	90: Wilt Chamberlain, vs. Roxborough, 2/17/55
Parkway	42: Stephen Stewart, vs. Central, 2/14/89
Robert Lamberton	55: Troy Daniel, vs. Engineering and Science, 2/23/84
Roxborough	55: Frank Stanczak, vs. Bok, 2/20/47
Simon Gratz	45: Bob Brooker, vs. Bok, 2/24/64 Brian Shorter, vs. Lincoln, 1/2/86; vs. King, 2/20/86
Southern	56: Lionel Simmons, vs. Bodine, 1/28/86
Strawberry Mansion	41: Chris Fletcher, vs. Franklin Learning Center, 12/3/85
Thomas Edison	37: Joe Jefferson, vs. Mastbaum, 2/24/87 Kevin Rideout, vs. Washington, 1/7/88
University City	41: Anthony "Juice" Williams, vs. Frankford, 1/14/85
West Philadelphia	52: Gene Banks, vs. Bok, 2/15/77
William Penn	50: Anthony "Bub" King, vs. Lincoln, 2/23/82
William Bodine	41: Monte Ross, vs. Northeast, 1/20/87

INTER-AC LEAGUE

Chestnut Hill Academy	36: Steve Harris, vs. Pennsylvania School for the Deaf, 1/13/65
Episcopal Academy **Episcopal Academy**	36: Bill Radcliffe, vs. Friends' Central, 2/27/62 36: Bill Radcliffe, vs. Friends' Central, 2/27/62 Eugene Burroughs, vs. Valley Forge, 2/15/89
Germantown Academy	48: Marvin Walters, vs. McDevitt, 1/13/86
Haverford School	44: Mike Edelman, vs. William Penn, 12/19/77
Malvern Prep	44: Charlie Floyd, vs. Carroll (D.C.), 12/26/73
Penn Charter	65: Billy Harris, vs. Germantown Lutheran, 3/2/71

SINGLE-GAME SCORING RECORDS

CATHOLIC LEAGUE NORTHERN DIVISION

Archbishop Ryan	37: Fran Ciliberti, vs. North Catholic, 2/19/84
Archbishop Wood	33: Jack Walsh, vs. Delhaas, 1980
Bishop Egan	37: Dave Gorlaski, vs. St. Joseph's Prep, 12/8/75
Bishop Kenrick	40: Jim Murphy, vs. Wood, 1/28/66
Bishop McDevitt	51: Bobby Haas, vs. Ryan, 1/28/68
Cardinal Dougherty	42: Lawrence Reid, vs. Egan, 2/29/76
Father Judge	34: Mike Krawczyk, vs. Dougherty, 2/11/68
La Salle	49: Joe Heyer, vs. St. Thomas More, 2/17/56
North Catholic	46: Bobby McNeill, vs. St. James, 1/27/56

CATHOLIC LEAGUE SOUTHERN DIVISION

Archbishop Carroll	41: Barry Bekkedam, vs. St. James, 2/23/86
Cardinal O'Hara	38: Mike O'Hara, vs. Roman, 3/1/87
Monsignor Bonner	35: Brian Daly, vs. West Catholic, 2/5/88
Roman Catholic	45: Lonnie McFarlan, vs. Kenrick, 12/11/79
St. James	42: Bill Lynch, vs. St. Joseph's Prep, 1/6/52
St. John Neumann	36: Billy Oakes, vs. West Catholic, 3/10/62
St. Joseph's Prep	45: Joe Ryan, vs. North Catholic, 1/26/55
St. Thomas More	45: Mike Jones, vs. St. James, 12/13/69
West Catholic	47: Pat Carey, vs. Roman, 2/13/55

Brian Daly, the school's single-game scoring leader, carried Bonner to the 1988 Catholic League championship

CAREER SCORING RECORDS

Player	School	Class	Points
Wilt Chamberlain	Overbrook	1955	2,252
Brian Shorter	Simon Gratz (Transferred following junior season)	1987	1,869
Reggie Jackson	St. Thomas More-Roman Catholic	1978	1,861
Lonnie McFarlan	Roman Catholic	1980	1,842
Steve Benton	St. John Neumann	1985	1,808
Clarence Tillman	West Philadelphia	1978	1,750
Charlie Floyd	Malvern Prep	1974	1,725
Gene Banks	West Philadelphia	1977	1,703
Andre Daniel	Robert Lamberton	1989	1,693
Troy Daniel	Robert Lamberton	1984	1,667
Michael Brooks	West Catholic	1976	1,651
Billy Harris	Penn Charter	1971	1,646
Greg Kimble	Murrell Dobbins	1985	1,596
Barry Brodzinski	North Catholic	1973	1,583
Charles Hickman	Episcopal Academy	1981	1,566
Mike Edelman	Haverford School	1978	1,550
Lionel Simmons	Southern	1986	1,539
Gary Duda	Malvern Prep	1988	1,535
Mark Stevenson	Dobbins-Roman Catholic	1985	1,519
Brian Leahy	Bishop Kenrick	1984	1,449
Craig White	Germantown Academy	1988	1,432
Otis Ellis	Germantown Academy	1985	1,421
Horace Owens	Murrell Dobbins	1979	1,420
Billy Hoy	St. Thomas More	1959	1,419
Tom Gola	La Salle	1951	1,392
Michael Anderson	Engineering and Science	1984	1,378
Rick Williams	Germantown Academy	1985	1,358
Eric Minkin	Germantown Academy	1968	1,358
Rodney Blake	Monsignor Bonner	1984	1,348
Howard Evans	West Philadelphia	1984	1,341
Glenn Welton	Roman Catholic	1981	1,323
Tony Costner	Overbrook	1980	1,292
Ron Schott	St. James	1972	1,285
Joe Ryan	St. Joseph's Prep	1955	1,273
Eric Ervin	Bishop McDevitt	1984	1,272
Marvin Walters	Germantown Academy	1986	1,254
Brian Daly	Monsignor Bonner	1988	1,253
Eric Gathers	Murrell Dobbins	1985	1,251

UNCONFIRMED NUMBERS			
Player	School	Class	Points
Paul Hutter	Germantown Academy	1970	1,550
Mike Kamen	Northeast	1967	1,400
Larry Cannon	Abraham Lincoln	1965	1,340
Doug Gray	Abraham Lincoln	1968	1,340
Mike Jones	St. Thomas More	1969	1,320
Joe Anderson	Simon Gratz	1971	1,260

FIFTY-POINT CLUB

90: Wilt Chamberlain, Overbrook, 1955.
84: Reggie Isaac, Bartram, 1986.
74: Chamberlain.
71: Chamberlain.
66: x-Michael Anderson, Engineering and Science, 1984.
65: x-Billy Harris, Penn Charter, 1971.
63: Bill Soens, Penn Charter, 1963; Willie Taylor, Olney, 1972.
59: Chamberlain.
57: Mike Moore, Bartram, 1968; Joe Bryant, Bartram, 1972.
56: Lionel Simmons, Southern, 1986.
55: Frank Stanczak, Roxborough, 1947; Troy Daniel, Lamberton, 1984.
54: Barry Love, Overbrook, 1947.
52: Ray Shiffner, Roxborough, 1950; Jim Muldoon, Southern, 1954; Frank Kunze, Bartram, 1964; Gene Banks, West Phila., 1977.
51: Joe Hindelang, Lincoln, 1963; Bobby Haas, McDevitt, 1968; x-Harris, 1971.
50: Richie Kohler, Penn Charter, 1955; Anthony King, Penn, 1982.
x: Non-league.

CITY TITLE RESULTS

1939 Simon Gratz 23, South Catholic 13
1940 South Phila. 33, South Catholic 26
1941 South Catholic 27, West Philadelphia 24
1942 West Philadelphia 38, La Salle 24
1943 West Philadelphia 29, Roman Catholic 28
1944 Bartram 36, South Catholic 27
1945 South Catholic 37, South Philadelphia 36
1946 La Salle 33, South Philadelphia 23
1947 St. Joseph's Prep 40, Bartram 38
1948 La Salle 39, Overbrook 38
1949 West Catholic 41, Overbrook 38
1950 La Salle 55, Overbrook 31
1951 St. Thomas More 39, West Philadelphia 36
1952 West Catholic 57, Ben Franklin 46
1953 West Catholic 54, Overbrook 42
1954 Overbrook 74, South Catholic 50
1955 Overbrook 83, West Catholic 42
1956 North Catholic 68, West Philadelphia 67
1957 Overbrook 56, North Catholic 41
1958 Overbrook 71, Bishop Neumann 54
1959 Overbrook 72, West Catholic 53
1960 Monsignor Bonner 55, West Philadelphia 46
1961 St. Thomas More 51, John Bartram 50
1962 West Philadelphia 61, St. Joseph's Prep 52
1963 West Philadelphia 65, La Salle 56
1964 Germantown 77, Cardinal Dougherty 62
1965 Bishop Neumann 75, Lincoln 66
1966 Thomas Edison 56, St. Thomas More 52
1967 North Catholic 50, Overbrook 45
1968 West Philadelphia 57, Cardinal O'Hara 50
1969 Thomas Edison 57, Roman Catholic 54
1970 Overbrook 70, Cardinal Dougherty 52
1971 Overbrook 76, St. Joseph's Prep 56
1972 St. Thomas More 53, John Bartram 45
1973 (Cancelled, public teachers on strike)
1974 Roman Catholic 48, West Philadelphia 35
1975 West Philadelphia 67, Father Judge 45
1976 West Philadelphia 71, Bishop Kenrick 61
1977 West Philadelphia 72, Father Judge 52
1978 West Philadelphia 67, Roman Catholic 64
1979 Overbrook 61, Roman Catholic 49
1980 Overbrook 65, Roman Catholic 56
　　　　(City Title Game Terminated)
　　Public Champ, Catholic Champ
1981 Ben Franklin, La Salle
1982 Jules Mastbaum, Roman Catholic
1983 Overbrook, Monsignor Bonner
1984 Ben Franklin, Monsignor Bonner
1985 Murrell Dobbins, St. John Neumann
1986 Southern, Roman Catholic
1987 Southern, North Catholic
1988 Frankford, Monsignor Bonner
1989 Frankford, Roman Catholic

Gene Banks and some of his high school memorabilia

HIGH SCHOOL

FOOTBALL

INDIVIDUAL RECORDS

	GAME
Rushing Yardage	379: Lawrence Reid, Dougherty, vs. Egan, 9/20/75
Rushing Attempts	49: Mike Elentrio, Judge, vs. Dougherty, 11/13/83
Rushing TDs	8: Hector Scott, Bartram, vs. Bok, 10/21/83
Passing Yardage	409: Mike Roche, Central, vs. Northeast, 11/27/86
Passes Attempted	55: Ed Hughes, Ryan, vs. Dougherty, 10/28/78
Passes Completed	25: Ed Hughes, Ryan, vs. Dougherty, 10/28/78 Dave Markowski, North Catholic, vs. Frankford, 11/26/87
Passing TDs	6: Jim Smink, Judge, vs. Washington, 11/27/69
Receiving Yardage	252: Don Clune, O'Hara, vs. Neumann, 10/19/69
Receptions	15: Don Clune, O'Hara, vs. Neumann, 10/19/69
Receiving TDs	4: Mike Casey, North Catholic, vs. Neumann, 9/18/66 Bob Smith, Neumann, vs. Southern, 11/26/70
Points	48: Hector Scott, Bartram, vs. Bok, 10/21/83
Touchdowns	8: Hector Scott, Bartram, vs. Bok, 10/21/83
PATs Made	9: Dave DeNofa, Frankford, vs. Roxborough, 11/19/81
Field Goals Made	4: Dan D'Orazio, O'Hara, vs. Bonner, 10/5/86

Central quarterback Mike Roche threw for a city-record 409 yards in a game against Northeast High in 1986

Dan D'Orazio: Cardinal O'Hara

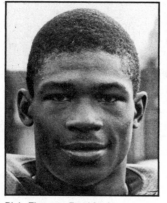
Blair Thomas: Frankford

Mike Elentrio: Father Judge

CITY TITLE GAMES

1938 St. Joseph's Prep 7, Central 0
1939 St. Joseph's Prep 27, Northeast 6
1940 Frankford 13, West Catholic 0
1941 (tie) West Phila. 0, West Catholic 0
1942 Northeast 7, St. Joseph's Prep 0
1943 West Catholic 21, Northeast 0
1944 South Phila. 13, West Catholic 7
1945 South Phila. 18, West Catholic 13
1946 Northeast 33, West Catholic 20
1947 Roman Catholic 40, Frankford 12
1948 (tie) Frankford 6, Southeast Catholic 6
1949 Northeast Catholic 21, Simon Gratz 6
1950 Edward Bok 13, Northeast Catholic 0
1951 West Catholic 42, Edward Bok 0
1952 North Catholic 25, Abraham Lincoln 0
1953 (tie) Northeast 20, St. James 20
1954 South Catholic 34, Frankford 0
1955 La Salle 26, Northeast 0
1956 North Catholic 12, Abraham Lincoln 0
1957 La Salle 19, Roxborough 0
1958 Abraham Lincoln 28, La Salle 20
1959 Monsignor Bonner 54, Central 0
1960 La Salle 24, Frankford 0
1961 Monsignor Bonner 20, South Phila. 13
1962 (tie) South Phila. 20, West Catholic 20
1963 (tie) Roxborough 16, Bishop Egan 16
1964 Father Judge 19, Frankford 18
1965 West Catholic 34, South Phila. 18
1966 Bishop Egan 27, Ben Franklin 0
1967 Bishop Egan 28, Central 12
1968 Cardinal Dougherty 48, Northeast 14
1969 Bishop Egan 29, Frankford 20
1970 Central 13, Bishop Egan 6
1971 Archbishop Carroll 15, Frankford 14
1972 St. James 42, Frankford 0
1973 Cardinal O'Hara 13, Frankford 6
1974 Archbishop Wood 20, Central 8
1975 Father Judge 9, Frankford 6
1976 Archbishop Carroll 21, John Bartram 6
1977 St. Joseph's 14, Abraham Lincoln 13
1978 Frankford 27, Archbishop Wood 7
1979 Cardinal O'Hara 28, Lincoln 7
    (City Title Game Terminated)
    Public Champion, Catholic Champion
1980 Frankford, Cardinal O'Hara
1981 Frankford, Father Judge
1982 Germantown, Cardinal Dougherty
1983 Northeast, Father Judge
1984 Frankford, Father Judge
1985 Central, Cardinal O'Hara
1986 Frankford, Bishop McDevitt
1987 Frankford, Bishop McDevitt
1988 Central, Archbishop Ryan

INDIVIDUAL RECORDS

	SEASON
Rushing Yardage	2,116: Bill Foley, Judge, 1968
Rushing Attempts	372: Mike Elentrio, Judge, 1983
Rushing TDs	28: Len Nelson, Neumann, 1983
Passing Yardage	2,012: Chris Fagan, Judge, 1987
Passes Attempted	293: Frank Costa, St. Joseph's Prep, 1988
Passes Completed	154: Frank Costa, St. Joseph's Prep, 1988
Passing TDs	23: Ray Capriotti, Dougherty, 1968
Receiving Yardage	1,142: Mike Saksa, Carroll, 1974
Receptions	59: Mike Saksa, Carroll, 1974
Receiving TDs	13: Kevin Mullen, Carroll, 1977
Points	180: Len Nelson, Neumann, 1983
Touchdowns	29: Len Nelson, Neumann, 1983
PATs Made	49: Chuck Wright, Egan, 1966
Field Goals Made	10: Chris Ellis, Judge, 1987

	CAREER
Rushing Yardage	3,941: Blair Thomas, Frankford, 1982-84
Rushing Attempts	626: Blair Thomas, Frankford, 1982-84
Rushing TDs	53: Blair Thomas, Frankford, 1982-84
Passing Yardage	4,074: Mike Bailey, Carroll, 1972-74
Passes Attempted	605: Mike Bailey, Carroll, 1972-74
Passes Completed	305: Mike Bailey, Carroll, 1972-74
Passing TDs	33: Ray Capriotti, Dougherty, 1966-68
Receiving Yardage	2,024: Jerry Riley, Egan, 1973-75
Receptions	120: Jerry Riley, Egan, 1973-75
Receiving TDs	22: Kevin Mullen, Carroll, 1975-77
Points	356: Blair Thomas, Frankford, 1982-84
Touchdowns	59: Blair Thomas, Frankford, 1982-84
PATs Made	95: Dan Ellis, Judge, 1981-83
Field Goals Made	25: Dan D'Orazio, O'Hara, 1984-87

SOCCER

CITY TITLE RESULTS

1957 Frankford 2, North Catholic 1
1958 Murrell Dobbins 3, North Catholic 2
1959 North Catholic 1, Olney 0
1960 Central 4, North Catholic 2
1961 Jules Mastbaum 2, North Catholic 0
1962 North Catholic 2, Jules Mastbaum 1
1963 Murrell Dobbins 3, North Catholic 1
1964 Frankford 2, North Catholic 1
1965 Frankford 3, North Catholic 1
1966 Murrell Dobbins 4, North Catholic 1
1967 Frankford 1, North Catholic 0
1968 Frankford 1, Cardinal Dougherty 0
1969 Cardinal Dougherty 2, Jules Mastbaum 0
1970 (tie) Frankford 0, North Catholic 0
1971 Roxborough 1, Cardinal Dougherty 0
1972 Cardinal Dougherty 1, Abraham Lincoln 0
1973 (tie) Cardinal Dougherty 0, Frankford 0

1974 Frankford 2, North Catholic 0
1975 North Catholic 4, Roxborough 0
1976 Frankford 3, Father Judge 0
1977 North Catholic 1, Abraham Lincoln 0
1978 North Catholic 1, Washington 0
1979 North Catholic 1, Washington 0
(City Title Game Terminated)
Public Champion, Catholic Champion
1980 Frankford, Cardinal Dougherty
1981 George Washington, Archbishop Ryan
1982 Northeast, Cardinal O'Hara
1983 Northeast/Frankford, Ryan
1984 George Washington, Archbishop Ryan
1985 Northeast, Archbishop Ryan
1986 George Washington, Archbishop Ryan
1987 Frankford, Archbishop Ryan
1988 Frankford, Archbishop Ryan

BASEBALL

CITY TITLE RESULTS

1945 North Catholic 1, South Philadelphia 0
1946 La Salle 3, Northeast 2
1947 South Philadelphia 5, North Catholic 4
1948 South Philadelphia 4, St. James 0
1949 South Philadelphia 5, North Catholic 2
1950 North Catholic 4, Overbrook 3
1951 Olney 6, La Salle 4
1952 South Catholic 4, Frankford 3
1953 South Catholic 5, Central 2
1954 South Philadelphia 4, North Catholic 1
1955 La Salle 2, Olney 1
1956 North Catholic 7, Central 1
1957 Abraham Lincoln 14, Father Judge 4
1958 Bishop Neumann 6, Abraham Lincoln 5 (10 inn.)
1959 South Philadelphia 6, La Salle 5
1960 John Bartram 5, Bishop Neumann 1
1961 John Bartram 12, St. James 2
1962 St. James 2, Abraham Lincoln 1
1963 John Bartram 4, St. James 3
1964 Father Judge 3, Frankford 2
1965 Abraham Lincoln 2, St. James 1
1966 South Philadelphia 2, West Catholic 0
1967 Father Judge 3, Roxborough 0
1968 Bishop Egan 1, South Phila. 0 (11 inn.)
1969 Cardinal Dougherty 10, Olney 0
1970 Monsignor Bonner 4, Abraham Lincoln 0
1971 St. James 5, Roxborough 1
1972 Frankford 6, St. James 5
1973 Father Judge 3, Frankford 2
1974 South Phila. 5, Archbishop Ryan 0
1975 South Philadelphia 7, Cardinal O'Hara 1
1976 Father Judge 14, Central 13
1977 North Catholic 13, Northeast 2
1978 Roman Catholic 10, George Washington 3
1979 West Catholic 6, Jules Mastbaum 2
(City Title Game Terminated)
Public Champion, Catholic Champion
1980 George Washington, Archbishop Ryan
1981 Frankford, North Catholic
1982 George Washington, Father Judge
1983 Ben Franklin, Cardinal O'Hara
1984 Northeast, Archbishop Ryan
1985 George Washington, Father Judge
1986 George Washington, North Catholic
1987 George Washington, Father Judge
1988 George Washington, La Salle
1989 Roxborough, Monsignor Bonner

Ken Mulderrig celebrates GW's 1988 Public League title

BOXING

Date	Weight Class	Site	Result	
5/19/09	Heavyweight	National A.C.	Jack Johnson def. Phila. Jack O'Brien	ND 6
6/ 2/24	Welterweight	Baker Bowl	Mickey Walker def. Lew Tendler	Dec. 10
10/ 1/24	Welterweight	Baker Bowl	Mickey Walker def. Bobby Barrett	KO (1:33) 6
4/ 1/25	Junior Lightweight	Armory A.A.	Mike Ballerino def. Kid Sullivan	Dec. 10
9/23/26	Heavyweight	Sesquicentennial Stadium (Now JFK Stadium)	Gene Tunney def. Jack Dempsey	Dec. 10
9/12/27	Featherweight	Municipal Stadium (Now JFK Stadium)	Benny Bass def. Red Chapman	Dec. 10
1/ 5/31	Junior Lightweight	Arena	Benny Bass def. Lew Massey	Dec. 10
7/15/31	Junior Lightweight	Baker Bowl	Kid Chocolate def. Benny Bass	TKO (2:58) 7
1/18/32	Junior Welterweight	Arena	Johnny Jadick def. Tony Canzoneri	Dec. 10
7/18/32	Junior Welterweight	Baker Bowl	Johnny Jadick def. Tony Canzoneri	Dec. 10
5/ 1/33	Junior Lightweight	Arena	Kid Chocolate def. Johnny Farr	Dec. 10
12/25/33	Junior Lightweight	Arena	Frankie Klick def. Kid Chocolate	TKO (2:58) 7
1/13/41	Bantamweight	Arena	Lou Salica def. Tommy Forte	Dec. 15
2/17/41	Heavyweight	Convention Hall	Joe Louis def. Gus Dorazio	KO (1:30) 2
6/16/41	Bantamweight	Shibe Park	Lou Salica def. Tommy Forte	Dec. 15
11/26/46	Lightweight	Convention Hall	Bob Montgomery def. Wesley Mouzon	KO (2:18) 8
8/ 4/47	Lightweight	Municipal Stadium	Ike Williams def. Bob Montgomery	KO (2:37) 6
7/12/48	Lightweight	Shibe Park	Ike Williams def. Beau Jack	TKO (0:33) 6
7/11/49	Welterweight	Municipal Stadium	Sugar Ray Robinson def. Kid Gavilan	Dec. 15
12/ 5/49	Lightweight	Convention Hall	Ike Williams def. Freddy Dawson	Dec. 15
6/ 5/50	Middleweight	Municipal Stadium	Sugar Ray Robinson def. Robert Villemain	Dec. 15
10/26/50	Middleweight	Convention Hall	Sugar Ray Robinson def. Carl "Bobo" Olson	KO (1:19) 12
6/ 5/52	Heavyweight	Municipal Stadium	Jersey Joe Walcott def. Ezzard Charles	Dec. 15
7/ 7/52	Welterweight	Municipal Stadium	Kid Gavilan def. Gil Turner	TKO (2:47) 11
9/23/52	Heavyweight	Municipal Stadium	Rocky Marciano def. Jersey Joe Walcott	KO (0:43) 13
10/20/54	Welterweight	Convention Hall	Johnny Saxton def. Kid Gavilan	Dec. 15
4/24/61	Light Heavyweight	Arena	Harold Johnson def. Von Clay	KO (2:23) 2
5/12/62	Light Heavyweight	Arena	Harold Johnson def. Doug Jones	Dec. 15
12/14/64	Middleweight	Convention Hall	Joey Giardello def. Ruben Carter	Dec. 15
12/10/68	Heavyweight	Spectrum	Joe Frazier def. Oscar Bonavena	Dec. 15
11/30/76	Junior Lightweight	Spectrum	Alfredo Escalera def. Tyrone Everett	Dec. 15
9/17/77	Lightweight	Spectrum	Roberto Duran def. Edwin Viruet	Dec. 15
12/ 5/78	Light Heavyweight	Spectrum	Mike Rossman def. Aldo Traversaro	TKO (1:15) 6
1/31/81	Bantamweight	Franklin Plaza	Jeff Chandler def. Jorge Lujan	Dec. 15
3/27/82	Bantamweight	Civic Center	Jeff Chandler def. Johnny Carter	TKO (2:28) 6
8/ 7/82	Light Heavyweight	Spectrum	Dwight Braxton def. Matthew Saad Muhammad	TKO (1:23) 6

LOCAL WORLD CHAMPIONS

PHILADELPHIA JACK O'BRIEN def. Bob Fitzsimmons (KO 13) to raise his record to 133-4-17 (44 KOs) and win the Light Heayweight title on Dec. 20, 1905 in San Francisco. O'Brien finished with a record of 148-12-19 (51 KOs).

HARRY LEWIS def. Frank Mantell (KO 3) to raise his record to 65-23-16 (21 KOs) and win the Welterweight title on Jan. 23, 1908 in New Haven. Lewis finished with a record of 110-36-24 (47 KOs).

BATTLING LEVINSKY def. Jack Dillon (W 12) to raise his record to 126-25-22 (27 KOs) and win the Light Heavyweight title on Dec. 24, 1916 in Boston. Levinsky finished with a record of 192-52-34 (34 KOs).

BENNY BASS def. Red Chapman (W 10) to raise his record to 78-13-6 (31 KOs) and win the Featherweight (NBA) title on Sept. 12, 1927 in Philadelphia. Bass finished with a record of 176-38-10 (63 KOs).

TOMMY LOUGHRAN def. Mike McTigue (W 15) to raise his record to 76-13-8 (15 KOs) and win the Light Heavyweight title on Oct. 7, 1927 in New York. Loughran finished with a record of 123-30-12 (17KOs).

MIDGET WOLGAST def. Black Bill (W 15) to raise his record to 70-4-1 (4 KOs) and win the Flyweight (New York) title on March 21, 1930 in New York. Wolgast finished with a record of 150-36-16 (15 KOs).

JOHNNY JADICK def. Tony Canzoneri (W 10) to raise his record to 59-16-4 (11 KOs) and win the Junior Welterweight title on Jan. 18, 1932 in Philadelphia. Jadick finished with a record of 85-57-9 (12 KOs).

BOB MONTGOMERY def. Beau Jack (W 15) to raise his record to 51-6-0 (28 KOs) and win the Lightweight (New York) title on May 21, 1943 in New York. Montgomery finished with a record of 75-19-3 (37 KOs).

JERSEY JOE WALCOTT def. Ezzard Charles (KO 7) to raise his record to 49-16-1 (30 KOs) and win the Heavyweight title on July 18, 1951 in Pittsburgh. Walcott finished with a record of 50-18-1 (30 KOs).

HAROLD JOHNSON def. Jesse Bowdry (TKO 9) to raise his record to 63-8 (28 KOs) and win the WBA Light Heavyweight title on Feb. 7, 1961 in Miami Beach.

JOHNSON def. Doug Jones (Dec. 15) to raise his record to 67-8 (29 KOs) and win the undisputed Light Heavyweight title on May 12, 1962 in Philadelphia. Johnson finished with a record of 76-11 (32 KOs).

JOEY GIARDELLO def. Dick Tiger (W 15) to raise his record to 94-22-7 (32 KOs) and win the Middleweight title on Dec. 7, 1963 in Atlantic City. Giardello finished with a record of 100-25-7 (32 KOs).

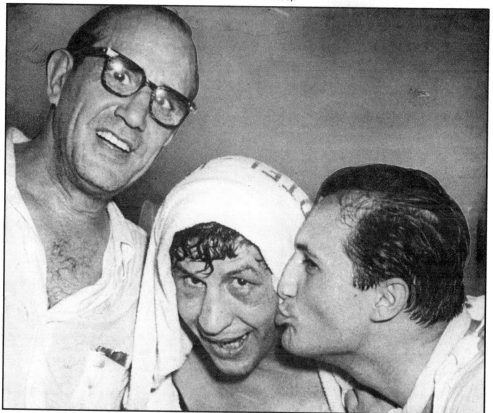

Joey Giardello is shown with trainer Joe Pollino (left) and handler Arnold Giovanetti after winning a fight at the Arena

LOCAL WORLD CHAMPIONS

A pair of Philadelphia champions, Jeff Chandler (left) and Matthew Saad Muhammad, talk at a charity function

JOE FRAZIER def. Buster Mathis (KO 11) to raise his record to 20-0-0 (18 KOs) and win the New York Heavyweight title on March 4, 1968 in New York.

FRAZIER def. Jimmy Ellis (TKO 5) to raise his record to 25-0-0 (22 KOs) and win the undisputed Heavyweight title on Feb. 16, 1970 in New York. Frazier finished with a record of 32-4-1 (27 KOs).

MIKE ROSSMAN def. Victor Galindez (TKO 13) to raise his record to 35-4-3 (22 KOs) and win the WBA Light Heavyweight title on Sept. 25, 1978 in New Orleans. Rossman finished with a record of 44-7-3 (27 KOs).

MATTHEW SAAD MUHAMMAD def. Marvin Johnson (TKO 8) to raise his record to 21-2-2 (15 KOs) and win the WBC Light Heavyweight title on April 22, 1979 in Indianapolis. Saad Muhammad finished with a record of 44-7-2 (28 KOs).

JEFF CHANDLER def. Julian Solis (TKO 14) to raise his record to 24-0-1 (12 KOs) and win the WBA Bantamweight title on Nov. 11, 1980 in Miami. Chandler finished with a record of 33-2-2 (18 KOs).

DWIGHT MUHAMMAD QAWI def. Matthew Saad Muhammad (TKO 10) to raise his record to 16-1-1 (9 KOs) and win the WBC Light Heavyweight title on Dec. 19, 1981 in Atlantic City.

MUHAMMAD QAWI def. Piet Crous (TKO 11) to raise his record to 24-2-1 (13 KOs) and win the WBA Cruiserweight title on July 27, 1985 in Sun City, South Afrcia. Muhammad Qawi finished with a record of 28-6-1 (17 KOs).

CHARLIE "CHOO CHOO" BROWN def. Melvin Paul (W 15) to raise his record to 23-2-1 (16 KOs) and win the IBF Lightweight title on Jan. 30, 1984 in Atlantic City. Brown finished with a record of 26-8-2 (18 KOs).

TIM WITHERSPOON def. Greg Page (W 12) to raise his record to 18-1 (12 KOs) and win the WBC Heavyweight title on March 9, 1984 in Las Vegas.

WITHERSPOON def. Tony Tubbs (W 15) to raise his record to 24-2 (16 KOs) and win the WBA Heavyweight title on Jan. 17, 1986 in Atlanta. Witherspoon's record is 28-3 (19 KOs).

GARY HINTON def. Reyes Cruz (Dec. 15) to raise his record to 25-3-2 (10 KOs) and win the IBF Junior Welterweight title on April 26, 1986 in Lucca, Italy. Hinton's record is 27-4-2 (11 KOs).

BUSTER DRAYTON def. Carlos Santos (Dec. 15) to raise his record to 28-9-1 (20 KOs) and win the IBF Junior Middleweight title on June 4, 1986, in East Rutherford. Drayton's record is 36-11-1 (28 KOs).

MELDRICK TAYLOR def. James "Buddy" McGirt (TKO 12) to raise his record to 21-0-1 (12 KOs) and win the IBF Junior Welterweight title on Sept. 3, 1988 in Atlantic City. Taylor's record is 21-0-1 (12 KOs).

ROBERT "BAM BAM" HINES def. Matthew Hilton (Dec. 12) to raise his record to 24-1-2 (16 KOs) and win the IBF Junior Middleweight title on Nov. 4, 1988 in Las Vegas. Hines's record is 24-2-2 (16 KOs).

Joe Frazier

In his fighting lifetime, Joe Frazier was known for his relentless attacking style, feared for his punishing left hook, and forever immortalized by a series of three fights with a single man.

Frazier, after seizing the heavyweight title that was stripped from Muhammad Ali when Ali refused to be drafted, fought Ali three times in a span of five years.

Frazier won the first in 1971, then lost the next two in 1974 and '75 in what is generally regarded as the greatest series in the history of boxing.

Born in Beaufort, S.C. on Jan. 12, 1944, Frazier began his climb to boxing's throne by winning an Olympic Gold Medal in 1964, then knocking out his first 11 professional opponents in a total of 28 rounds.

By the time Ali had lost his title in 1967, Frazier was 16-0 with 14 knockouts and obviously a prime championship contender. In Ali's absence, Frazier won the title by knocking out Jimmy Ellis in the fifth round.

It wouldn't be until March 8, 1971 that Ali would get a chance at the title by getting into the ring with Frazier. By then, Frazier was 26-0 with 23 knockouts.

In that furious first fight at Madison Square Garden, Frazier defended his belt by decisioning Ali, winning it with a vicious knockdown in the last round.

Ali came out rusty, but held on and held off to survive through 14 rounds. But in the 15th, as both fighters neared exhaustion, Frazier caught Ali in the jaw with his famous left, sending Ali to the canvas. Ali got up and went the distance, but the fight was won with that typical Frazier attack. It would be the only fight in the series he would win.

In their second fight, considered the tamest of the three, again at the Garden, on Jan. 28, 1974, Ali took the decision and the championship.

But it was their third bout, the so-called "Thrilla in Manila" on Oct. 1, 1975, that crowned the series. By then, beginning the downside of their careers, Ali was 33, Frazier 31.

The two fighters fired away at each other for 14 full rounds before Frazier's cornermen forced him to quit because he was half-blind from injury.

After the fight, Ali said that he had never been closer to death than in the ring with Frazier.

After the last Ali fight, Frazier was knocked out for the second time by George Foreman, and retired after taking an enormous amount of punishment. He made a belated comeback in 1981 before retiring once and for all.

He retired with a career record of 32-4-1.

BOX SCORES

PHILLIES 6, METS 0
JUNE 21, 1964, AT NEW YORK

PHILLIES	ab r h bi	NEW YORK	ab r h bi
Briggs, cf	4 1 0 0	Hickman, cf	3 0 0 0
Herrnstein, 1b	4 0 0 0	Hunt, 2b	3 0 0 0
Callison, rf	4 1 2 1	Kranepool, 1b	3 0 0 0
Allen, 3b	3 0 1 1	Christopher, rf	3 0 0 0
Covington, lf	2 0 0 0	Gonder, c	3 0 0 0
a-Wine, ss	1 1 0 0	R. Taylor, lf	3 0 0 0
T. Taylor, 2b	3 2 1 0	C. Smith, ss	3 0 0 0
Rojas, ss-lf	3 0 1 0	Samuel, 3b	2 0 0 0
Triandos, c	4 1 2 2	c-Altman	1 0 0 0
Bunning, p	4 0 1 2	Stallard, p	1 0 0 0
		Wakefield, p	0 0 0 0
		b-Kanehl	1 0 0 0
		Sturdivant, p	0 0 0 0
		d-Stephenson	1 0 0 0
Totals	32 6 8 6		27 0 0 0

a — Ran for Covington in 6th.
b — Grounded out for Wakefield in 6th.
c — Struck out for Samuel in 9th.
d — Struck out for Sturdivant in 9th.

Phillies	110 004 000 — 6
New York	000 000 000 — 0

LOB — Phillies 5, New York 0. 2B — Triandos, Bunning. HR — Callison. S — Herrnstein, Rojas.

	IP	H	R	ER	BB	SO
Phillies						
Bunning (W, 7-2)	9	0	0	0	0	10
New York						
Stallard (L, 4-3)	5⅔	7	6	6	4	3
Wakefield	⅓	0	0	0	0	0
Sturdivant	3	1	0	0	0	3

Umpires — Sudol, Pryor, Secory, Burkhart.
Time — 2:19. Attendance — 32,036.

PHILLIES 4, REDS 0
JUNE 23, 1971, AT CINCINNATI

PHILLIES	ab r h bi	CINCINNATI	ab r h bi
Harmon, 2b	4 0 0 0	Rose, rf	4 0 0 0
Bowa, ss	4 0 0 0	Foster, cf	3 0 0 0
McCarver, c	3 0 2 0	May, 1b	3 0 0 0
Johnson, 1b	2 0 0 0	Bench, c	3 0 0 0
Lis, lf	2 1 0 0	Perez, 3b	3 0 0 0
Stone, lf	1 0 0 0	McRae, lf	3 0 0 0
Montanez, cf	4 0 1 0	Granger, p	0 0 0 0
Freed, rf	4 1 1 1	Helms, 2b	3 0 0 0
Vukovich, 3b	4 0 1 0	Concepcion, ss	1 0 0 0
Wise, p	4 2 2 3	Stewart, ph	1 0 0 0
		Grimsley, p	1 0 0 0
		Carbo, ph	1 0 0 0
		Carroll, p	0 0 0 0
		Cline, lf	1 0 0 0
Totals	32 4 7 4	Totals	27 0 0 0

Phillies	010 020 010 — 4
Cincinnati	000 000 000 — 0

DP — Cincinnati 2. LOB — Phillies 5, Cincinnati 1. 2B — Montanez, Freed. HR — Wise 2 (4).

	IP	H	R	ER	BB	SO
Phillies						
Wise (W, 8-4)	9	0	0	0	1	3
Cincinnati						
Grimsley (L, 4-3)	6	4	3	3	2	1
Carroll	2	2	1	1	1	1
Granger	1	1	0	0	0	1

HBP — Lis by Grimsley.
Umpires — Dale, Gorman, Pelekoudas, Harvey.
T — 1:53. A — 13,329.

Rick Wise held the Reds hitless . . .

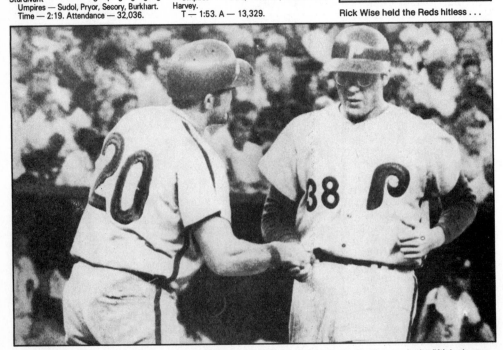

. . . and managed to hit two home runs himself. Roger Freed greets Wise after his first homer, in the fifth inning.

SLUGFEST

PHILLIES 23, CUBS 22

MAY 17, 1979, AT CHICAGO

PHILLIES	ab r h bi	CHICAGO	ab r h bi
McBride, rf	8 2 3 1	DeJesus, ss	6 4 3 1
Bowa, ss	8 4 5 1	Vail, rf	5 2 3 1
Rose, 1b	7 4 3 4	Burris, p	0 0 0 0
Schmidt, 3b	4 3 2 4	Thompson, cf	2 1 1 0
Unser, lf	7 1 1 2	Buckner, 1b	7 3 4 7
Maddox, cf	4 3 4 4	Kingman, lf	6 4 3 6
Gross, cf	2 1 1 1	Ontiveros, 3b	7 1 1 1
Boone, c	4 2 3 5	Martin, cf	6 2 3 3
Meoli, 2b	5 0 1 0	Sutter, p	0 0 0 0
Lerch, p	1 1 1 1	Foote, c	6 1 3 1
Bird, p	1 1 0 0	Sizemore, 2b	4 2 2 1
Luzinski, ph	0 0 0 0	Caudill, p	0 0 0 0
Espinosa, pr	1 1 0 0	Murcer, rf	2 0 1 0
McGraw, p	0 0 0 0	Lamp, p	0 0 0 0
Reed, p	0 0 0 0	Moore, p	1 0 1 1
McCarver, ph	1 0 0 0	Hernandez, p	1 0 0 0
Eastwick, p	0 0 0 0	Dillard, 2b	1 2 1 0
		Biitner, ph	1 0 0 0
		Kelleher, 2b	1 0 0 0
Totals	53 23 24 23	Totals	56 22 26 22

Phillies	**708 240 100 1 — 23**
Chicago	**600 373 030 0 — 22**

E — Schmidt 2, Kingman, DeJesus. DP — Phillies 2. LOB — Phillies 15, Chicago 7. 2B — Bowa 2, Maddox 2, Rose 2, Foote, Martin, DeJesus, Boone. 3B — Moore, Gross. HR — Kingman 3 (12), Schmidt 2 (14), Boone (2), Lerch (1), Maddox (6), Ontiveros (1), Buckner (4), Martin (3). SB — Bowa, Meoli. SF — Unser, Gross.

	IP	H	R	ER	BB	SO
Phillies						
Lerch	⅓	5	5	5	0	0
Bird	3⅔	8	4	4	0	2
McGraw	⅔	4	7	4	3	1
Reed	3⅓	9	6	6	0	0
Eastwick (W, 1-0)	2	0	0	0	0	1
Cincinnati						
Lamp	⅓	6	6	6	0	0
Moore	2	6	7	7	2	1
Hernandez	2⅔	7	8	6	7	1
Caudill	1⅓	3	1	1	2	3
Burris	1⅔	1	0	0	0	1
Sutter (L, 1-1)	2	1	1	1	1	0

HBP — Boone by Hernandez.
T — 4:03. A — 14,952.

Randy Lerch scores after his homer

1980 WORLD SERIES

GAME 1

OCTOBER 14, AT VETERANS STADIUM

PHILLIES 7, ROYALS 6

KANSAS CITY

	AB	R	H	BI	O	A	E
Wilson, lf	5	0	0	0	2	1	0
McRae, dh	3	1	1	0	0	0	0
G. Brett, 3b	4	1	1	0	0	2	0
Aikens, 1b	4	2	2	4	13	0	0
Porter, c	2	1	0	0	5	1	0
Otis, cf	4	1	3	2	1	0	0
Hurdle, rf	3	0	1	0	1	0	0
a-Wathan, rf	1	0	0	0	1	0	0
White, 2b	4	0	1	0	0	5	0
Washington, ss	4	0	0	0	1	6	0
Leonard, p	0	0	0	0	0	0	1
Martin, p	0	0	0	0	0	0	0
Quisenberry, p	0	0	0	0	0	0	0
Totals	34	6	9	6	24	15	1

PHILLIES

	AB	R	H	BI	O	A	E
Smith, lf	4	0	2	0	3	1	0
Gross, lf	1	0	0	0	1	0	0
Rose, 1b	3	1	0	0	7	2	0
Schmidt, 3b	2	2	1	0	2	3	0
McBride, rf	4	1	3	3	3	0	0
Luzinski, dh	3	0	0	0	0	0	0
Maddox, cf	3	0	0	1	2	0	0
Trillo, 2b	4	1	1	0	1	2	0
Bowa, ss	4	1	1	0	0	3	0
Boone, c	4	1	3	2	6	0	0
Walk, p	0	0	0	0	2	0	0
McGraw, p	0	0	0	0	0	0	0
Totals	32	7	11	6	27	11	0

a — Hit into doubleplay for Hurdle in 8th.

Kansas City	**022 000 020 — 6**
Phillies	**005 110 00x — 7**

Game-winning RBI — McBride.

DP — Phils 1. LOB — Kansas City 4, Phils 6. 2B — Boone 2, Brett. HR — Otis, Aikens 2, McBride. SB — Bowa, White. SF — Maddox.

	IP	H	R	ER	BB	SO
Kansas City						
Leonard (L)	3⅔	6	6	6	1	3
Martin	4	5	1	1	1	1
Quisenberry	⅓	0	0	0	0	0
Phillies						
Walk (W)	7	8	6	6	3	3
McGraw (S)	2	1	0	0	0	2

Walk faced two batters in 8th.

HBP — By Leonard (Rose), by Martin (Luzinski). WP — Walk.

Umpires — Home: Wendelstedt (NL); First: Kunkel (AL); Second: Pryor (NL); Third: Denkinger (AL); Left: Rennert (NL); Right: Bremigan (AL). Time — 3:01. Attendance — 65,791.

HOW THEY SCORED

ROYALS SECOND (2): Porter walked. Otis homered to left, Porter also scoring.

ROYALS THIRD (2): With one out, McRae singled to center. Brett struck out. Aikens homered to right-center, McRae also scoring.

PHILLIES THIRD (5): With one out, Bowa singled and stole second. Boone doubled down the leftfield line, Bowa scoring. Smith singled to left, Boone stopping at third, then scoring when Smith was caught in a rundown between first and second. Rose was hit by a pitch. Schmidt walked. McBride homered, Rose and Schmidt also scoring.

PHILLIES FOURTH (1): With one out, Trillo singled and went to second on Leonard's error on a pickoff attempt. Bowa grounded out, Trillo going to third. Boone doubled down the rightfield line, Trillo scoring.

PHILLIES FIFTH (1): With one out, Schmidt walked. McBride singled to left, Schmidt stopping at second. Luzinski was hit a pitch, Schmidt going to third and McBride to second. Maddox hit a sacrifice fly to left, Schmidt scoring.

ROYALS EIGHTH (2): Brett doubled to left-center and went to third on Walk's wild pitch. Aikens homered, Brett also scoring.

GAME 2

OCTOBER 15, AT VETERANS STADIUM

PHILLIES 6, ROYALS 4

KANSAS CITY

	AB	R	H	BI	O	A	E
Wilson, lf	4	1	1	0	1	0	0
Washington, ss	4	0	1	0	0	3	0
G. Brett, 3b	2	0	2	0	2	2	0
Chalk, 3b	0	1	0	0	0	1	0
c-Porter	1	0	0	0	0	0	0
McRae, dh	4	1	3	0	0	0	0
Otis, cf	5	1	2	2	5	0	0
Wathan, c	3	0	0	1	2	0	0
Aikens, 1b	3	0	1	0	6	0	0
LaCock, 1b	0	0	0	0	2	0	0
Cardenal, rf	4	0	0	0	3	0	0
White, 2b	4	0	1	0	3	3	0
Gura, p	0	0	0	0	0	0	0
Quisenberry, p	0	0	0	0	0	0	0
Totals	34	4	11	3	24	9	0

PHILLIES

	AB	R	H	BI	O	A	E
Smith, lf	3	0	0	0	0	0	0
a-Unser, cf	1	1	1	1	0	0	0
Rose, 1b	4	0	0	0	7	1	0
McBride, rf	3	1	1	1	2	0	0
Schmidt, 3b	4	1	2	1	1	1	0
Moreland, dh	4	1	2	1	0	0	0
Maddox, cf	3	1	1	0	1	1	0
b-Gross, lf	1	0	0	0	0	0	0
Trillo, 2b	2	0	0	1	6	3	1
Bowa, ss	3	0	1	1	0	6	0
Boone, c	1	1	0	0	10	1	0
Carlton, p	0	0	0	0	0	1	0
Reed, p	0	0	0	0	0	0	0
Totals	29	6	8	6	27	14	1

a — Doubled for Smith in 8th.
b — Hit into doubleplay for Maddox in 8th.
c — Struck out for Chalk in 9th.

Kansas City	**000 001 300 — 4**
Phillies	**000 020 04x — 6**

Game-winning RBI — Schmidt.

DP — Kansas City 2, Phillies 4. LOB — Kansas City 11, Phillies 3. 2B — Maddox, Otis, Unser, Schmidt. SB — Wilson, Chalk. SH — Washington. SF — Trillo, Wathan.

	IP	H	R	ER	BB	SO
Kansas City						
Gura	6	4	2	2	2	2
Quisenberry (L)	2	4	4	4	1	0
Phillies						
Carlton (W)	8	10	4	3	6	10
Reed (S)	1	1	0	0	0	2

WP — Carlton.

Umpires — Home: Kunkel (AL); First: Pryor (NL); Second: Denkinger (AL); Third: Rennert (NL); Left: Bremigan (AL); Right: Wendelstedt (NL). Time — 3:01. Attendance — 65,775.

HOW THEY SCORED

PHILLIES FIFTH (2): With one out, Moreland singled. Maddox doubled, Moreland stopping at third. Trillo hit a sacrifice fly, Moreland scoring and Maddox going to third. Bowa singled to left, Maddox scoring.

ROYALS SIXTH (1): Otis singled to center. Wathan walked, Otis going to second. Aikens reached first on Trillo's throwing error, Otis scoring.

ROYALS SEVENTH (3): Wilson walked. Washington sacrificed to pitcher, Wilson going to second. Wilson stole third. Chalk walked and stole second. McRae walked, loading the bases. Otis doubled down the leftfield line, Washington and Chalk scoring and McRae stopping at third. Wathan hit a sacrifice fly to center, McRae scoring.

PHILLIES EIGHTH (4): Boone walked. Unser, batting for Smith, doubled to left-center, Boone scoring. Rose grounded out to first, Unser going to third. McBride singled to right, Unser scoring. Schmidt doubled to right, McBride scoring and Schmidt going to third on the throw home. Moreland singled to center, Schmidt scoring.

1980 WORLD SERIES

GAME 3
OCTOBER 17, AT KANSAS CITY
ROYALS 4, PHILLIES 3
(10 Innings)

PHILLIES

	AB	R	H	BI	O	A	E
Smith, lf	4	0	2	1	0	0	0
b-Gross, lf	0	0	0	0	0	0	0
Rose, 1b	4	0	1	1	11	0	0
Schmidt, 3b	5	1	1	1	3	3	0
McBride, rf	5	0	2	0	1	0	0
Moreland, dh	5	0	1	0	0	0	0
Maddox, cf	4	0	1	0	3	0	0
Trillo, 2b	5	1	2	0	2	6	0
Bowa, ss	5	1	3	0	1	3	0
Boone, c	4	0	1	0	8	1	0
Ruthven, p	0	0	0	0	0	0	0
McGraw, p	0	0	0	0	0	0	0
Totals	41	3	14	3	29	13	0

KANSAS CITY

	AB	R	H	BI	O	A	E
Wilson, lf	4	1	0	0	3	0	0
White, 2b	5	0	0	0	4	2	0
G. Brett, 3b	4	1	2	1	0	3	0
Aikens, 1b	5	1	2	1	7	1	0
McRae, dh	4	0	2	1	0	0	0
Otis, cf	4	1	2	1	9	0	0
Hurdle, rf	4	0	2	0	1	0	0
a-Concepcion	0	0	0	0	0	0	0
Cardenal, rf	0	0	0	0	0	0	0
Porter, c	4	0	0	0	6	0	0
Washington, ss	4	0	1	0	1	2	0
Gale, p	0	0	0	0	0	1	0
Martin, p	0	0	0	0	0	0	0
Quisenberry, p	0	0	0	0	1	1	0
Totals	38	4	11	4	30	10	0

a — Ran for Hurdle in 9th.
b — Sacrificed for Smith in 10th.

Phillies	010	010	010	0	—	3
Kansas City	100	100	100	1	—	4

Game-winning RBI — Aikens.
Two outs when winning run scored.
DP — Phillies 1, Kansas City 2. LOB — Phillies 15, Kansas City 7. 2B — Trillo, G. Brett. 3B — Aikens. HR — G. Brett, Schmidt, Otis. SB — Hurdle, Bowa, Wilson. SH — Gross.

Phillies

	IP	H	R	ER	BB	SO
Ruthven	9	9	3	3	0	7
McGraw (L)	⅔	2	1	1	2	1

Kansas City

	IP	H	R	ER	BB	SO
Gale	4⅓	7	2	2	3	3
Martin	3⅓	5	1	1	1	1
Quisenberry (W)	2⅓	2	0	0	2	0

Umpires — Home: Pryor (NL); First: Denkinger (AL); Second: Rennert (NL); Third: Bremigan (AL); Left: Wendelstedt (NL); Right: Kunkel (AL).
Time — 3:19. Attendance — 42,380.

HOW THEY SCORED

ROYALS FIRST (1): With two outs, Brett homered to right.

PHILLIES SECOND (1): With one out, Trillo singled to pitcher. Bowa singled to right, Trillo stopping at second. Boone walked, Trillo going to third and Bowa to second. Smith grounded out to pitcher, Trillo scoring.

ROYALS FOURTH (1): With one out, Aikens tripled to left. McRae singled to center, Aikens scoring.

PHILLIES FIFTH (1): Schmidt homered to left.

ROYALS SEVENTH (1): With one out, Otis homered to right-center.

PHILLIES EIGHTH (1): With one out, Bowa singled. Boone flied to center. Bowa stole second. Smith walked. Rose singled to right-center, Bowa scoring.

ROYALS TENTH (1): Washington singled to left. Wilson walked, Washington going to second. Washington was thrown out attempting to steal third. White struck out. Wilson stole second. Brett was intentionally walked. Aikens singled to left-center, Wilson scoring.

GAME 4
OCTOBER 18, AT KANSAS CITY
ROYALS 5, PHILLIES 3

PHILLIES

	AB	R	H	BI	O	A	E
Smith, dh	4	0	0	0	0	0	0
Rose, 1b	4	1	2	0	8	2	0
McBride, rf	3	0	1	0	3	0	0
Schmidt, lf	3	0	1	1	2	0	0
Unser, lf	4	0	1	0	1	0	0
Maddox, cf	4	0	1	0	2	0	0
Trillo, 2b	4	2	1	0	2	6	0
Bowa, ss	4	0	2	1	1	1	0
Boone, c	3	0	1	1	6	0	0
Christenson, p	0	0	0	0	0	0	1
Noles, p	0	0	0	0	0	1	0
Saucier, p	0	0	0	0	0	0	0
Brusstar, p	0	0	0	0	0	0	0
Totals	33	3	10	3	24	9	1

KANSAS CITY

	AB	R	H	BI	O	A	E
Wilson, lf	4	1	1	0	4	0	0
White, 2b	5	0	0	0	2	4	1
G. Brett, 3b	5	1	1	1	0	7	0
Aikens, lf	3	2	2	3	13	0	0
McRae, dh	4	1	2	0	0	0	0
Otis, cf	4	0	2	1	1	0	0
Hurdle, rf	2	0	1	0	3	0	0
Porter, c	3	0	0	0	2	1	0
Washington, ss	4	0	1	0	2	3	1
Leonard, p	0	0	0	0	0	0	0
Quisenberry, p	0	0	0	0	0	0	0
Totals	34	5	10	5	27	15	2

Phillies	010	000	110	—	3
Kansas City	401	000	00x	—	5

Game-winning RBI — G. Brett.
DP — Kansas City 1. LOB — Phillies 6, Kansas City 10. 2B — McRae 2, Otis, Hurdle, McBride, Trillo, Rose. 3B — G. Brett. HR — Aikens 2. SB — Bowa. SF — Boone, Schmidt.

Phillies

	IP	H	R	ER	BB	SO
Christenson (L)	⅓	5	4	4	0	0
Noles	4⅔	5	1	1	2	6
Saucier	⅔	0	0	0	0	0
Brusstar	2⅓	0	0	0	0	1

Kansas City

	IP	H	R	ER	BB	SO
Leonard (W)	7	9	3	2	1	2
Quisenberry (S)	2	1	0	0	0	0

Leonard faced 1 batter in 8th.
WP — Leonard, Saucier.
Umpires — Home: Denkinger (AL); First: Rennert (NL); Second: Bremigan (AL); Third: Wendelstedt (NL); Left: Kunkel (AL); Right: Pryor (NL).
Time — 2:37. Attendance — 42,363.

HOW THEY SCORED

ROYALS FIRST (4): Wilson singled to center and went to third on Christenson's error on a pickoff attempt. White flied to right. Brett tripled down the rightfield line, Wilson scoring. Aikens homered to right, Brett also scoring. McRae doubled to center. Otis doubled to right-center, McRae scoring.

PHILLIES SECOND (1): With one out, Maddox singled to right. Trillo reached first on a fielder's choice, Maddox out at second, Trillo going to second on Washington's throwing error. Bowa singled to left, Trillo scoring.

ROYALS SECOND (1): With two outs, Aikens homered to right.

PHILLIES SEVENTH (1): With one out, Trillo doubled to right. Bowa singled to left, Trillo stopping at third. Boone hit a sacrifice fly to left, Trillo scoring.

PHILLIES EIGHTH (1): Rose doubled to left. Quisenberry relieved Leonard. McBride grounded out to second, Rose going to third. Schmidt hit a sacrifice fly to right, Rose scoring.

GAME 5
OCTOBER 19, AT KANSAS CITY
PHILLIES 4, ROYALS 3

PHILLIES

	AB	R	H	BI	O	A	E
Rose, 1b	4	0	0	0	7	1	0
McBride, rf	4	1	0	0	1	0	0
Schmidt, 3b	4	2	2	2	1	1	0
Luzinski, lf	2	0	0	0	1	0	0
a-Smith, lf	0	0	0	0	0	0	0
c-Unser, lf	1	1	1	1	0	0	0
Moreland, dh	3	0	1	0	0	0	0
Maddox, cf	4	0	0	0	2	0	0
Trillo, 2b	4	0	1	1	3	5	0
Bowa, ss	4	0	1	0	2	2	0
Boone, c	3	0	1	0	10	0	0
Bystrom, p	0	0	0	0	1	1	0
Reed, p	0	0	0	0	0	0	0
McGraw, p	0	0	0	0	1	0	0
Totals	33	4	7	4	27	12	0

KANSAS CITY

	AB	R	H	BI	O	A	E
Wilson, lf	5	0	2	0	2	0	0
White, 2b	3	0	0	0	2	6	0
G. Brett, 3b	5	0	1	1	1	2	1
d-Concepcion	0	0	0	0	0	0	0
Aikens, 1b	3	0	1	0	10	1	1
McRae, dh	5	0	1	0	0	0	0
Otis, cf	3	1	2	1	3	0	0
Hurdle, rf	3	1	1	0	3	0	0
b-Cardenal, rf	2	0	0	0	0	0	0
Porter, c	4	0	2	0	2	0	0
Washington, ss	3	1	2	1	2	2	0
Gura, p	0	0	0	0	2	4	0
Quisenberry, p	0	0	0	0	0	0	0
Totals	36	3	12	3	27	15	2

a — Ran for Luzinski in 8th.
b — Flied out for Hurdle in 7th.
c — Doubled for Smith in 9th.
d — Ran for Aikens in 9th.

Phillies	000	200	002	—	4
Kansas City	000	001	200	—	3

Game-winning RBI — Trillo.
DP — Kansas City 2. LOB — Phillies 4, Kansas City 13. 2B — Wilson, McRae, Unser. HR — Schmidt, Otis. SB — G. Brett. SH — White, Moreland. SF — Washington.

Phillies

	IP	H	R	ER	BB	SO
Bystrom	5	10	3	3	1	4
Reed	1	1	0	0	0	0
McGraw (W)	3	1	0	0	4	5

Kansas City

	IP	H	R	ER	BB	SO
Gura	6⅓	4	2	1	1	2
Quisenberry (L)	2⅔	3	2	2	0	0

Bystrom faced 3 batters in 6th.
Umpires — Home: Rennert (NL); First: Bremigan (AL); Second: Wendelstedt (NL); Third: Kunkel (AL); Left: Pryor (NL); Right: Denkinger (AL).
Time — 2:51. Attendance — 42,369.

HOW THEY SCORED

PHILLIES FOURTH (2): With one out, McBride reached first on Aikens' error. Schmidt homered to center, McBride also scoring.

ROYALS FIFTH (1): Washington singled to center. Wilson singled to third, Washington stopping at second. White sacrificed to third, Washington going to third and Wilson to second. Brett grounded out to Trillo, Washington scoring.

ROYALS SIXTH (2): Otis homered to left. Hurdle singled to center. Porter singled to right, Hurdle going to third. Reed relieved Bystrom. Washington hit a sacrifice fly to left, Hurdle scoring.

PHILLIES NINTH (2): Schmidt singled to third. Unser, batting for Smith, doubled down the rightfield line, Schmidt scoring. Moreland sacrificed to first, Unser going to third. Maddox grounded out to third. Trillo singled to pitcher, Unser scoring.

118

1980 WORLD SERIES

GAME 6
OCTOBER 21, AT VETERANS STADIUM
PHILLIES 4, ROYALS 1

KANSAS CITY

	AB	R	H	BI	O	A	E
Wilson, lf	4	0	0	0	3	0	0
Washington, ss	3	0	1	1	2	4	0
G. Brett, 3b	4	0	2	0	1	1	0
McRae, dh	4	0	0	0	0	0	0
Otis, cf	3	0	0	0	2	0	0
Aikens, 1b	2	0	0	0	6	0	1
a-Concepcion	0	0	0	0	0	0	0
Wathan, c	3	1	2	0	4	1	0
Cardenal, rf	4	0	2	0	4	0	0
White, 2b	4	0	0	0	2	1	1
Gale, p	0	0	0	0	0	0	0
Martin, p	0	0	0	0	0	0	0
Splittorff, p	0	0	0	0	0	1	0
Pattin, p	0	0	0	0	0	0	0
Quisenberry, p	0	0	0	0	0	0	0
Totals	31	1	7	1	24	8	2

PHILLIES

	AB	R	H	BI	O	A	E
Smith, lf	4	2	1	0	1	0	0
Gross, lf	0	0	0	0	0	0	0
Rose, 1b	4	0	3	0	9	0	0
Schmidt, 3b	3	0	1	2	0	0	0
McBride, rf	4	0	0	1	2	0	0
Luzinski, dh	4	0	0	0	0	0	0
Maddox, cf	4	0	2	0	1	0	0
Trillo, 2b	4	0	0	0	2	3	0
Bowa, ss	4	1	1	0	3	3	0
Boone, c	2	1	1	1	9	1	0
Carlton, p	0	0	0	0	0	2	0
McGraw, p	0	0	0	0	0	0	0
Totals	33	4	9	4	27	9	0

a — Ran for Aikens in 9th.

Kansas City	000 000 010	— 1
Phillies	002 011 00x	— 4

Game-winning RBI — Schmidt.
DP — Kansas City 1, Phillies 2. LOB — Kansas City 9, Phillies 7. 2B — Maddox, Smith, Bowa. SF — Washington.

	IP	H	R	ER	BB	SO
Kansas City						
Gale (L)	2	4	2	1	1	1
Martin	2⅓	1	1	1	1	0
Splittorff	1⅔	4	1	1	0	0
Pattin	1	0	0	0	0	2
Quisenberry	1	0	0	0	0	0
Phillies						
Carlton (W)	7	4	1	1	3	7
McGraw (S)	2	3	0	0	2	2

Gale faced 4 batters in 3rd; Splittorff faced 1 batter in 7th; Carlton faced 2 batters in 8th.

Umpires — Home: Bremigan (AL); First: Wendelstedt (NL); Second: Kunkel (AL); Third: Pryor (NL); Left: Denkinger (AL); Right: Rennert (NL).

Time — 3:00. Attendance — 65,838.

HOW THEY SCORED

PHILLIES THIRD (2): Boone walked. Smith reached first on Washington's error, Boone going to second. Rose reached first on a bunt single to third, Boone going to third and Smith to second. Schmidt singled to right, Boone and Smith scoring.

PHILLIES FIFTH (1): Smith doubled to center. Rose flied to center, Smith going to third. Schmidt walked. Splittorff relieved Martin. McBride grounded out to short, Smith scoring.

PHILLIES SIXTH (1): With two outs, Bowa doubled to left. Boone singled to center, Bowa scoring.

ROYALS EIGHT (1): Wathan walked. Cardenal singled to left, Wathan stopping at second. McGraw relieved Carlton. White fouled to Rose. Wilson walked, Wathan going to third and Cardenal to second. Washington hit a sacrifice fly to center, Wathan scoring.

Tug McGraw holds up newspaper at celebration for 1980 World Series victory

1948 NFL TITLE

DEC. 19, 1948, AT SHIBE PARK

EAGLES 7, CARDINALS 0

Chicago Cardinals	0	0	0	0 —	0
Eagles	0	0	7 —		7

HOW THEY SCORED
Fourth Quarter
Eagles 7, Cardinals 0: Steve Van Buren scored on a 5-yard run three plays into the final period. Key play: Frank Kilroy's recovery of a fumble by the Cardinals' Elmer Angsman on the Chicago 17-yard line. Cliff Patton PAT.

TEAM STATISTICS

	Cardinals	Eagles
First downs	6	16
Rushing	3	15
Passing	3	0
Penalty	0	1
Total net yards	131	232
Net yards rushing	96	225
Rushing plays	34	57
Avg./play	2.8	3.9
Net yards passing	35	7
Comp.-att.-int.	3-11-1	2-12-2
Punting avg.	37.4	37
Fumbles-lost	3-2	1-1
Yards penalized	33	17

INDIVIDUAL STATISTICS
RUSHING — CARDINALS: Angsman 10-33, Harder 11-30, Trippi 9-26, Mallouf 2-5, Clatt 1-2, Schwall 1-0. **EAGLES:** Van Buren 26-98, Pritchard 16-67, Thompson 11-50, Myers 2-7, Muha 2-3.
PASSING — CARDINALS: Mallouf 3-7 — 35, Trippi 0-2 — 0, Eikenberg 0-2 — 0. **EAGLES:** Thompson 2-12 — 7.

1949 NFL TITLE

DEC. 18, 1949, AT LOS ANGELES

EAGLES 14, RAMS 0

Eagles	0	7	7	0 —	14
Los Angeles	0	0	0	0 —	0

HOW THEY SCORED
Second Quarter
Eagles 7, Rams 0: Tommy Thompson hit Pete Pihos with a 31-yard touchdown pass. Cliff Patton PAT.
Third Quarter
Eagles 14, Rams 0: Leo Skladany blocked Bob Waterfield's punt at the Rams' 5-yard line, recovered at the 2 and scored. Patton PAT.

TEAM STATISTICS

	Eagles	Rams
First downs	17	7
Rushing	12	0
Passing	4	6
Penalty	1	1
Total net yards	342	119
Net yards rushing	274	21
Rushing plays	61	24
Net yards passing	68	98
Comp.-att.-int.	5-9-1	10-27-2
Fumbles-Lost	1-0	4-1

INDIVIDUAL STATISTICS
RUSHING — EAGLES: Van Buren 31-196, Parmer 15-41, Scott 6-23, Thompson 4-7, Ziegler 3-4, Pritchard 1-2, Myers 1-1. **RAMS:** Gehrke 3-13, Smith 6-11, Hoerner 7-10, Waterfield 2-3, Kalmanir 2-0, Hirsch 2-0, Van Brocklin 2-minus 16.
PASSING — EAGLES: Thompson 5-9 — 68. **RAMS:** Waterfield 5-13 — 43, Van Brocklin 5-14 — 55.

1960 NFL TITLE

DEC. 26, 1960, AT FRANKLIN FIELD

EAGLES 17, PACKERS 13

Packers	3	3	0	7 —	13
Eagles	0	10	0	7 —	17

HOW THEY SCORED
First Quarter
Packers 3, Eagles 0: Paul Hornung hits a 20-yard field goal with 8:40 left. Key play: Bill Forester's recovery of a Ted Dean fumble on the Eagles' 22.
Second Quarter
Packers 6, Eagles 0: Hornung hits a FG from 23 yards out with 13:12 left.
Eagles 7, Packers 6: Norm Van Brocklin hits Tommy McDonald for a 35-yard TD pass with 6:52 remaining. Key play: Van Brocklin's 22-yard pass to McDonald from Eagles' 43 on only other play. Bob Walston PAT.
Eagles 10, Packers 6: Walston connects on a 15-yard field goal with 3:12 left. Key plays: Van Brocklin's 41-yard pass to Pete Retzlaff and 22-yard swing pass to Ted Dean on a third-and-7 from Packers' 30.
Fourth Quarter
Packers 13, Eagles 10: Max McGee scores on a 7-yard TD pass from Bart Starr with 13:07 remaining, capping a 12-play, 80-yard drive. Key plays: McGee's 35-yard run out of punt formation on fourth-and-10 from the Packers' 20. Starr's 17-yard pass to Gary Knafelc on a third-and-16. McGee PAT.
Eagles 17, Packers 13: Dean goes around the left end for a 5-yard TD run with 9:39 to go. Key plays: Dean's 58-yard kickoff return, Van Brocklin's 13-yard safety valve pass to Billy Barnes following a 7-yard loss on a sack. Walston PAT.

INDIVIDUAL STATISTICS

Rushing

Packers	Att.	Yds.	Avg.	Lg	TD
Taylor	24	105	4.4	16	0
Hornung	11	61	5.5	16	0
Starr	1	0	0.0	0	0
McGee	1	35	35.0	35	0
Moore	5	22	4.4	12	0
Eagles					
Dean	13	54	4.2	8	1
Barnes	13	42	3.2	7	0
Van Brocklin	2	3	1.5	4	0

Receiving

Packers	No.	Yds.	Avg.	Lg	TD
Knafelc	6	76	12.7	20	0
Hornung	4	14	3.5	8	0
Taylor	6	46	7.7	15	0
Dowler	1	14	14.0	14	0
McGee	2	19	9.5	12	1
Moore	2	9	4.5	5	0
Eagles					
Walston	3	38	12.7	35	0
McDonald	3	90	30.0	t35	1
Retzlaff	1	41	41.0	41	0
Dean	1	22	22.0	22	0
Barnes	1	13	13.0	13	0

Passing

Packers	Cmp.	Att.	Yds.	TD	Int.
Starr	21	34	178	1	0
Hornung	0	1	0	0	0
Eagles					
Van Brocklin	9	20	204	1	1

TEAM STATISTICS

	Packers	Eagles
First downs	22	13
Total net yards	401	296
Offensive plays	77	49
Net yards rushing	223	99
Rushing plays	42	28
Net yards passing	178	197
Sacked-yds. lost	0-0	1-7
Gross yds. passing	178	204
Comp.-att.-int.	21-35-0	9-20-1
Punts-average	5-45.2	6-39.5
Total return yardage	67	101
Penalties-yards	4-27	0-0
Fumbles-Lost	1-1	3-2
PAT made-att.	1-1	2-2
FG made-att.	2-3	1-1

Steve Van Buren signs NFL title game ball for coach Greasy Neale in 1948

1980 NFC CHAMPIONSHIP

JAN. 11, 1981, AT VETERANS STADIUM

EAGLES 20, COWBOYS 7

Dallas	0	7	0	0 —	7
Eagles	7	0	10	3 —	20

HOW THEY SCORED
First Quarter

Eagles 7, Cowboys 0: Wilbert Montgomery scores on the Eagles' second play from scrimmage, a 42-yard run with 12:49 left, after the Cowboys punted following their first possession. Tony Franklin PAT.

Second Quarter

Eagles 7, Cowboys 7: Tony Dorsett scores on a 3-yard run with 5:50 left, capping a 10-play, 68-yard drive. Key plays: Dorsett's 18-yard gain on a pass from the Cowboys' 47 and Dorsett's five-yard gain on a third-and-1 from the Eagles' 11. Rafael Septien PAT.

Third Quarter

Eagles 10, Cowboys 7: Franklin connects on a 26-yard field goal with 7:42 left. Dennis Harrison had recovered a Danny White fumble on the Cowboys' 11-yard line, but the Eagles could gain just 2 yards on three plays.

Eagles 17, Cowboys 7: Leroy Harris scores on a 9-yard run with 1:47 left, capping a six-play, 38-yard drive following Jerry Robinson's 22-yard return of a Dorsett fumble to the Cowboy 38. Key plays: Montgomery's 3-yard gain on a third-and-2 from the Cowboys's 30 and Harris's 12-yard run on first down from the 27. Franklin PAT.

Fourth Quarter

Eagles 20, Cowboys 7: Franklin makes a 20-yard field goal with 2:10 left, capping a 12-play, 62-yard drive covering 6:48. Key plays: Harris' 3-yard run on third-and-1 from the Eagles' 44; a Cowboys offside penalty on third-and-2 from the Dallas 45; Jaworski's 17-yard pass to Keith Krepfle from the Cowboys' 40; Guy Morriss' recovery of Montgomery's fumble at Cowboys' 18 and Montgomery's 11-yard run on second-and-5 from the Cowboys' 18.

TEAM STATISTICS

	Cowboys	Eagles
First downs	11	19
Total net yards	202	340
Offensive plays	55	71
Net yards rushing	86	263
Rushes	22	40
Net yards passing	116	77
Sacked-yds. lost	1-11	2-14
Att.-comp.-int.	32-12-1	29-9-2
Punts-average	7-33.7	4.34.3
Total return yardage	108	114
Punt returns-yds.	3-4	6-69
Kickoff returns-yds.	5-104	2-40
Interception-yds.	2-0	1-5
Penalties-yds.	5-40	5-45
Fumbles-lost	5-3	4-0
PAT made-att.	1-1	2-2
FG made-att.	0-0	2-3
Time of possession	24:01	35:59

INDIVIDUAL STATISTICS

Rushing

Cowboys	Att.	Yds.	Avg.	Lg	TD
Dorsett	13	41	3.2	11	1
Newhouse	7	44	6.3	11	0
Johnson	1	5	5.0	5	0
White	1	-4	-4.0	-4	0
Eagles					
Montgomery	26	194	7.5	55	1
Jaworski	2	2	1.0	3	0
Harris	10	60	6.0	12	1
Harrington	1	4	4.0	4	0
Campfield	1	3	3.0	3	0

Passing

Cowboys	Cmp.	Att.	Yds.	TD	Int.
White	12	31	127	0	1
D.Pearson	0	1	0	0	0
Eagles					
Jaworski	9	29	91	0	2

Receiving

Cowboys	No.	Yds.	Avg.	Lg	TD
Dorsett	3	27	9.0	18	0
P. Pearson	2	32	16.0	23	0
Johnson	2	27	13.5	21	0
D. Pearson	2	15	7.5	12	0
Springs	2	-2	-1.0	4	0
Saldi	1	28	28.0	28	0
Eagles					
Parker	4	31	7.8	15	0
Krepfle	2	22	11.0	17	0
Campfield	1	17	17.0	17	0
Montgomery	1	14	14.0	14	0
Carmichael	1	7	7.0	7	0

Wilbert Montgomery scores on a 42-yard run in the Eagles' 1980 NFC Championship Game victory over Dallas

WILT CHAMBERLAIN'S 100-POINT GAME

WARRIORS 169, KNICKS 147
MARCH 2, 1962, AT HERSHEY, PA.
WARRIORS

	Min	FG-A	FT-A	R	A	PF	Pts.
Arizin	31	7-18	2-2	5	4	0	16
Meschery	40	7-12	2-2	7	3	4	16
Chamberlain	48	36-63	28-32	25	2	2	100
Rodgers	48	1-4	9-12	7	20	5	11
Attles	34	8-8	1-1	5	6	4	17
Conlin	14	0-4	0-0	4	1	1	0
Ruklick	8	0-1	0-2	2	1	2	0
Luckenbill	3	0-0	0-0	1	0	2	0
Larese	14	4-5	1-1	1	2	5	9
Totals	240	63-115	43-52	57	39	25	169

Field Goal Percentage: 54.8
Free Throw Percentage: 82.7
Team Rebounds: 3

NEW YORK

	Min	FG-A	FT-A	R	A	PF	Pts.
Naulls	43	9-22	13-15	7	2	5	31
Green	21	3-7	0-0	7	1	5	6
Imhoff	20	3-7	1-1	6	0	6	7
Guerin	46	13-29	13-17	8	6	5	39
Butler	32	4-13	0-0	7	3	1	8
Buckner	33	16-26	1-1	8	0	4	33
Budd	27	6-8	1-1	10	1	1	13
Butcher	18	3-6	4-6	3	4	5	10
Totals	240	57-118	33-41	56	17	32	147

Field Goal Percentage: 48.3
Free Throw Percentage: 80.5
Team Rebounds: 4.

Warriors	42	37	46	44 —	169
New York	26	42	38	41 —	147

Officials: Willie Smith, Pete D'Ambrosio.
Attendance: 4,124.

WILT: QUARTER BY QUARTER

	Min	FG-A	FT-A	R	A	PF	Pts.
First	12	7-14	9-9	10	0	0	23
Second	12	7-12	4-5	4	1	1	18
Third	12	10-16	8-8	6	1	0	28
Fourth	12	12-21	7-10	5	0	1	31

Wilt Chamberlain's number came up in Hershey on March 2, 1962

1967 NBA CHAMPIONSHIP SERIES

GAME 1
APRIL 14, 1967, AT SAN FRANCISCO
SIXERS 141, WARRIORS 135
SIXERS

	FG-A	FT-A	R	A	PF	Pts.
Walker	8-18	7-12	8	4	5	23
Jackson	3-9	2-3	10	3	6	8
Chamberlain	6-8	4-9	33	10	2	16
Greer	13-29	6-9	10	6	5	32
Jones	13-26	4-5	10	8	3	30
Cunningham	11-22	4-8	5	3	4	26
Guokas	3-4	0-0	3	1	2	6
Totals	57-116	27-46	79	35	27	141

Field Goal Percentage: 49.1
Free Throw Percentage: 58.7

SAN FRANCISCO

	FG-A	FT-A	R	A	PF	Pts.
Barry	15-43	7-8	8	7	3	37
Hetzel	4-12	4-4	5	1	4	12
Thurmond	10-20	4-5	31	3	3	24
Neumann	2-9	3-4	2	1	2	7
Mullins	7-18	2-2	7	6	6	16
Meschery	9-22	2-4	12	0	6	20
Attles	2-5	0-1	7	4	3	4
King	6-11	3-4	5	3	2	15
Olsen	0-0	0-2	3	0	2	0
Totals	55-140	25-34	80	25	31	135

Field Goal Percentage: 39.3
Free Throw Percentage: 73.5

Sixers	43	30	34	21	13 — 141
San Francisco	30	35	28	33	7 — 135

Officials: Earl Strom and Richie Powers.
Attendance: 9,283.

GAME 2
APRIL 16, 1967, AT CONVENTION HALL
SIXERS 126, WARRIORS 95
SAN FRANCISCO

	FG-A	FT-A	R	A	PF	Pts.
Barry	10-28	10-12	10	1	4	30
Hetzel	1-4	1-1	2	0	1	3
Thurmond	3-14	1-3	29	2	0	7
Neumann	2-7	1-2	1	2	3	5
Mullins	6-16	0-1	3	3	2	12
King	4-15	3-5	10	6	1	11
Meschery	4-13	2-2	7	1	5	10
Attles	1-4	0-0	0	2	2	2
Lee	4-17	1-3	8	1	4	9
Ellis	1-4	0-0	1	2	2	2
Warlick	0-0	0-0	0	0	0	0
Olsen	2-7	0-0	5	0	4	4
Totals	38-129	19-29	76	20	24	95

FG Pct.: 29.5. FT Pct.: 65.5.

SIXERS

	FG-A	FT-A	R	A	PF	Pts.
Walker	7-17	4-4	8	3	4	18
Jackson	2-10	2-4	15	1	3	6
Chamberlain	4-10	2-17	38	10	2	10
Greer	13-30	4-4	12	9	4	30
Jones	8-16	0-1	5	3	5	16
Cunningham	13-24	2-4	6	2	4	28
Guokas	4-5	0-0	5	3	2	8
Gambee	2-3	2-2	2	1	1	6
Weiss	2-3	0-0	2	2	1	4
Totals	55-118	16-36	93	34	26	126

FG Pct.: 46.6. FT Pct.: 44.4.

San Francisco	17	29	23	26 —	95
Sixers	26	31	28	41 —	126

Officials: Norm Drucker, Mendy Rudolph.
Attendance: 9,426.

GAME 3
APRIL 18, 1967, AT SAN FRANCISCO
WARRIORS 130, SIXERS 124
SAN FRANCISCO

	FG-A	FT-A	R	A	PF	Pts.
Attles	2-4	0-0	5	1	5	4
Barry	22-48	11-19	12	5	4	55
King	11-19	6-6	9	6	4	28
Lee	4-9	0-1	8	1	4	8
Meschery	5-13	0-0	7	2	5	10
Mullins	3-8	0-0	4	5	4	6
Neumann	0-3	2-2	1	3	3	2
Thurmond	6-13	5-6	25	4	5	17
Totals	53-117	24-34	71	27	34	130

Field Goal Percentage: 45.3
Free Throw Percentage: 70.6

SIXERS

	FG-A	FT-A	R	A	PF	Pts.
Chamberlain	12-23	2-9	26	5	3	26
Cunningham	7-14	5-10	5	3	6	19
Gambee	2-4	4-4	3	0	3	8
Greer	6-19	9-10	7	4	3	21
Guokas	1-4	0-0	0	1	4	2
Jackson	4-11	1-2	11	2	4	9
Jones	8-18	2-3	1	7	4	18
Walker	7-16	7-7	6	6	3	21
Totals	47-109	30-45	59	28	30	124

Field Goal Percentage: 43.1
Free Throw Percentage: 66.7

Sixers	35	28	29	32 —	124
San Francisco	32	37	29	32 —	130

Officials: Earl Strom and John Vanak.
Attendance: 14,773.

1967 NBA CHAMPIONSHIP SERIES

GAME 4
APRIL 20, 1967, AT SAN FRANCISCO
SIXERS 122, WARRIORS 108

SAN FRANCISCO

	FG-A	FT-A	R	A	PF	Pts.
Attles	1-5	1-3	7	4	5	3
Barry	17-41	9-12	7	3	5	43
King	9-20	5-7	6	3	2	23
Lee	5-14	1-4	18	3	1	11
Meschery	1-7	0-0	5	0	6	2
Mullins	6-15	2-2	6	2	6	14
Neumann	1-5	2-3	1	0	1	4
Thurmond	4-18	0-2	25	5	2	8
Totals	44-125	20-33	75	20	28	108

Field Goal Percentage: 35.2
Free Throw Percentage: 60.6

SIXERS

	FG-A	FT-A	R	A	PF	Pts.
Chamberlain	3-6	4-9	27	8	2	10
Cunningham	7-21	1-1	9	3	5	15
Greer	15-35	8-9	9	4	3	38
Guokas	1-5	2-4	5	3	4	4
Jackson	3-5	2-2	4	3	4	8
Jones	6-10	2-2	5	2	4	14
Walker	10-18	13-18	11	2	1	33
Totals	45-100	32-45	68	25	23	122

Field Goal Percentage: 45.0
Free Throw Percentage: 71.1

Sixers	34	26	31	31	— 122
San Francisco	27	22	29	30	— 108

Officials: Mendy Rudolph and Joe Gushue.
Attendance: 15,117.

GAME 5
APRIL 23, 1967, AT CONVENTION HALL
WARRIORS 117, SIXERS 109

SIXERS

	FG-A	FT-A	R	A	PF	Pts.
Walker	6-16	13-16	13	3	5	25
Jackson	4-9	3-4	14	0	4	11
Chamberlain	9-15	2-12	24	4	4	20
Greer	7-19	6-7	5	7	6	20
Jones	7-22	2-2	1	6	2	16
Cunningham	6-13	1-5	7	4	3	13
Guokas	1-3	0-0	1	1	0	2
Gambee	1-1	0-0	1	1	1	2
Totals	41-98	27-46	66	26	25	109

Field Goal Percentage: 41.8
Free Throw Percentage: 58.7

SAN FRANCISCO

	FG-A	FT-A	R	A	PF	Pts.
Barry	14-37	8-8	10	2	4	36
Hetzel	6-13	2-3	6	0	3	14
Thurmond	7-21	3-7	28	1	4	17
Attles	2-3	0-0	9	6	4	4
Neumann	0-1	0-0	1	3	1	0
King	6-16	2-3	5	2	4	14
Mullins	4-12	5-6	3	5	3	13
Lee	1-2	0-0	0	1	0	2
Meschery	7-14	3-4	7	2	6	17
Totals	47-119	23-31	69	22	29	117

Field Goal Percentage: 39.5
Free Throw Percentage: 74.2

Sixers	32	32	32	13	— 109
San Francisco	31	30	23	33	— 117

Officials: Mendy Rudolph, Norm Drucker.
Attendance: 10,229.

GAME 6
APRIL 24, 1967, AT SAN FRANCISCO
SIXERS 125, WARRIORS 122

SIXERS

	FG-A	FT-A	R	A	PF	Pts.
Chamberlain	8-13	8-16	23	4	3	24
Cunningham	4-13	9-13	2	3	5	17
Gambee	0-2	0-0	0	0	1	0
Greer	5-16	5-7	5	7	2	15
Guokas	4-6	1-2	1	1	1	9
Jackson	5-13	3-6	21	2	4	13
Jones	8-18	11-15	1	6	4	27
Walker	8-17	4-5	7	2	5	20
Totals	42-98	41-64	60	25	25	125

Field Goal Percentage: 42.9
Free Throw Percentage: 64.1

SAN FRANCISCO

	FG-A	FT-A	R	A	PF	Pts.
Attles	3-4	0-0	5	3	5	6
Barry	16-38	12-13	6	2	5	44
Hetzel	4-11	0-0	3	1	3	8
King	9-16	1-1	14	7	3	19
Meschery	3-9	0-0	5	2	5	6
Lee	1-2	0-0	2	1	4	2
Mullins	9-19	5-7	3	3	3	23
Neumann	1-1	0-0	0	4	2	2
Thurmond	4-13	4-8	22	5	6	12
Totals	50-113	22-29	64	28	36	122

Field Goal Percentage: 44.2
Free Throw Percentage: 75.9

Sixers	43	25	29	29	— 125
San Francisco	41	31	30	20	— 122

Officials: Earl Strom, John Vanak.
Attendance: 15,612.

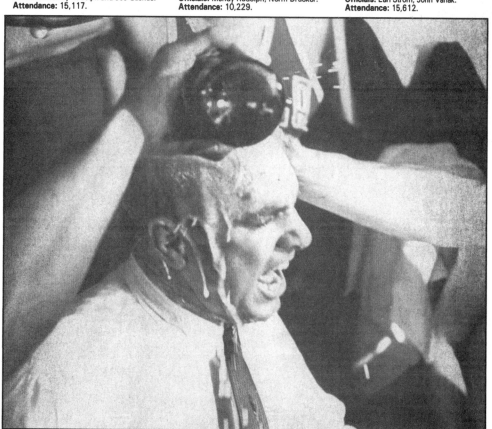

Coach Alex Hannum gets doused with champagne after the Sixers won the 1967 NBA Championship in San Francisco

123

1983 NBA CHAMPIONSHIP SERIES

GAME 1: SIXERS 113, LAKERS 107
MAY 22, 1983, AT THE SPECTRUM

LOS ANGELES

	Min	FG-A	FT-A	R	A	PF	Pts.
Rambis	19	0-4	5-6	6	0	2	5
Wilkes	34	8-15	0-0	5	1	4	16
Jabbar	39	8-15	4-6	4	3	4	20
Nixon	41	12-23	2-3	4	3	3	26
E. Johnson	43	8-15	3-3	9	11	4	19
Cooper	28	4-11	3-4	5	1	5	11
Landsberger	19	1-6	2-2	10	0	4	4
D. Jones	9	0-3	0-2	2	0	1	0
C. Johnson	7	3-4	0-0	2	1	2	6
Mix	1	0-0	0-0	0	0	0	0
Totals	240	44-96	19-26	47	20	29	107

SIXERS

	Min	FG-A	FT-A	R	A	PF	Pts.
Erving	39	8-18	4-6	10	9	2	20
Iavaroni	26	3-4	0-0	7	0	2	6
Malone	41	9-20	9-12	18	0	3	27
Cheeks	25	5-11	0-0	3	5	4	10
Toney	39	9-18	7-7	1	4	3	25
Richardson	31	7-12	1-2	4	3	4	15
Jones	28	2-7	0-2	4	5	2	4
C. Johnson	9	2-5	0-0	5	0	2	4
Edwards	1	0-1	2-2	1	0	0	2
R. Johnson	1	0-0	0-0	0	0	0	0
Totals	240	45-96	23-31	53	26	22	113

Los Angeles   20 37 26 24 — 107
Sixers   30 24 31 28 — 113

Team rebounds: Los Angeles 9, Sixers 9.
Three-point attempts: Los Angeles 0-2 (Cooper 0-1, Wilkes 0-1), Sixers 0-0.
Blocked shots: Los Angeles 8 (Jabbar 3, Lansberger 2, Rambis 2, Cooper 1), Sixers 13 (Erving 5, Jones 4, Malone 3, Iavaroni 1).
Steals: Los Angeles 7 (Cooper 2, Nixon 2, Wilkes 1, E. Johnson 1, C. Johnson 1), Sixers 11 (Richardson 4, Cheeks 2, Malone 2, Iavaroni 1, Erving 1, B. Jones 1).
Turnovers: Los Angeles 15, Sixers 14.
Officials: Jack Madden and Ed Rush.
Time: 2:23. **Attendance:** 18,482.

GAME 2: SIXERS 103, LAKERS 93
MAY 26, 1983, AT THE SPECTRUM

LOS ANGELES

	Min	FG-A	FT-A	R	A	PF	Pts.
Rambis	21	4-7	1-1	5	0	3	9
Wilkes	41	8-21	1-2	7	2	2	17
Jabbar	34	11-17	1-2	4	3	5	23
Nixon	38	4-13	0-0	2	6	4	8
E. Johnson	44	6-14	0-0	8	13	3	12
Landsberger	12	1-2	0-0	3	0	3	2
Cooper	28	6-7	0-0	4	1	4	12
McAdoo	19	4-10	0-0	7	1	5	10
C. Johnson	2	0-0	0-0	0	0	0	0
McGee	1	0-0	0-0	0	0	0	0
Totals	240	44-91	3-5	40	26	29	93

SIXERS

	Min	FG-A	FT-A	R	A	PF	Pts.
Erving	39	6-17	2-2	7	2	3	14
Iavaroni	29	3-6	3-4	6	2	2	9
Malone	31	8-10	8-13	12	1	5	24
Cheeks	37	8-14	3-5	2	8	0	19
Toney	37	7-18	5-6	4	5	2	19
B. Jones	28	6-11	2-2	5	2	0	14
Richardson	21	1-4	0-0	5	1	4	2
Cureton	17	1-3	0-0	3	1	3	2
Edwards	1	0-0	0-0	0	0	0	0
Totals	240	40-83	23-32	44	22	16	103

Los Angeles   29 26 20 18 — 93
Sixers   26 25 28 24 — 103

Team rebounds: Los Angeles 6, Sixers 11.
Three-point attempts: Los Angeles 2-7 (McAdoo 2-3, Nixon 0-2, E. Johnson 0-1, Landsberger 0-1), Sixers 0-1 (Toney 0-1).
Blocked shots: Los Angeles 10 (Jabbar 3, McAdoo 2, Wilkes 2, C. Johnson 1, Nixon 1, Rambis 1), Sixers 6 (Erving 3, B. Jones 3).
Steals: Los Angeles 10 (Wilkes 3, E. Johnson 3, McAdoo 2, Rambis 1, Jabbar 1), Sixers 10 (Cheeks 3, Toney 2, B. Jones 2, Cureton 2, Erving 1).
Turnovers: Los Angeles 20, Sixers 18.
Officials: Darrell Garretson, John Vanak.
Time: 2:23. **Attendance:** 18,482.

GAME 3: SIXERS 111, LAKERS 94
MAY 29, 1983, AT LOS ANGELES

SIXERS

	Min	FG-A	FT-A	R	A	PF	Pts.
Erving	39	8-16	5-7	12	3	3	21
Iavaroni	26	2-2	0-2	6	4	5	4
Malone	40	10-19	8-13	19	6	4	28
Cheeks	43	6-12	0-2	3	5	3	12
Toney	32	8-19	5-8	2	5	4	21
C. Johnson	10	1-5	0-0	2	1	0	2
Richardson	20	1-7	0-0	2	1	1	2
Jones	26	7-12	3-3	7	2	3	17
Cureton	2	0-0	0-0	0	0	0	0
Edwards	1	0-0	0-0	0	0	0	0
McNamara	1	2-2	0-0	1	0	0	4
Totals	240	45-94	21-35	54	27	23	111

LOS ANGELES

	Min	FG-A	FT-A	R	A	PF	Pts.
Rambis	19	5-5	0-0	2	1	4	10
Wilkes	43	10-20	0-0	6	3	4	20
Jabbar	42	8-20	7-8	15	3	4	23
E. Johnson	44	3-12	12-13	7	13	4	18
Nixon	31	1-6	5-8	2	5	3	7
McAdoo	23	5-12	2-2	7	0	3	12
Cooper	30	2-6	0-0	2	1	6	4
Landsberger	4	0-0	0-0	0	0	3	0
C. Johnson	3	0-1	0-0	0	0	0	0
McGee	1	0-0	0-0	0	0	0	0
Totals	240	34-82	26-31	41	26	31	94

Sixers   21 28 23 39 — 111
Los Angeles   32 20 20 22 — 94

Team rebounds: Sixers 12, Los Angeles 9.
Three-point attempts: Sixers 0-1 (Jones 0-1), Los Angeles 0-3 (C. Johnson 0-1, E. Johnson 0-1, McAdoo 0-1).
Blocked shots: Sixers 2 (Erving 1, Richardson 1), Los Angeles 8 (Wilkes 3, Abdul-Jabbar 2, Rambis 2, E. Johnson 1).
Steals: Sixers 14 (Cheeks 4, Malone 3, Erving 2, Toney 2, Johnson 1, Richardson 1, Jones 1), Los Angeles 12 (Wilkes 3, McAdoo 3, E. Johnson 2, Nixon 2, Rambis 1, Abdul-Jabbar 1).
Turnovers: Sixers 19, Los Angeles 25.
Officials: Jake O'Donnell and Jess Kersey.
Time: 2:26. **Attendance:** 17,505.

GAME 4: SIXERS 115, LAKERS 108
MAY 31, 1983, AT LOS ANGELES

SIXERS

	Min	FG-A	FT-A	R	A	PF	Pts.
Erving	36	8-13	5-5	5	6	3	21
Iavaroni	18	2-5	0-2	3	2	6	4
Malone	45	9-22	6-9	23	1	3	24
Cheeks	38	7-10	6-8	1	7	3	20
Toney	39	6-16	11-12	2	9	2	23
C. Johnson	19	2-3	0-0	2	0	4	4
Richardson	20	2-5	2-2	2	2	3	6
B. Jones	25	6-7	1-2	3	2	4	13
Totals	240	42-81	31-40	41	29	28	115

LOS ANGELES

	Min	FG-A	FT-A	R	A	PF	Pts.
Rambis	26	3-9	1-2	5	2	4	7
Wilkes	39	9-20	3-5	5	1	4	21
Jabbar	40	10-15	8-10	7	3	5	28
Cooper	40	5-11	2-2	3	4	5	13
E. Johnson	48	8-21	11-12	7	13	5	27
McGee	18	3-9	0-0	7	1	3	6
Landsberger	21	2-2	0-0	7	2	2	4
D. Jones	8	1-5	0-0	2	0	3	2
Totals	240	41-92	25-31	43	26	31	108

Sixers   24 27 31 33 — 115
Los Angeles   26 39 28 15 — 108

Team rebounds: Sixers 9, Los Angeles 12.
Three-point attempts: Sixers 0-1 (Toney 0-1), Los Angeles 1-3 (Cooper 1-2, E. Johnson 0-1).
Blocked shots: Sixers 11 (Malone 3, Erving 2, Iavaroni 2, B. Jones 2, C. Johnson 1, Toney 1), Los Angeles 3 (Abdul-Jabbar 1, E. Johnson 1, Rambis 1).
Steals: Sixers 9 (B. Jones 4, Cheeks 2, Erving 1, Malone 1, Toney 1), Los Angeles 7 (Cooper 4, Wilkes 1, Abdul-Jabbar 1, E. Johnson 1).
Turnovers: Sixers 17, Los Angeles 20.
Officials: Earl Strom and Hugh Evans.
Time: 2:37. **Attendance:** 17,505.

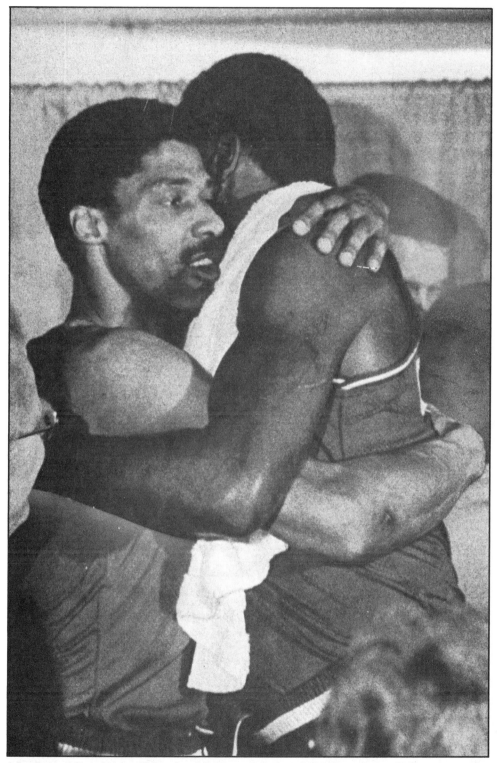

Julius Erving (left) and Moses Malone hug following presentation of NBA Championship Trophy

1974 STANLEY CUP FINALS

GAME 1: BRUINS 3, FLYERS 2
(MAY 7, 1974, AT BOSTON)

Flyers	0	1	1—2
Boston	2	0	1—3

FIRST PERIOD — 1, Boston, Cashman 4 (Orr, Vadnais), 12:08; 2, Boston, Sheppard 10 (Forbes, Smith), 13.01. Penalties — Sims, Boston (elbowing), 1:07; Dupont, Flyers (holding), 3:24; Barber, Flyers (interference), 10:52; Smith, Boston (tripping), 15:00; Dupont, Flyers and Hodge, Boston (roughing), 17:51; Van Impe, Flyers (hooking) 18:28.

SECOND PERIOD — 2, Flyers, Kindrachuk 4 (Joe Watson, Saleski) 7:47. Penalties — Bladon, Flyers (holding), 4:45; Van Impe, Flyers (high sticking and fighting) Cashman, Boston (high sticking and fighting) and Jim Watson, Flyers (high sticking and fighting), 6:46; Clarke, Flyers and Sheppard, Boston (slashing), 10:20; Dupont, Flyers (hooking) 16:31.

THIRD PERIOD — 4, Flyers, Clarke 3 (Joe Watson, Nolet), 5:32; 5, Boston, Orr 2 (Hodge, Cashman), 19:30. Penalties — Clarke, Flyers (slashing) Vadnais, Boston (hooking), 11:07.

Shots on Goal — Flyers 9-12-7 — 28. Boston 11-2-8 — 31.

GAME 2: FLYERS 3, BRUINS 2
(MAY 9, 1974, AT BOSTON)
(Overtime)

Flyers	0	1	1	1—3
Boston	2	0	0	0—2

FIRST PERIOD — 1, Boston, Cashman 8 (Esposito, Vadnais), 14:24; 2, Boston, Esposito 8 (Hodge, Cashman), 17:22. Penalties — Savard, Boston (tripping), 4:06; Cashman, Boston (elbowing), 7:43; Bladon, Flyers (interference) Shultz (elbowing and fighting) and O'Reilly, Boston (fighting), 12:21.

SECOND PERIOD — 3, Flyers, Clarke 4 (Flett, Schultz), 1:00. Penalties — Parent, Flyers (interference), 10:49; Kindrachuk, Flyers and Savard, Boston (elbowing and roughing), 14:42; Smith, Boston (holding), 18:13; Kindrachuk, Flyers and Gilbert, Boston (roughing) and Cashman, Boston (game misconduct), 20:00.

THIRD PERIOD — 4, Flyers, Dupont 3 (MacLeish, Clarke), 19:02. Penalties — Saleski, Flyers and Savard, Boston (roughing), 6:03; Jim Watson, Flyers (holding), 10:30; Esposito, Boston (tripping), 10:46; Jim Watson, Flyers (holding), 14:13.

OVERTIME — 5, Flyers, Clarke 6 (Flett, Schultz), 12:01.

Shots on Goal — Flyers 12-5-7-6 — 30. Boston 10-14-8-7 — 39. Attendance — 15,003.

GAME 3: FLYERS 4, BRUINS 1
(MAY 12, 1974, AT THE SPECTRUM)

Boston	1	0	0—1
Flyers	2	0	2—4

FIRST PERIOD — 1, Boston, Bucyk 6 (Sheppard, Orr), 1:03; 2, Flyers, Bladon 4 (Clarke, MacLeish), 10:27; 3 Flyers, Crisp 2 (unassisted), 15.43. Penalties — Vadnais, Boston (elbowing), 3:52; Bladon, Flyers (elbowing) 5:25; Joe Watson, Flyers (tripping), 7:30; Cashman, Boston (interference), 9:36; Schmautz, Boston (interference), 10:03; Van Impe, Flyers (tripping), 13:19; Saleski, Flyers (holding), 16:34.

SECOND PERIOD — None. Penalties — Orr, Boston and Clarke, Flyers (high sticking), 2:24; Cashman, Boston (interference), 2:57; Bladon, Flyers (hooking), 3:43; MacLeish, Flyers (hooking) 9:50; Hodge, Boston (holding), 9:35; Jim Watson, Flyers (holding) 18:49.

THIRD PERIOD — 4, Flyers, Kindrachuck 5 (Saleski, Barber), 7:53; 5, Flyers, Lonsberry 4 (MacLeish), 14:19. Penalties — None.

Shots on Goal — Boston 11-6-8 — 25. Flyers 7-12-8 — 27. Attendance — 17,007.

GAME 4: FLYERS 4, BRUINS 2
(MAY 14, 1974, AT THE SPECTRUM)

Boston	2	0	0—2
Flyers	2	0	2—4

FIRST PERIOD — 1, Flyers, MacLeish 12 (Bladon), 4:40; 2, Flyers, Schultz 2 (Saleski, Van Impe), 5:30; 3, Boston, Esposito 9, (Bucyk, Hodge), 7:12; 4, Boston, Savard 3 (Orr, Vadnais), 11:24. Penalties — Savard, Boston and Kindrachuk, Flyers (fighting), 2:43; Leach, Flyers (holding), 3:21; Joe Watson, Flyers (holding), 6:09; Cashman, Boston and Jim Watson, Flyers (high sticking and fighting), 6:17; Schultz, Flyers and O'Reilly, Boston (fighting), 7:56; Esposito, Boston (slashing), Smith, Boston (high sticking), Bladon, Flyers (elbowing) and Saleski, Flyers (roughing), 9:43; Vadnais, Boston (cross-checking) and Flett, Flyers (slashing), 13:03; Leduc, Boston (holding) and Clarke, Flyers (slashing), 13:16; O'Reilly, Boston (charging), 16:10; Shultz, Flyers and Savard, Boston (roughing), 19:15.

SECOND PERIOD — None. Penalties — MacLeish, Flyers (holding), 6:19; Schmautz, Boston and Joe Watson, Flyers (roughing), 11:48; Esposito, Boston (roughing) and Bladon, Flyers (elbowing), 19:26.

THIRD PERIOD — 5, Flyers, Barber 3 (Lonsberry, Jim Watson), 14:25; 6, Flyers, Dupont 4 (Clarke, Crisp), 16:40. Penalties — Marcotte, Boston and Joe Watson, Flyers (roughing), 6:16.

Shots on Goal — Boston 11-8-11 — 30. Flyers 9-9-13 — 31. Attendance — 17,007.

GAME 5: BRUINS 5, FLYERS 1
(MAY 16, 1974, AT BOSTON)

Flyers	0	1	0—1
Boston	1	2	2—5

FIRST PERIOD — 1, Boston, Sheppard 11 (Orr), 8;14. Penalties — Schultz, Flyers and Vadnais, Boston (fighting), 0:24; Schmautz, Boston (cross-checking); 0:45; Bladon, Flyers (holding), 1:11; Van Impe, Flyers (roughing) and Cashman, Boston (high sticking), 1:37; Dupont, Flyers (elbowing), 2:28; Joe Watson, Flyers (tripping), 4:00; Orr, Boston (high sticking), 6:01; Dupont, Flyers (fighting) and O'Reilly, Boston (kneeing and fighting), 7:58; Jim Watson, Flyers and Savard, Boston (fighting), 11:15; Dupont, Flyers (holding), 15:47; Lonsberry, Flyers (hooking), 18:21.

SECOND PERIOD — 2, Flyers, Clement 1 (Flett, Van Impe), 6:04; 3, Boston, Orr 3 (Shepard, Bucyk), 12:06; 4, Boston, Orr 4 (Hodge, Smith), 16:55. Penalties — Cashman, Boston and Flett, Flyers (roughing), 3:52; Esposito, Boston and Bladon, Flyers (roughing), 5:00; Esposito, Boston and Jim Watson, Flyers (high sticking), 13:40; Joe Watson, Flyers (holding), 14:23; Cashman, Boston and Schultz, Flyers (fighting), 17:48; Dupont, Flyers (butt ending), 19:16.

THIRD PERIOD — 5, Boston, Hodge (Shepard, Bucyk), 0:39; 6, Boston, Marcotte 4 (Savard, O'Reilly), 18:59. Penalties — Cashman, Boston (spearing), 4:30; Clarke, Flyers and Vadnais, Boston (high sticking), 4:37; Crisp, Flyers and Edestrand, Boston (high sticking), 6:47; Smith, Boston (slashing), 7:02; O'Reilly, Boston (hooking), 10:37; Schultz, Flyers (roughing and misconduct) Schmautz, Boston (roughing and game misconduct) and Vadnais, Boston (roughing), 13:58; Clarke, Flyers (cross-checking), 14:47; Leduc, Boston, Vadnais, Boston, Cowick, Flyers, Bladon, Flyers (fighting), 18:47.

Shots on Goal — Flyers 8-9-10 — 27. Boston 17-9-12 — 38.

GAME 6: FLYERS 1, BRUINS 0
(MAY 19, 1974, AT THE SPECTRUM)

Boston	0	0	0—0
Flyers	1	0	1—1

FIRST PERIOD — 1, Flyers, MacLeish 13 (Dupont), 14:38. Penalties — Dupont, Flyers (interference), 0:32; Forbes, Boston (roughing), Cowick, Flyers (elbowing) and Clement, Flyers (roughing), 10:18; O'Reilly, Boston (hooking), 13:50; Orr, Boston and Clarke, Flyers (roughing), 14:22.

SECOND PERIOD — No scoring. Penalties — Dupont, Flyers (tripping), 4:01; Hodge, Boston (hooking), 1:13; Joe Watson, Flyers (holding), 9:22; Joe Watson, Flyers (tripping), 15:02; Vadnais, Boston (tripping), 17:46.

THIRD PERIOD — No scoring. Penalties — O'Reilly, Boston (hooking), 8:12; Schultz, Flyers (holding), 11:15; Bucyk, Boston (tripping), 14:54; Orr, Boston (holding); 17:38.

Shots on Goal — Boston 16-9-5 — 30. Flyers 8-14-4 — 26. Attendance — 17,007.

Flyers mob Rich MacLeish after his Cup-winning goal

1975 STANLEY CUP FINALS

GAME 1: FLYERS 4, SABRES 1
(MAY 15, 1975, AT THE SPECTRUM)

Buffalo	0	0	1 — 1
Flyers	0	0	4 — 4

FIRST PERIOD — None. Penalties — Saleski, Flyers (elbowing), 3:17; Hajt, Buffalo (tripping), 4:25; Perreault, Buffalo (hooking), 7:36; Dornhoefer, Flyers (cross-checking), 11:39; Dupont, Flyers (cross-checking), 11:39; Spencer, Buffalo (high sticking), 18:43; MacLeish, Flyers (high sticking), 18:43.

SECOND PERIOD — None. Penalties — Bladon, Flyers (hooking), 2:56; Dornhoefer, Flyers (elbowing) 5:38; Gare, Buffalo (roughing) 9:47; Schultz, Flyers (slashing, roughing), 9:47.

THIRD PERIOD — 1, Flyers, Barber 5 (Van Impe, MacLeish), 3:42; 2, Flyers, Lonsberry 3 (Bladon, Clarke), 7:29; 3, Buffalo, Martin 6 (Lorentz), 11:07; 4, Flyers, Clarke 3 (unassisted), 11:41; 5, Barber 6 (Clarke), 19:02. Penalties — Schoenfeld, Buffalo (holding), 4:28; Bladon, Flyers (interference) 9:20; Korab, Buffalo (slashing), 11:36.

Shots on Goal — Buffalo 8-14-6 — 28. Flyers 3-8-13 — 22. **Attendance** — 17,077.

GAME 2: FLYERS 2, SABRES 1
(MAY 18, 1975, AT THE SPECTRUM)

Buffalo	0	0	1 — 1
Flyers	0	1	1 — 2

FIRST PERIOD — None. Penalties — Clarke, Flyers (cross-checking), 0:52; Martin, Buffalo (holding), 8:07; Joe Watson, Flyers (tripping), 11:26; Bladon, Flyers (elbowing), 13:56; Carriere, Buffalo (charging), 19:01; Luce, Bufalo (misconduct), 19:05.

SECOND PERIOD — 1, Flyers, Leach 6 (Clarke, Lonsberry), 8:24. Penalties — Bladon, Flyers (charging), 3:57; Robert, Buffalo (roughing) 17:05; Saleski, Flyers (roughing), 17:05.

THIRD PERIOD — 2, Buffalo, Korab 2 (Lorentz, Spencer), 2:18; 3, Flyers, Clarke 4 (Barber, MacLeish), 6:43. Penalites — Luce, Buffalo (hooking), 6:15.

Shots on Goal — Buffalo 8-8-3 — 19. Flyers 12-5-7 — 24. **Attendance** — 17,077.

GAME 3: SABRES 5, FLYERS 4
(MAY 20, 1975, AT BUFFALO)
(Overtime)

Flyers	3	1	0	0 — 4
Buffalo	2	1	1	1 — 5

FIRST PERIOD — 1, Flyers, Dornhoefer 4 (Barber), 0:39; 2, Flyers, Saleski 2 (Ramsey), 3:09; 3, Buffalo, Gare 6 (Ramsey, Luce); 11:46; 4, Buffalo, Martin 7 (Guevremont), 12:03; 5, Flyers, MacLeish 11 (Barber), 14:13. Penalties — Kelly, Buffalo (slashing), 8:07; Dupont, Flyers (charging) 10:47; Schultz, Flyers (roughing), 15:03; Gare, Buffalo (roughing), 15:03.

SECOND PERIOD — 6, Buffalo, Luce 4 (Korab), 0:29; 7, Flyers, Leach 7 (Crisp, Kelly), 14:30. Penalties — Dornhoefer, Flyers (elbowing), 5:15; Schoenfeld, Buffalo (interference), 7:48; Guevremont, Buffalo (tripping), 11:57.

THIRD PERIOD — 8, Buffalo, Hajt 1 (Martin, Luce), 9:56; Penalties — Van Impe, Flyers (tripping), 1:59; Dudley, Buffalo (roughing), 8:19; Dornhoefer, Flyers (roughing), 8:19.

OVERTIME — 9, Robert 5 (Perrault, Martin), 18:29. Penalties — Dupont, Flyers (hooking), 4:18.

Shots on Goal — Flyers 6-14-7-6 — 33. Buffalo 18-9-10-7 — 46. **Attendance** — 15,863.

GAME 4: SABRES 4, FLYERS 2
(MAY 22, 1975, AT BUFFALO)

Flyers	1	1	0 — 2
Buffalo	0	3	1 — 4

FIRST PERIOD — None. 1, Flyers, Dupont 3 (Kelly, Crisp), 11:28. Penalties — Van Impe, Flyers (interference), 3:26; Perreault, Buffalo (tripping), 4:16; Saleski, Flyers (holding), 4:29; Robert, Buffalo (hooking), 18:15.

SECOND PERIOD — 2, Buffalo, Korab 3 (Robert, Martin), 3:46; 3, Flyers, Lonsberry 4 (MacLeish), 4:20; 4, Buffalo, Perreault 6 (Robert, Martin), 10:07. Penalties — Saleski, Flyers (interference), 0:17; Dupont, Flyers (charging), 2:26; Van Impe, Flyers (roughing), 3:26; Dudley, Buffalo (roughing), 3:26; Schultz, Flyers (fighting), 5:38; Schoenfeld, Buffalo (fighting), 5:38; Dudley, Buffalo (fighting), 5:38; Kelly, Flyers (fighting), 5:38; Lonsberry, Flyers (cross-checking), 9:15; Guevremont, Buffalo (holding) 12:14; Perreault, Buffalo (holding), 18:42.

THIRD PERIOD — 6, Buffalo, Gare 7 (Luce), 19:28. Penalties — None.

Shots on Goal — Flyers 7-11-7 — 25. Buffalo 8-14-5 — 27. **Attendance** — 15,863.

GAME 5: FLYERS 5, SABRES 1
(MAY 25, 1975, AT THE SPECTRUM)

Buffalo	0	0	1 — 1
Flyers	3	2	0 — 5

FIRST PERIOD — 1, Flyers, Schultz 1 (Saleski, Kindrachuk), 3:12; 2, Flyers, Schultz 2 (Van Impe), 5:38; 3, Flyers, Kelly 2 (Crisp, Joe Watson), 12:50. Penalties — Goodenough, Flyers (interference), 10:17; Dornhoefer, Flyers (tripping), 14:47; Spencer, Buffalo (tripping) 17:16.

SECOND PERIOD — 4, Flyers, Leach 8 (Barber, Goodenough), 1:55; 5, Flyers, Schultz 2 (Goodenough, Harris), 9:56. Penalties — Guevremont, Buffalo (hooking) 0:40; Dornhoefer, Flyers (interference), 2:16.

THIRD PERIOD — 6, Buffalo, Luce 5 (Ramsey). Penalties — Dornhoefer, Flyers (holding), 14:50; Lorentz, Buffalo (holding), 17:50.

Shots on Goal — Buffalo 10-6-8 — 24. Flyers 9-7-10 — 26. **Attendance** — 17,077.

GAME 6: FLYERS 2, SABRES 0
(MAY 27, 1975, AT BUFFALO)

Flyers	0	0	2 — 2
Buffalo	0	0	0 — 0

FIRST PERIOD — None. Penalties — Korab, Buffalo (charging), 2:29; Clement, Flyers (holding), 8:53; Dupont, Flyers (holding), 11:41; Van Impe, Flyers (interference), 14:19; Robert, Buffalo (holding), 15:24; Schultz, Flyers (interference), 19:21.

SECOND PERIOD — None. Penalties — Korab, Buffalo (holding), 5:19; Harris, Flyers (cross-checking), 7:29; Guevremont, Buffalo (holding), 13:53.

THIRD PERIOD — 1, Flyers, Kelly 3 (Leach, Jim Watson), 0:11; 2, Flyers, Clement 1 (Kindrachuk), 17:13. Penalties — Martin, Buffalo (tripping) 1:11; Carriere, Buffalo (slashing), 3:25; Kindrachuk, Flyers (holding), 10:32.

Shots on Goal — Flyers 6-12-13 — 31. Buffalo 13-13-6 — 32. **Attendance** — 15,863.

Fans surround flatbed trucks carrying Flyers during the 1975 Stanley Cup championship parade through Center City

Eddie Pinckney snips down net after Villanova's 66-64 victory over Georgetown in 1985 NCAA Championship game

1954 FINAL FOUR

NATIONAL SEMIFINAL
MARCH 19, 1954, AT KANSAS CITY
LA SALLE 69, PENN ST. 54

LA SALLE	FG	FT	Pt	PENN STATE	FG	FT	Pt
Singley	4	2	10	Weidenhammer	1	1	3
Maples	3	1	7	Haag	2	0	4
Blatcher	7	5	19	Fields	2	1	5
Gola	5	9	19	Brewer	3	0	6
O'Malley	3	3	9	Arnelle	5	8	18
O'Hara	2	1	5	Rohrland	2	0	4
				Blocker	2	0	4
				Sherry	1	4	6
				Edwards	2	0	4
Totals	24	21	69	Totals	20	14	54

NATIONAL CHAMPIONSHIP
MARCH 20, 1954, AT KANSAS CITY
LA SALLE 92, BRADLEY 76

LA SALLE	FG	FT-A	Pt	BRADLEY	FG	FT-A	Pt
Singley	8	7-10	23	Petersen	4	2-2	10
Greenberg	2	1-2	5	Babetch	0	0-0	0
Maples	2	0-0	4	King	3	6-7	12
Blatcher	11	1-2	23	Gower	0	1-2	1
Gola	7	5-5	19	Estergald	3	11-12	17
O'Malley	5	1-1	11	Carney	3	11-17	17
O'Hara	2	3-4	7	Utt	0	0-0	0
				Kent	8	0-2	16
				Riley	1	1-2	3
Totals	37	18-24	92	Totals	22	32-44	76

1985 NCAA TOURNAMENT

FIRST ROUND
MARCH 15, AT DAYTON, OHIO
VILLANOVA 51, DAYTON 49

DAYTON

	Min	FG-A	FT-A	R	A	Pts.
Grant	21	1-5	0-0	8	0	2
Goodwin	38	4-8	8-8	9	2	16
Colbert	39	2-5	1-1	6	1	5
Schellenbrg	40	3-6	6-6	5	4	12
Toney	37	5-16	2-2	0	4	12
Zern	17	1-2	0-0	1	0	2
Christie	7	0-1	0-0	1	1	0
Harris	1	0-0	0-0	0	0	0
Totals	200	16-43	17-17	30	12	49

VILLANOVA

	Min	FG-A	FT-A	R	A	Pts.
Pressley	38	4-9	0-1	5	1	8
McClain	36	5-9	1-1	5	3	11
Pinckney	40	6-10	8-13	6	1	20
Wilbur	23	1-5	0-0	1	1	2
McLain	37	1-4	0-0	2	1	2
Jensen	24	3-5	2-2	0	1	8
Plansky	1	0-0	0-0	1	0	0
Everson	1	0-0	0-0	0	0	0
Totals	200	20-42	11-17	20	8	51

Dayton	23 26	— 49
Villanova	21 30	— 51

Blocked shots: Dayton 2 (Grant 1, Zern 1), Villanova 7 (Pinckney 4, Pressley 2, McClain 1).
Steals: Dayton 5, Villanova 8.
Turnovers: Dayton 16, Villanova 12.
Officials: Joe Sylvester, Robert Garibaldi, Phil Bova.

SECOND ROUND
MARCH 17, AT DAYTON, OHIO
VILLANOVA 59, MICHIGAN 55

VILLANOVA

	Min	FG-A	FT-A	R	A	Pts.
Pressley	34	3-10	3-5	7	2	9
McClain	36	8-12	4-4	4	1	20
Pinckney	40	2-4	10-11	7	1	14
Wilbur	15	0-2	0-0	0	1	0
McLain	37	3-5	3-5	0	3	9
Jensen	27	0-1	3-4	2	1	3
Plansky	9	1-1	2-2	1	1	4
Everson	2	0-0	0-0	0	0	0
Totals	200	17-35	25-31	21	10	59

MICHIGAN

	Min	FG-A	FT-A	R	A	Pts.
Rellford	28	5-7	1-2	2	0	11
Wade	25	0-1	0-0	8	3	0
Tarpley	40	7-14	0-0	13	1	14
Joubert	30	6-13	0-0	1	3	12
Grant	33	0-4	0-0	0	1	0
Thompson	18	3-5	2-3	1	2	8
Henderson	15	2-3	0-0	2	1	4
Rockymore	11	3-4	0-0	1	1	6
Totals	200	26-51	3-5	28	12	55

Villanova	30 29	— 59
Michigan	26 29	— 55

Blocked shots: Villanova 0, Michigan 0.
Steals: Villanova 7, Michigan 8.
Turnovers: Villanova 10, Michigan 13.
Technicals: Wade.
Officials: Joe Sylvester, Robert Garibaldi, Phil Bova.

REGIONAL SEMIFINAL
MARCH 22, AT BIRMINGHAM, ALA.
VILLANOVA 46, MARYLAND 43

VILLANOVA

	Min	FG-A	FT-A	R	A	Pts.
Pressley	35	3-12	1-4	10	1	7
McClain	40	5-9	2-2	4	2	12
Pinckney	36	5-7	6-7	13	1	16
Wilbur	25	1-5	2-2	4	3	4
McLain	36	1-5	1-2	2	1	3
Plansky	13	2-3	0-0	4	2	4
Jensen	11	0-5	0-1	0	1	0
Everson	4	0-0	0-0	0	0	0
Totals	200	17-46	12-18	37	11	46

MARYLAND

	Min	FG-A	FT-A	R	A	Pts.
Branch	39	9-19	3-5	5	2	21
Bias	40	4-13	0-0	5	1	8
Lewis	24	0-2	0-0	5	0	0
Gatlin	30	2-7	0-0	4	2	4
Adkins	29	2-7	0-0	4	4	4
Baxter	10	2-2	0-0	0	0	4
Long	16	0-1	2-2	4	0	2
Jones	12	0-2	0-0	2	1	0
Totals	200	19-53	5-7	29	10	43

Villanova	19 27	— 46
Maryland	20 23	— 43

Blocked shots: Villanova 2 (Pressley 1, Pinckney 1), Maryland 3 (Lewis 2, Long 1).
Steals: Villanova 1, Maryland 3.
Turnovers: Villanova 12, Maryland 6.
Officials: Mike Tanko, Bob Showalter, Rick Wulcow.

REGIONAL FINAL
MARCH 24, AT BIRMINGHAM, ALA.
VILLANOVA 56, N. CAROLINA 44

VILLANOVA

	Min	FG-A	FT-A	R	A	Pts.
Pressley	38	7-13	1-2	3	1	15
McClain	36	4-11	3-3	5	2	11
Pinckney	38	3-6	3-6	7	3	9
Wilbur	9	0-3	0-0	2	1	0
McLain	39	3-5	5-6	2	2	11
Plansky	7	0-1	0-0	1	1	0
Jensen	31	5-7	0-0	3	3	10
Everson	2	0-1	0-0	0	0	0
Totals	200	22-47	12-17	23	13	56

NORTH CAROLINA

	Min	FG-A	FT-A	R	A	Pts.
Popson	14	2-3	1-1	2	0	5
Daugherty	38	7-9	3-6	12	0	17
Wolf	34	2-6	0-0	4	5	4
Peterson	20	0-3	0-0	0	0	0
K. Smith	40	2-7	0-0	3	5	4
Morris	2	0-0	0-0	0	0	0
R. Smith	20	3-10	0-0	4	3	6
Hunter	16	3-4	0-0	2	0	6
Martin	16	1-2	0-0	1	1	2
Totals	200	20-44	4-7	28	11	44

Villanova	17 39	— 56
North Carolina	22 22	— 44

Blocked shots: Villanova 2 (Pinckney 2), North Carolina 2 (Martin 2).
Steals: Villanova 13, North Carolina 3.
Turnovers: Villanova 10, North Carolina 19.
Officials: Tim Higgins, Jim Burr, J.C. Leimbach.

NATIONAL SEMIFINAL
MARCH 30, AT LEXINGTON, KY.
VILLANOVA 52, MEMPHIS ST. 45

VILLANOVA

	Min	FG-A	FT-A	R	A	Pts.
Pressley	29	1-8	1-2	6	1	3
McClain	40	6-9	7-7	4	2	19
Pinckney	39	3-7	6-9	9	1	12
Wilbur	6	0-2	0-0	1	0	0
McLain	39	2-5	5-5	2	2	9
Jensen	35	3-6	0-0	4	1	6
Plansky	11	1-1	1-3	0	2	3
Everson	1	0-0	0-0	1	0	0
Totals	200	16-38	20-26	27	9	52

MEMPHIS ST.

	Min	FG-A	FT-A	R	A	Pts.
Lee	23	3-9	4-4	7	1	10
Holmes	31	4-9	0-0	7	0	8
Bedford	32	4-9	0-0	7	0	8
Askew	40	1-3	0-1	7	7	2
Turner	40	5-13	1-2	4	3	11
Bailey	8	1-1	0-0	0	0	2
Becton	22	1-4	2-2	5	1	4
Boyd	3	0-2	0-0	0	0	0
Wilfong	1	0-1	0-0	1	0	0
Totals	200	19-50	7-9	34	12	45

Villanova	23 29	— 52
Memphis St.	23 22	— 45

Blocked shots: Villanova 4 (Pinckney 3, McLain 1), Memphis St. 2 (Lee 1, Bedford 1).
Steals: Villanova 5, Memphis St. 4.
Turnovers: Villanova 11, Memphis St. 11.
Technicals: Bedford.
Officials: John Clougherty, Bob Dibler, Willie McJunkin.

NATIONAL CHAMPIONSHIP
APRIL 1, AT LEXINGTON, KY.
VILLANOVA 66, GEORGETOWN 64

VILLANOVA

	Min	FG-A	FT-A	R	A	Pts.
Pressley	40	4-6	3-4	4	1	11
McClain	40	5-7	7-8	1	3	17
Pinckney	37	5-7	6-7	6	5	16
Wilbur	5	0-0	0-0	0	1	0
McLain	40	3-3	2-2	2	2	8
Jensen	34	5-5	4-5	1	2	14
Plansky	1	0-0	0-1	0	0	0
Everson	3	0-0	0-0	0	0	0
Totals	200	22-28	22-27	17	14	66

GEORGETOWN

	Min	FG-A	FT-A	R	A	Pts.
Martin	37	4-6	2-2	5	1	10
Williams	29	5-9	0-2	4	2	10
Ewing	39	7-13	0-0	5	2	14
Jackson	37	4-7	0-0	0	9	8
Wingate	39	8-14	0-0	2	2	16
McDonald	2	0-1	0-0	0	1	0
Broadnax	13	1-2	2-2	0	0	4
Dalton	4	0-1	2-2	0	0	2
Totals	200	29-53	6-8	17	18	64

Villanova	29 37	— 66
Georgetown	28 36	— 64

Blocked shots: Villanova 1 (Pressley 1), Georgetown 1 (Ewing 1).
Steals: Villanova 8, Georgetown 6.
Turnovers: Villanova 17, Georgetown 11.
Officials: Don Rutledge, John Clougherty, Bob Dibler.

NCAA CHAMPIONS

MEN'S INDOOR

Team
1968: Villanova (Coach: Jumbo Elliott)
1971: Villanova (Coach: Jumbo Elliott)
1979: Villanova (Coach: Jumbo Elliott)

Individual 60-Yard High Hurdles
1969: Erv Hall, Villanova
1980: Rodney Wilson, Villanova

Individual 440-Yard Dash
1968: Larry James, Villanova
1969: Larry James, Villanova
1970: Larry James, Villanova
1983: Carlton Young, Villanova

Individual 600-Yard Run
1979: Anthony Tufariello, Villanova

Individual 880-Yard Run
1967: Dave Patrick, Villanova
1968: Dave Patrick, Villanova
1969: Frank Murphy, Villanova
1973: Ken Schappert, Villanova
1977: Mark Belger, Villanova
1978: Mark Belger, Villanova
1983: John Marshall, Villanova

Individual 1,000-Yard Run
1976: Mark Belger, Villanova
1978: Don Paige, Villanova
1979: Don Paige, Villanova
1980: Don Paige, Villanova

Individual Mile Run
1971: Marty Liquori, Villanova
1975: Eamonn Coghlan, Villanova
1976: Eamonn Coghlan, Villanova

Individual Two-Mile Run
1971: Marty Liquori, Villanova
1974: John Harnett, Villanova

One-Mile Relay
1968: Villanova (Hal Nichter, Hardge Davis, Ken Prince, Larry James)
1970: Villanova (Lamotte Hyman, Greg Govan, Hardge Davis, Larry James)
1979: Villanova (Keith Brown, Derrek Harbour, Anthony Tufariello, Tim Dale)

Two-Mile Relay
1983: Villanova (John Borgese, John Keyworth, Mike England, Marcus O'Sullivan)

Distance Medley Relay
1968: Villanova (Charles Messenger, Bob Whitehead, Tom Donnelly, Frank Murphy)
1969: Villanova (Andy O'Reilly, Ernie Bradshaw, Chris Mason, Frank Murphy)
1980: Villanova (John Hunter, Tim Robinson, Mike England, Sydney Maree)

MEN'S OUTDOOR

Team
1957: Villanova (Coach: Jumbo Elliott)

Individual 100-Meter Dash
1961: Frank Budd, Villanova
1962: Frank Budd, Villanova

Individual 200-Meter Dash
1958: Ed Collymore, Villanova
1961: Frank Budd, Villanova
1965: Earl Horner, Villanova

Individual 400-Meter Dash
1970: Larry James, Villanova

Individual 800-Meter Run
1921: Earl Eby, Penn
1958: Ron Delany, Villanova
1979: Don Paige, Villanova
1980: Don Paige, Villanova

Individual 1,500-Meter Run
1956: Ron Delany, Villanova
1957: Ron Delany, Villanova
1958: Ron Delany, Villanova
1966: Dave Patrick, Villanova
1968: Dave Patrick, Villanova
1969: Marty Liquori, Villanova
1970: Marty Liquori, Villanova
1971: Marty Liquori, Villanova
1975: Eamonn Coghlan, Villanova
1976: Eamonn Coghlan, Villanova
1979: Don Paige, Villanova
1980: Sydney Maree, Villanova
1981: Sydney Maree, Villanova

Individual 3,000-Meter Steeplechase
1948: Browning Ross, Villanova
1962: Pat Traynor, Villanova
1963: Vic Zwolak, Villanova
1964: Vic Zwolak, Villanova

Individual 5,000-Meter Run
1979: Sydney Maree, Villanova

Individual 110-Meter High Hurdles
1969: Erv Hall, Villanova

Individual 400-Meter Hurdles
1972: Bruce Collins, Penn
1974: Bruce Collins, Penn

Individual High Jump
1956: Phil Reavis, Villanova (Three-way tie)

Individual Pole Vault
1955: Don Bragg, Villanova
1964: John Uelses, La Salle

Individual Triple Jump
1956: Bill Sharpe, West Chester
1979: Nate Cooper, Villanova

Individual Shot Put
1959: Carl Shine, Penn

Individual Hammer Throw
1932: Grant McDougall, Penn

Individual Javelin Throw
1981: Mike Juskus, Glassboro St.

1,600-Meter Relay
1968: Villanova (Hardge Davis, Ken Prince, Hal Nichter, Larry James)
1978: Villanova (Keith Brown, Anthony Tufariello, Glenn Bogue, Tim Dale)

WOMEN'S INDOOR

800 Meters
1984: Veronica McIntosh, Villanova

3,000 Meters
1987: Vicki Huber, Villanova
1988: Vicki Huber, Villanova
1989: Vicki Huber, Villanova

Mile
1988: Vicki Huber, Villanova

3,200-Meter Relay
1985: Villanova (Kelly Toole, Debbie Grant, Joanne Kehs, Veronica McIntosh)
1987: Villanova (Kathy Franey, Colleen Gallagher, Michelle DiMuro, Gina Procaccio)
1989: Villanova (Meg Moisen, Michelle Bennett, Kim Certain, Michelle DiMuro)

WOMEN'S OUTDOOR

3,000 Meters
1987: Vicki Huber, Villanova
1988: Vicki Huber, Villanova
1989: Vicki Huber, Villanova

BASKETBALL

MEN
1954: La Salle (Coach: Ken Loeffler)
1985: Villanova (Coach: Rollie Massimino)
NATIONAL INVITATION TOURNAMENT
1938: Temple (Coach: Jimmy Usilton)
1952: La Salle (Coach: Ken Loeffler)
1969: Temple (Coach: Harry Litwack)

FENCING

MEN
Team
1953: Penn (Coach: Lajos Csiszar)
1969: Penn (Coach: Lajos Csiszar)
1981: Penn (Coach: Dave Micahnik)
Individual Foil
1954: Robert Goldman, Penn
1969: Norman Braslow, Penn
1973: Brooke Makler, Penn
Individual Sabre
1947: Oscar Parsons, Temple
1953: Robert Parmacek, Penn
1967: Todd Makler, Penn
1968: Todd Makler, Penn
1980: Paul Friedberg, Penn
1981: Paul Friedberg, Penn
Individual Epee
1953: Jack Tori, Penn
1969: James Wetzler, Penn
1972: Ernesto Fernandez, Penn
1976: Randy Eggleton, Penn
1986: Chris O'Loughlin, Penn
WOMEN
Team
1986: Penn (Coach: Dave Micahnik)
Individual
1984: Mary Jane O'Neill, Penn

WRESTLING

MEN
123 Pounds
1969: Wayne Boyd, Temple
175 Pounds
1941: Richard DiBattista, Penn
1942: Richard DiBattista, Penn
Heavyweight
1985: Bill Hyman, Temple

MEN'S SOCCER
1961: West Chester (Coach: Mel Lorback)

LACROSSE

WOMEN
1984: Temple (Coach: Tina Sloan Green)
1988: Temple (Coach: Tina Sloan Green)

SWIMMING

MEN
Individual 200-Yard Butterfly
1947: Joe Verdeur, La Salle
1948: Joe Verdeur, La Salle
1963: Dick McDonough, Villanova
Individual 150-Yard Medley
1949: Joe Verdeur, La Salle
1950: Joe Verdeur, La Salle

TENNIS

MEN
Singles
1903: E.B. Dewhurst, Penn
1905: E.B. Dewhurst, Penn
1909: W.F. Johnson, Penn
1922: Carl Fischer, Phila. Osteo.
Doubles
1905: E.B. Dewhurst, H.B. Register, Penn
1908: H.M. Tilden, A. Thayer, Penn
1909: W.F. Johnson, A. Thayer, Penn

GYMNASTICS

MEN
Team
1949: Temple (Coach: Max Younger)
Individual Floor Exercise
1988: Chris Wyatt, Temple
Individual Pommel Horse
1949: Joe Berenato, Temple
Individual Horizontal Bar
1939: Adam Walters, Temple
1940: Norm Boardman, Temple
1942: Norm Boardman, Temple
1949: Bob Stout, Temple
Individual Tumbling
1942: George Szypula, Temple
Individual Flying Rings
1948: George Hayes, Temple

Temple's Bill Hyman captured the NCAA Heavyweight wrestling crown at Oklahoma City, Okla. on March 16, 1985

OLYMPICS

LOUIS ABELL (Vesper Boat Club): 1900 and 1904, rowing (eights with coxswain).
JOSEPH AMLONG (Vesper Boat Club): 1964, rowing (eights with coxswain).
THOMAS AMLONG (Vesper Boat Club): 1964, rowing (eights with coxswain).
CHARLES ARMSTRONG (Vesper Boat Club): 1904, rowing (eights with coxswain).
HORACE ASHENFELTER (Phoenixville, Pa.): 1952, track and field (3,000-meter steeplechase).
JANE BARKMAN (Bryn Mawr, Pa.): 1968 and 1972, swimming (4 x 100-meter freestyle swimming).
IRVING BAXTER (University of Pennsylvania): 1900, track and field (high jump, pole vault).
DAVID BERKOFF (Huntingdon Valley): 1988, swimming (400 medley relay)
ALDIS BERZINS (Wilmington, Del.): 1984, volleyball.
TYRELL BIGGS (Philadelphia): 1984, boxing (super-heavyweight).
DON BRAGG (Villanova University): 1960, track and field (pole vault).
HAROLD BUDD (Vesper Boat Club): 1964, rowing (eights with coxswain).
WILLIAM A. CARR (University of Pennsylvania): 1932, track and field (400 meters, 4 x 400-meter relay).
WILLIAM J. CARR SR. (Vesper Boat Club): 1900, rowing (eights with coxswain).
NATHANIEL CARTMELL (University of Pennsylvania): 1908, track and field (4 x 400-meter relay).
EMERY CLARK (Vesper Boat Club): 1964, rowing (eights with coxswain).
PAUL COSTELLO SR. (Philadelphia): 1920, 1924 and 1928, rowing (double sculls).
FREDERICK CRESSAR (Vesper Boat Club): 1904, rowing (eights with coxswain).
STANLEY CWIKLINSKI (Vesper Boat Club): 1964, rowing (eights with coxswain).
BRUCE DAVIDSON (Unionville, Pa.): 1976 and 1984, equestrian (three-day team event).
HARRY DEBAECKE (Vesper Boat Club): 1900, rowing (eights with coxswain).
RON DELANY (Villanova University): 1956, track and field (1,500 meters).
JOSEPH DEMPSEY (Vesper Boat Club): 1904, rowing (eights with coxswain).
BARNEY EWELL (Lancaster, Pa.): 1948, track and field (4 x 100-meter relay).
JOHN EXLEY (Vesper Boat Club): 1900 and 1904, rowing (eights with coxswain).
JAMES FLANIGAN (Vesper Boat Club): 1904, rowing (eights with coxswain).
HUGH FOLEY (Vesper Boat Club): 1964, rowing (eights with coxswain).
JOE FRAZIER (Philadelphia): 1964, boxing (heavyweight).
JOHN GEIGER (Vesper Boat Club): 1900, rowing (eights with coxswain).
MICHAEL GLEASON (Vesper Boat Club): 1904, rowing (eights with coxswain).
DONALD HALDEMAN (Souderton, Pa.): 1976, shooting (trap shooting).
SCOTT HAMILTON (Philadelphia Skating Club): 1984, figure skating.
BRUCE HARLAN (Lansdownce, Pa.): 1948, diving (springboard).
WALT HAZZARD (Philadelphia): 1964, basketball.
EDWARD HEDLEY (Vesper Boat Club): 1900, rowing (eights with coxswain).
LARRY JAMES (Villanova University): 1968, track and field (4 x 400-meter relay).
CHARLES JENKINS (Villanova University): 1956, track and field (400 meters, 4 x 400-meter relay).
JAMES JUVENAL (Vesper Boat Club): 1900, rowing (eights with coxswain).
JACK KELLY SR. (Philadelphia): 1920, rowing (single sculls); 1920 and 1924 rowing (double sculls).
WILLIAM KNECHT (Vesper Boat Club): 1964, rowing (eights with coxswain).
ALVIN KRAENZLEIN (University of Pennsylvania): 1900, track and field (60 meters, 110-meter hurdles, 200-meter hurdles, long jump).
CARL LEWIS (Willingboro, N.J.): 1984, track and field (100 meters, 200 meters, 4 x 100-meter relay, long jump), 1988, track and field (100 meters, long jump).
ROSCOE LOCKWOOD (Vesper Boat Club): 1900, rowing (eights with coxswain).
HARRY LOTT (Vesper Boat Club): 1904, rowing (eights with coxswain).
OLIVER MacDONALD (University of Pennsylvania): 1924, track and field (4 x 400-meter relay).
EDWARD MARSH (Vesper Boat Club): 1900, rowing (eights with coxswain).
JOHN MEDICA (Philadelphia): 1936, swimming (400-meter freestyle).
JAMES MEREDITH (University of Pennsylvania): 1912, track and field (800 meters, 4 x 400-meter relay).
RICHARD MURPHY (Oaklyn, N.J.): 1952, rowing (eights with coxswain).
GEORGE ORTON (University of Pennsylvania): 1900, track and field (3,000-meter steeplechase).
STEPHEN RERYCH (Philadelphia): 1968, swimming (4 x 100- and 4 x 400-meter freestyle relay).
STEVE RIDDICK (Philadelphia Pioneers): 1976, track and field (4 x 100-meter relay).
JOSEPH SCHAUERS (Drexel): 1932, rowing (pairs with coxswain).
FRANK SCHELL (Vesper Boat Club): 1904, rowing (eights with coxswain).
MARK SCHULTZ (Rosemont, Pa.): 1984, freestyle wrestling (middleweight).
JEAN SHILEY (Haverford, Pa.; Temple): 1932, track and field (high jump).
WILLIAM STOWE (Vesper Boat Club): 1964, rowing (eights with coxswain).
JOHN TAYLOR (University of Pennsylvania): 1908, track and field (4 x 400-meter relay).
MELDRICK TAYLOR (Philadelphia): 1984, boxing (featherweight).
JOHN TEWKSBURY (University of Pennsylvania): 1900, track and field (200 meters, 400-meter hurdles).
BOBBY WEAVER (Lehigh): 1984, freestyle wrestling (light-flyweight).
JOE VERDEUR (La Salle): 1948, swimming (200-meter breaststroke).
ROBERT ZIMONYI (Vesper Boat Club): 1964, rowing (eights with coxswain).

HALL OF FAMERS
(Year inducted in parentheses)

BASEBALL

GROVER ALEXANDER (1938): Phillies 1911-17
FRANK BAKER (1955): Athletics 1908-14
DAVE BANCROFT (1971): Phillies 1915-20
CHIEF BENDER (1953): Athletics 1903-14; Phillies 1916-17
DAN BROUTHERS (1945): Phillies 1896
ROY CAMPENELLA (1969): Born in Philadelphia on 11/19/21
TY COBB (1936): Athletics 1927-28
MICKEY COCHRANE (1947): Athletics 1925-33
EDDIE COLLINS (1939): Athletics 1906-14, '27-30
JIMMY COLLINS (1945): Athletics 1907-08
EARLE COMBS (1970): Phillies coach 1954
ROGER CONNOR (1976): Phillies 1892
STAN COVELESKI (1969): Athletics 1912
ED DELAHANTY (1945): Phillies 1888-89, '91-1901
HUGH DUFFY (1945): Phillies 1904-06
JOHNNY EVERS (1946): Phillies 1917
ELMER FLICK (1963): Phillies 1898-1901; Athletics 1901
JIMMIE FOXX (1951): Athletics 1925-35; Phillies 1945
LEFTY GROVE (1947): Athletics 1925-33
BILLY HAMILTON (1961): Phillies 1890-95
BUCKY HARRIS (1974): Phillies manager 1943
WAITE HOYT (1969): Athletics 1931
HUGHIE JENNINGS (1945): Phillies 1901-02
TIM KEEFE (1964): Phillies 1891-93
GEORGE KELL (1983): Athletics 1943-46
CHUCK KLEIN (1980): Phillies 1928-33, '36-44
NAP LAJOIE (1937): Phillies 1896-1900; Athletics 1901-02, '15-16
BOB LEMON (1976): Phillies coach 1961
CONNIE MACK (1937): Athletics manager 1901-50
JOE McCARTHY (1957): Born in Philadelphia on 4/21/1887
TOMMY McCARTHY (1946): Phillies 1886-87
KID NICHOLS (1949): Phillies 1905-06
HERB PENNOCK (1948): Athletics 1912-15; Born in Kennett Square, Pa., on 2/10/94
EDDIE PLANK (1946): Athletics 1901-14

EPPA RIXEY (1963): Phillies 1912-17, '19-20
ROBIN ROBERTS (1976): Phillies 1948-61
WILBERT ROBINSON (1945): Philadelphia (American Association), 1886-90
AL SIMMONS (1953): Athletics 1924-32, '40-41, '44
TRIS SPEAKER (1937): Athletics 1928
CASEY STENGEL (1966): Phillies 1920-21
SAM THOMPSON (1974): Phillies 1889-98
RUBE WADDELL (1946): Athletics 1902-07
LLOYD WANER (1967): Phillies 1942
ZACK WHEAT (1959): Athletics 1927
HACK WILSON (1979): Phillies 1934
HARRY WRIGHT (1953): Phillies manager 1884-93

PHILADELPHIA BASEBALL

GROVER ALEXANDER (1981): Phillies 1911-17, '30
RICHIE ASHBURN (1979): Phillies 1948-59
JIM BUNNING (1984): Phillies 1964-67, '70-71
MICKEY COCHRANE (1982): Athletics 1925-33
EDDIE COLLINS (1987): Athletics 1906-14, '27-30
ED DELAHANTY (1985): Phillies 1888-89, '91-1901
JIMMY DYKES (1984): Athletics 1918-32
DEL ENNIS (1982): Phillies 1946-56
JIMMIE FOXX (1979): Athletics 1925-35; Phillies 1945
LEFTY GROVE (1980): Athletics 1925-33
GRANNY HAMNER (1987): Phillies 1944-59
CHUCK KLEIN (1980): Phillies 1928-33, '36-44
CONNIE MACK (1978): Athletics manager 1901-50
WALLY MOSES (1988): Athletics 1935-41, '49-51
PAUL OWENS (1988): Phillies general manager 1972; manager 1972, '83-84
EDDIE PLANK (1985): Athletics 1901-14
ROBIN ROBERTS (1978): Phillies 1948-61
AL SIMMONS (1981): Athletics 1924-32, '40-41, '44
RUBE WADDELL (1986): Athletics 1923-33
CY WILLIAMS (1986): Phillies 1918-30

HOCKEY

BOBBY CLARKE (1984): Flyers 1969-84
BERNIE PARENT (1986): Flyers 1967-71, '73-79
ED SNIDER (1988): Flyers' founder and owner

Richie Ashburn

Paul Owens

Ed Snider

BIG 5

CLIFF ANDERSON (1973): St. Joseph's 1965-67
MIKE BANTOM (1979): St. Joseph's 1971-73
JOHN BAUM (1978): Temple 1966-69
GEORGE BERTELSMAN (1976): St. Joseph's athletic director at formation of Big 5
BOB BIGELOW (1989): Penn 1972-75
STEVE BILSKY (1988): Penn 1969-71
NORMAN BLACK (1985): St. Joseph's 1976-79
ALEX BRADLEY (1987): Villanova 1977-81
CLARENCE BROOKINS (1984): Temple 1965-68
MICHAEL BROOKS (1986): La Salle 1976-80
JOE BRYANT (1981): La Salle 1973-75
CORKY CALHOUN (1976): Penn 1970-72
LARRY CANNON (1973): La Salle 1966-69
ERNIE CASALE (1982): Temple athletic director 1958-82
DICK CENSITS (1981): Penn 1956-68
TIM CLAXTON (1987): Temple 1974-78
JOSH CODY (1976): Temple athletic director at formation of Big 5
FRANK CORACE (1974): La Salle 1961-64
STEVE COURTIN (1980): St. Joseph's 1962-64
ANDY DOUGHERTY (1989): St. Joseph's administration
BRUCE DRYSDALE (1977): Temple 1959-62
BUD DUDLEY (1976): Villanova athletic director at formation of Big 5
KEN DURRETT (1975): La Salle 1968-71
KURT ENGELBERT (1986): St. Joseph's 1955-57
BOB FIELDS (1984): La Salle 1969-71
CHRIS FORD (1977): Villanova 1969-72
JERRY FORD (1976): Penn athletic director at formation of Big 5
TOM GOLA (1986): La Salle coach 1968-70
MATT GUOKAS (1976): St. Joseph's 1965-66
RON HAIGLER (1982): Penn 1973-75
PHIL HANKINSON (1980): Penn 1971-73
MIKE HAUER (1977): St. Joseph's 68-70
JIM HENRY (1976): La Salle athletic director at formation of Big 5
KEITH HERRON (1984): Villanova 1974-78
JIM HUGGARD (1978): Villanova 1958-61
TOM INGELSBY (1979): Villanova 1970-73
OLLIE JOHNSON (1979): Temple 1969-72
WALLY JONES (1973): Villanova 61-64
JOHN JONES (1981): Villanova 1966-69
DAN KELLY (1980): St. Joseph's 1968-70
"PICKLES" KENNEDY (1975): Temple 1957-60
JACK KRAFT (1987): Villanova coach 1961-73
HAL LEAR (1974): Temple 1953-56
ALONZO LEWIS (1980): La Salle 1954-57
HARRY LITWACK (1978): Temple coach 1952-73
JIM LYNAM (1975): St. Joseph's 1961-63
HUBIE MARSHALL (1977): La Salle 1964-67
BILL MELCHIONNI (1974): Villanova 63-66

BOBBY MORSE (1977): Penn 1970-72
BOB McATEER (1976): La Salle 1959-62
KEVEN McDONALD (1985): Penn 1976-78
PAT McFARLAND (1984): St. Joseph's 1971-73
BOB McNEILL (1974): St. Joseph's 1958-60
JEFF NEUMAN (1984): Penn 1964-66
JAKE NEVIN (1985): Villanova trainer 1939-1985
JAY NORMAN (1976): Temple 1955-58
JIM O'BRIEN (1989): St. Joseph's 1972-74
STAN PAWLAK (1973): Penn 1964-66
JOHN PINONE (1989): Villanova 1979-83
HOWARD PORTER (1981): Villanova 1968-71
TONY PRICE (1985): Penn 1977-79
JACK RAMSAY (1983): St. Joseph's coach 1955-66
GUY RODGERS (1973): Temple 1955-58
JOHN ROSSITER (1975): Original Big 5 business manager
CHARLES SCOTT (1981): Penn assistant athletic director and Big 5 manager 1955-81
AL SHRIER (1984): Temple sports information director 1953-88
HANK SIEMIONTKOWSKI (1988): Villanova 1969-72
RORY SPARROW (1986): Villanova 1976-80
JOE SPRATT (1983): St. Joseph's 1957-79
JOE STURGIS (1983): Penn 1954-56
BILLY TAYLOR (1989): La Salle 1972-75
BOB VETRONE (1988): Sports writer, publicist
BRYAN WARRICK (1988): St. Joseph's 1979-82
JIM WASHINGTON (1975): Villanova 62-65
HUBIE WHITE (1976): Villanova 1959-62
JOHN WIDEMAN (1974): Penn 1961-63
BERNIE WILLIAMS (1982): La Salle 1966-69
JIM WILLIAMS (1983): Temple 1963-66
MARCELLUS "BOO" WILLIAMS (1987): St. Joseph's 1978-81
CHARLIE WISE (1982): La Salle 1972-76
DAVE WOHL (1975): Penn 1969-71
TOM WYNNE (1978): St. Joseph's 1961-63

COLLEGE FOOTBALL

CHUCK BEDNARIK: Penn 1946-48
GEORGE BROOKE: Penn 1893-95
CHARLES GELBERT: Penn 1894-96
T. TRUXTON HARE: Penn 1897-1900
WILLIAM M. HOLLENBACK: Penn 1904, '06-08
LOUIS L. LITTLE Villanova coach 1921-22
E. LEROY MERCER: Penn 1910-12
JOHN H. MINDS Penn 1895-97
J. RAY MORRISON Temple coach 1940-48
WINCHESTER D. OSGOOD Penn 1890-94
HUNTER SCARLETT Penn 1906-08
ANDREW L. SMITH Penn coach 1909-12
VINCENT M. STEVENSON Penn 1903-05
GLENN S. "POP" WARNER Temple coach 1933-38
CHARLES "BUCK" WHARTON Penn 1894-96
GEORGE W. WOODRUFF Penn coach 1892-00

BASKETBALL

PAUL ARIZIN (1977): Born in Philadelphia on 4/9/28; Villanova 1946-50; Warriors 1950-62
AL CERVI (1984): Nationals/Sixers 1948-53
WILT CHAMBERLAIN (1978): Born in Philadelpha on 8/21/36; Overbrook High School 1951-55; Warriors 1959-64; Sixers 1964-68
BILLY CUNNINGHAM (1985): Sixers 1965-74
JOE FULKS (1977): Warriors 1946-54.
TOM GOLA (1975) Born in Philadelphia on 1/13/33; La Salle High School 1947-51; La Salle College 1951-55; Warriors 1955-63
EDDIE GOTTLIEB (1971) Warriors owner, coach 1946-55
HAL GREER (1981): Sixers 1958-73
HARRY LITWACK (1975): Temple coach 1952-73
DOLPH SCHAYES (1972): Nationals/Sixers 1948-64

PRO FOOTBALL

HERB ADDERLY (1980): Born in Philadelphia on 6/8/39
CHUCK BEDNARIK (1967): Penn 1945-48; Eagles 1949-62
BERT BELL (1963): Eagles founder, head coach 1936-40
BILL HEWITT (1971): Eagles 1936-39, '43
SONNY JURGENSEN (1983): Eagles 1957-63
OLLIE MATSON (1972): Eagles 1964-66
GREASY NEALE (1969): Eagles head coach 1941-50
PETE PIHOS (1970): Eagles 1947-55
JIM RINGO (1981): Eagles 1964-67
NORM VAN BROCKLIN (1971): Eagles 1958-60
STEVE VAN BUREN (1965): Eagles 1944-51
ALEX WOJCIECHOWICZ (1968): Eagles 1946-50

Index